T3-BSC-059

The Logic of Social Control

The Logic of Social Control

Allan V. Horwitz
Rutgers University
New Brunswick, New Jersey

Plenum Press • New York and London

Library of Congress Cataloging-in-Publication Data

Horwitz, Allan V.
The logic of social control / Allan V. Horwitz.
p. cm.
Includes bibliographical references and index.
ISBN 0-306-43475-X
1. Social control. I. Title.
HM291.H67 1990
303.3'3--dc20
90-39719
CIP

ISBN 0-306-43475-X

A Division of Plenum Publishing Corporation
233 Spring Street, New York, N.Y. 10013

Printed in the United States of America

To Colleen

Foreword

Historians of the future might justifiably call our century the "Century of Science." Most scientific knowledge has come into being since 1900, and most of the scientists who have ever lived are presently alive. While our understanding of old problems everywhere expands, we continually identify new problems for investigation and broaden the jurisdiction of science. Social science is thus largely a twentieth-century invention, and even scientific behavior itself is a subject of scientific inquiry.

We have learned, for example, that scientific knowledge advances primarily through the establishment of what Thomas Kuhn calls "paradigms"—frameworks that identify problems for research, organize findings, and guide the elaboration of theory. We have also learned that scientific ideas, including the paradigms themselves, do not arise and proliferate by logic alone but rather by what another student of science, Derek de Solla Price, calls "invisible colleges"—social networks of scientists who participate jointly in building a common body of knowledge. *The Logic of Social Control,* by Allan V. Horwitz, beautifully illustrates the nature of scientific progress. Indeed, it is a model of modern sociology.

The investigation of social control—how people define and respond to deviant behavior—began at the turn of the century and has continued at a steadily increasing rate across a broadening range of phenomena. First came inquiries into the evolution of law—one of the most sophisticated and controversial forms of social control in modern societies. Anthropologists discovered, however, that simpler societies often handle deviant behavior entirely without governmental institutions such as the police, courts, or legislatures, in fact, without government or law at all.

Now we also recognize that even in the most complex and differentiated societies of the modern world, legal activity constitutes only a small fraction of the social control in everyday life. All settings—whether families, organizations, occupations, neighborhoods, friendships, or gatherings of strangers—have their own forms of social control. It includes everything from rebukes to homicides, avoidance and exclusion, gossip, negotiation, and various modes of third-party intervention such as mediation, psychotherapy, and adjudication. Social control mirrors the diversity of social life itself.

A number of sociologists have explored this diversity across the social universe, past and present, seeking always to discover precisely how social control varies with its location and direction in social space. Professor Horwitz, a leading figure in this movement, previously devoted most of his attention to the handling of deviant personalities (those known as insane) and wrote what may be the most important published work on that subject: *The Social Control of Mental Illness* (New York: Academic Press, 1982). But the present volume reaches far beyond his previous work.

The Logic of Social Control is the most comprehensive study of social control ever written. It offers at once a statement of the paradigm guiding the field, an inventory of existing knowledge, and a wide array of new formulations extending the theoretical frontiers of the field. The book is truly breathtaking in its ambition and scope, and will provide a starting point for empirical and theoretical studies of social control for many years to come. Moreover, with the publication of *The Logic of Social Control*, a major field of social science comes of age. The sociology of social control may now be regarded as one of the scientific accomplishments of the twentieth century.

DONALD BLACK

Charlottesville, Virginia

Preface

Over the past two decades, interest in social control has greatly expanded. Researchers from many disciplines, including sociology, anthropology, history, political science, and law, have produced numerous empirical and theoretical studies of many types of social control systems. Especially noteworthy is the range and scope of these studies. Investigations include detailed ethnographies of tribal societies, archival studies of historical settings, and intensive case studies, as well as large survey research projects of social control systems in modern societies. This book attempts to synthesize the findings from many of these diverse inquiries and develop a number of generalizations about social control systems that explain and predict social control efforts in a wide variety of times and places.

Two basic assumptions guide this undertaking. The first is that it is possible to create general propositions that illuminate the most basic properties of social control systems out of the mass of diverse empirical detail. The second is that the relationships between people—whether they are intimates or strangers, allies or enemies, isolates or group members, dependents or dominates—underlie the variation in social control systems.

Both of these assumptions are controversial. The first involves abstracting social control efforts from the particular social and historical contexts in which they emerge. The contextual, richly textured nature of these efforts is inevitably lost. This book, then, will have more appeal to those who seek the general, abstract, and principled nature of social life than to those who look toward its specific, detailed, and contextual aspects. The second leads to a focus on the purely social features of human behavior. It considers society through the lens of social relationships rather than through the myriad of biological, psychological, political, or economic factors that also influence social control systems. The resulting generalizations will be more attractive to people who prefer a consistent and selective viewpoint than to ones who would use many variables from multiple approaches to explain as much variance in human behavior as possible. The emphasis on social relationships also extracts bivariate relationships from multivariate situations. Because my aim is to contribute toward a purely social theory, I feel that the benefits of a clear and consistent focus on the social underpinnings of social control outweigh the costs of oversimplifying a more complex reality.

The approach taken here is embedded in the pioneering work of Donald Black. Black's work (see especially 1976, 1989a) provides a model for how general characteristics of social structure can be used to predict and explain features of social control systems. I am grateful to Professor Black for his comments on the manuscript. Mary Pat Baumgartner and Mark Cooney also made numerous contributions to improving the manuscript. I am also indebted to all of the authors on whose work this book heavily relies. David Mechanic, the director of the Institute for Health, Health Care Policy, and Aging Research, as well as Diane Alington and Eileen Lanno at the Institute created an unsurpassed working environment for writing the manuscript. My wife, Colleen, and children, Becky, Jessica, and Stephanie, provided the diversion from academic concerns necessary to complete a book.

ALLAN V. HORWITZ

Contents

PART III. THE EFFECTIVENESS OF SOCIAL CONTROL

1

Introduction

At the heart of any social order are conceptions of right and wrong. People may sometimes sacrifice their lives, yet at other times remain quiescent or even blame themselves when they have suffered an injury. People might seek vengeance for an inequity or settle with those they see as responsible; internalize their hostility or mobilize courts of law; demand compensation or seek psychiatric help. Whatever the response, the definition and defense of the moral order is a fundamental aspect of all social organization. Social control is the aspect of society that protects the moral order of the group.

Studies of social control explain the variation in responses to violations of the normative order. Norms are the standards of right and wrong that prescribe and proscribe what conduct ought or ought not occur (Blake & Davis, 1964). Every social action, relationship, or arrangement is permeated by normative qualities that indicate moral conduct. What people consider to be right and wrong and how they act when their notions of justice are violated constitute the study of social control. Understanding these perceptions goes to the heart of the question, "What makes social order possible?" (Parsons, 1937).

The Evolution of Social Control

The study of social control has traditionally been a central aspect of the sociological enterprise. The classical view of social control emphasizes how law and other forms of state-centered social control emerged as the central guarantors of social order over the course of social evolution. Accounts as divergent as those found in Marx (1890), Weber (1925), Durkheim (1893), and Parsons (1966) view the rise of the state and the legal process as the key development in the evolution of social control. In these accounts social control was transformed from an undifferentiated group process to a specialized application of rules and sanctions by designated agents of the state.

In the classical view of social control, members of premodern societies apply generally shared norms to sanction offenders. These norms are learned through socialization, legitimated by deeply rooted religious authority, and enforced by informal sanctions such as scorn, ridicule, anger, and violence. Social control is rooted in status relationships between individuals so the critical determinant of the response to deviance is whether the victim is a spouse, uncle, clansman, age-mate, neighbor, or stranger (Maine, 1861).

In technologically simple societies, no state or specific agents of social control exists to stand above the particular interests of contesting parties. Male elders or heads of families, not organized and designated authoritative third-party agents, apply sanctions. The pursuit of justice rests on the actions of the particular people who believe they have been wronged. Yet, the pursuit of private justice poses a great threat to the order of small, homogeneous groups because it creates recurring cycles of violation and vengeance. The fundamental tension between the efforts of private parties to obtain justice and the public need for group harmony leads the community to bring strong normative pressure to bear on disputants to settle their disputes peaceably.

Social evolution produces increasing group size, growing division of labor, greater social heterogeneity, and more elaborate systems of social stratification. Societies become more complex and divide into many units performing specialized functions. The basis of social control shifts from status relationships ascribed at birth to contracts between individuals (Maine, 1861). The central problem in maintaining moral order changes from the control of private vengeance to the creation of moral systems that culturally, socially, and economically diverse groups can share.

In these classical accounts, the development of the legal order solves the problem of creating shared morality in modern societies. Law becomes the distinctive form of social control as the state emerges to seek revenge or recompense, public forums replace private settlements of disputes, and legitimate force moves from private to public hands.

In contrast to the particularistic character of informal norms, laws are *general* rules that apply to broadly defined classes of individuals without personal or class favoritism (Berman, 1983; Unger, 1976). All citizens are, in theory, formally equal under the law. Law is also *autonomous* from other social institutions. Legal norms and legal culture maintain their own logic distinct from economic, political, religious, or scientific norms and interests. Finally, laws are *centralized* instead of diffused throughout the whole society. A distinct legal profession trained in legal culture administers the law, applies legal reasoning, and staffs legal institutions, whereas a public police force is given the sole authority to use legitimate force (Weber, 1925).

These characteristics render law uniquely suited to solve the problem of maintaining a shared moral order in complex societies. Because law is general it does not reflect the particular interests of competing groups and individuals so provides legitimacy to the decisions of legal officials. The autonomy of law further insures that contesting parties will respect the authority of legal decision makers. The concentration of legitimate force in the hands of specially trained officials insures that private groups cannot impose their own interests on less powerful parties. Social order is possible because citizens maintain allegiance to an autonomous legal order that stands above contesting private interests.

Schools of thought such as functionalism and Marxism that are otherwise widely divergent accept the movement from particularistic, indistinct, and diffuse norms to general, autonomous, and centralized legal institutions. Parsons (1966), for example, emphasizes how growing social differentiation creates the need for an overarching symbolic system that can integrate political, economic, and social institutions. An autonomous legal order is ideally suited to legitimate the practices of authorities who guide these bodies.

Marxists and conflict theorists, as well, emphasize the compelling power of law in capitalist societies (e.g., Beirne & Quinney, 1982). In Diamond's (1971, p. 320) view: "We live in a law-ridden society; law has cannibalized the institutions which it presumably reinforces or with which it interacts." Societies relying on the private ownership of the means of production inevitably generate class conflict that is incapable of resolution in the absence of state agencies of social control. Widely shared beliefs in general rules applied equally to all and autonomous legal institutions that do not favor particular groups allow ruling elites to justify their self-interest through claims of universal morality. For Marxists, definitions of moral wrongs reflect the sorts of behaviors that threaten the exploiting class but are justified through appeals to the general good.[1]

[1]According to the Marxist view, the need to uphold the rule of law can at times work against elite interests in the short run (Balbus, 1973). Sometimes elite members must be punished to maintain the legitimacy of the system, criminals set free to uphold general rules, or laws passed that work against the interest of elites in order to forestall more fundamental change. The problem in such explanations is the difficulty of falsifying them.

The focus on law and other formal institutions of social control leads most empirical studies of social control to focus on state institutions. A dominant theme of historical work has been to trace how formal institutions of social control such as the police (Lane, 1967; Monkkonen, 1981); juvenile courts (Platt, 1969); mental hospitals (Foucault, 1965; Grob, 1973, 1983), or reformatories (Rafter, 1984) developed over the course of the eighteenth and nineteenth centuries to replace family and community-based forms of care or neglect. The focus of work on contemporary social control systems also has been to scrutinize the social control processes of formal institutions such as police arrest practices, the sentencing patterns of courts, or psychiatric therapy. The central dynamics of social control in modern societies are presumed to lie in those agencies of social control that are staffed by specially trained professionals. Contemporary trends toward providing more services and care to deviants indicate the expansion of state control over wayward behavior (Cohen, 1985). As the number of social workers, psychologists, probation officers, alcohol counselors, mental health workers, and the like expands, growing numbers of deviants are captured in the net of formal agencies of social control. State bureaucracies and professional services are thought to have replaced families, neighbors, friends, and other community members as the primary caretakers of deviants (Donzelet, 1979; Lasch, 1977).

A further tendency in studies of social control has been to emphasize repressive forms of social control. All responses to deviance represent the imposition of one set of standards either in the interest of the general good or in the self-interest of particular groups. The criminal law, in particular, is seen as of preeminent importance in enforcing social order (Sparks, 1980). The wide variety of responses to normative violations such as self-help, avoidance, negotiation, or compensation are relegated to a secondary position or ignored completely.

Studies concerned with the question of why people obey social norms also assume that official sanctions are the major generators of conformity. Potential or actual deviants are seen as primarily responsive to sanctions of legal bodies or to the therapeutic efforts of professionals. Studies of criminal sanctions examine how raising the certainty and severity of legal punishments influences rates of offending behavior (e.g., Ehrlich, 1973). The binding power of sanctions is assumed to arise from state authority. Correspondingly, research about the effectiveness of psychotherapy concentrates on formal therapeutic efforts, rather than the help informal caretakers provide (e.g., Smith, Glass, & Miller, 1980). The possible influence of informal groups in maintaining conformity is largely neglected.

Whether the movement in social evolution is viewed as from

gemeinshaft to gesellschaft (Tonnies, 1887), status to contract (Maine, 1861), mechanical to organic (Durkheim, 1893), undifferentiated to differentiated (Parsons, 1966), or feudal to capitalist to socialist (Marx, 1890), the central dynamic of social control is seen as the transformation from diffuse mechanisms of informal social control to the dominance of law and other formal institutions of control. Although they have produced many penetrating analysis of how these formal institutions and professions develop and operate, these studies have tended to ignore the continuing power of informal social control in modern life.

THE APPROACH OF THIS WORK

Because of the law-centered focus in the study of social control, the role of informal norms and practices in upholding the moral order of modern societies has been neglected. My assumption is that the logic of social control is based on informal norms that govern interpersonal relationships. Social control emerges out of and serves to maintain the ways of life and social practices of groups. It varies from society to society and place to place according to the dominant modes of social relations. Various forms of social control are embedded in concrete social relationships (Gluckman, 1967). Regardless of time or place, when the social location and direction of social control efforts are the same, similar types of social control should result. For example, most cases of social control in tribal societies involve closely related persons. In modern societies, strangers typically confront each other. The social control of strangers in tribal groups or of intimates in modern settings should resemble those efforts in the other setting. The evolutionary dynamic found in the movement of law may represent less an evolution of social control to more developed and impersonal forms than a change in the relational context of the disputes that control systems are called upon to handle (Falk-Moore, 1972).

Legal rules are only one of many sorts of guides people use in responding to normative violations. Informal norms based on common sense notions of morality, rather than legal rules, usually determine whether people define acts as morally wrong, how they respond to them, and if they mobilize formal control agencies. In practice, people are typically ignorant of the formal law and use practical senses of right and wrong to react to deviance (Ellickson, 1986). If they are aware of legal rules, people are often hesitant about using legal procedures against their adversaries. Even in the absence of any state institutions for enforcing law, people will often respect fundamental rules of morality (Reid, 1980).

The result is that the vast majority of disputes, conflicts, altercations, grievances, and crimes remain embedded in interpersonal networks and never enter the realm of formal institutions (Galanter, 1983).

The prevailing focus in the study of social control also overstates the role of criminal law and penal sanctions. Punishment-oriented responses are but one style of responding to norm violations. Often, an apology or payment will suffice to set matters straight between disputants. In other instances, two contesting parties may compromise their differences and jointly agree to a solution. Still other cases of deviance may be defined as sickness that is beyond the control of the individual. A prominent feature of social control is the variety of styles through which it can be exercised.

Another deficiency of state-centered approaches is their neglect of how the preferences of complainants drives the responses of official systems. Most formal systems of social control are reactive systems that depend upon citizens to observe and mobilize cases (Black, 1971). Although political authority establishes what actions are illegal, laws are dormant until victims demand justice. Likewise, psychiatrists do not seek out cases in the community but respond to individuals who use their own definitions of when they and their intimates need psychiatric help.

Even those cases that do enter formal systems of social control are often handled in ways that more closely correspond to the particularistic grounding of disputes in role relationships than to formal principles of legal reasoning. Official control agents closely attend to victim preferences and the relationships between contesting parties. Their decision-making practices in many ways more closely resemble everyday moral standards that are grounded in basic aspects of social relationships than universalistic legal rules (Black, 1989a; Sudnow, 1965). The result is that legal institutions such as criminal, family, or small claims courts often mediate the claims of contesting parties rather than apply sanctions to them (Falk-Moore, 1972). The imposition of general and autonomous legal rules is usually limited to cases that arise between unrelated individuals who have no social ties that could serve as the basis for alternative resolutions.

Even legal principles themselves are grounded in commonsense notions of right and wrong. Legal standards often serve to ratify and codify existing moral belief and customs (Bohannon, 1965). Fundamental terms of legal culture such as *reasonableness, recklessness,* or *intention* are incapable of interpretation apart from their grounding in everyday moralities. Analogously, basic terms such as *inappropriate, excessive,* or *voluntary* that define psychiatric categories must rely on concepts that are permeated by notions of ordinary behavior.

I also depart from traditional notions of the sources of the effectiveness of social control. People are responsive to control efforts that affect their reputations, disturb their interpersonal networks, or appeal to their senses of morality (Braithwaite, 1989). The success of social control efforts in modern societies stems less from the efforts of state authority than from the ability to mobilize and change relational networks. Only formal control efforts that coincide with or can change the norms and behaviors of informal networks should accomplish their objectives.

To emphasize the power of informal social control in modern life is not to deny the importance of state social control. The explicit or implicit threat of using law to settle disputes stands behind many informal settlements. Legal rules often provide the context for informal bargaining, even if cases never actually enter the legal system (Mnookin & Kornhauser, 1979). Therefore, the small proportion of conflicts that actually enter the legal system does not totally reflect the influence of law on dispute resolution.

Moreover, although law may not directly settle many cases in modern societies, it still has a large symbolic presence. Legal cases often set the boundaries of acceptable and unacceptable behavior and speak to issues of great social significance. In this way, they have a normative influence far beyond the number of cases that actually enter legal systems and reach formal resolutions.

Finally, law and other forms of official control are coming to penetrate more and more relational and institutional boundaries. Private forums such as families, schools, clubs, and businesses that were immune to law in the past are now subject to more legal control than ever before. This has resulted in the perception of a "litigation crisis" where people are becoming ever more likely to bring lawsuits to realize their goals (Lieberman, 1981). At the same time, legal resources and professional forms of help giving have become more accessible to growing numbers of people. Therefore, the symbolic and actual presence of law and other formal control in everyday life has greatly expanded in recent decades.

Nevertheless, the dominant focus on law and governmental social control systems and the peripheral place allocated to the extralegal handling of disputes in the study of social control is unjustified. Private forms of settlement still prevail in most disputing situations. Most conflicts are ignored or tolerated. Others result in negotiated settlements between the parties involved. Even the small proportion of cases that do enter formal systems are typically resolved through informal bargaining rather than imposed decisions. Those that do result in official resolutions are but a small proportion of initial grievances. Although formal systems of social control hold a critical place in modern life, they cannot be understood apart from informal norms and control systems that retain their importance in the contemporary world.

THE SCIENTIFIC STUDY OF SOCIAL CONTROL

The goal of this work is to contribute to a theory of social control that explains the conditions under which various types of social control systems emerge, the principles under which they operate, and the degree to which they are effective. It develops generalizations about the behavior of social control in social space by using evidence from sociological, anthropological, and historical studies.

The principle that social control can be studied in ways no different than other social phenomena guides this study. I use the theory of law and other social control developed by Donald Black (1976, 1984, 1989a) to order a wide variety of empirical material. Black's theory stems from a tradition in the natural sciences known as the "covering-law" or "hypothetical-deductive" view of theory (Black, 1979; Horwitz, 1982—83; Lenski, 1988). In this view, a theory is a restricted set of propositions that yields deductive implications that can be confirmed or refuted through empirical tests. Unlike most types of classical and contemporary sociological theories, this approach does not develop a comprehensive, discursive system of inquiry or an interpretative world view but rather a set of testable propositions.

The Concept of Social Control

The purpose of a theory is to order, predict, and explain variation. Ordering occurs through concepts that organize and categorize phenomena that are considered important for the purpose of the theory.[2] The first task in the study of social control is to define the appropriate field of study. A concept of social control must be broad enough to embrace the wide variety of styles and forms that respond to norm violations yet precise enough to create a manageable field of study.

The concept of "social control" has been used in many diverse ways.

[2]One issue that arises in the study of social control is how phenomena that are themselves normative can be studied through objective scientific methods. Social norms are not objectively given in nature but are social creations. Yet, whereas normative phenomena are the object of studies, these studies themselves need not be normative. The object of study must not be confused with the method of study. The study of normative phenomena, because of its subject matter, need not be less scientific than the study of any other social phenomenon.

For the early American sociologists, the meaning of social control was extremely broad. Initially, the concept of social control referred to the capacity of society to regulate itself according to values and principles of proper behavior (see Janowitz, 1975). For sociologists such as Ross (1901), Cooley (1909), and Thomas and Znaniecki (1918), the central problem of moral order was how to regulate the individualism that forces of industrialization, urbanization, and modernization had created. They studied all social forms that allow groups to achieve legitimate moral aims under the rubric of *social control*. For example, Ross' *Social Control* (1901) included chapters on public opinion, education, social suggestion, and ethics.

In many ways the broad conception of social control inverts the common contemporary usage of this concept. Social control now is often used to indicate a coercive process imposed upon individuals to enforce normative conformity (e.g., Murashin, 1976; Quinney, 1974).[3] In this view, social norms are never consensual but reflect the efforts of particular groups to impose their views of morality on other groups. Processes of social control are inevitably grounded in group conflict, manipulation, and coercion.

The perspective that regards social control as all influences that contribute to social order is too broad to serve as a useful basis of study. On the other hand, the equation of social control with coercive processes is too constrictive. Many responses to norm violations are neither coercive nor manipulative but are oriented toward reconciliation, therapy, or compensation.

I adopt a *normative conception* that defines social control as specific attempts to influence deviance and conformity (e.g., Clark & Gibbs, 1965; Parsons, 1951; Pitts, 1961). In this conception, social control is limited to purposive actions that define, respond to, and control deviant behavior. In contrast to the broad usage, the normative concept identifies social control with intentional efforts to respond to deviant behavior, not with all processes that contribute to social order. In contrast to the narrow usage, it encompasses all sorts of intentional responses to normative violations, rather than solely coercive ones.

The normative conception of social control does not require the existence of consensus regarding definitions of appropriate behavior. Depending on the situation, social norms are more or less deeply rooted and widely shared. Nor need social control involve coercion applied to

[3]Indeed, in historical studies, the "social control thesis" refers to studies that uncover the coercive and manipulative underpinnings of seemingly benign efforts of the helping professions (Murashin, 1976).

unwilling or unwitting groups. I make no assumptions about the extent to which the norms that social control defends are consensual or conflictual but regard this as an empirical question.

Central to the normative conception is deviant behavior—the phenomenon that elicits social control. Deviant behavior is any action that is regarded as undesirable from a normative standpoint (Black, 1984a). Judgment from a normative standpoint means that the behavior in question is evaluated on the basis of right and wrong conduct. Deviance is behavior that *ought not* occur. Social control is the resulting effort to respond to normative violations.

Social norms are often ambiguous. The extent to which actions are evaluated through normative criteria varies across societies, historical eras, groups, and individuals. Homosexuality, for example, may be regarded as a sign of immorality, a disease, or a freely chosen life-style. Severe mental illness may appear as an affliction of the gods, sickness, badness, or a sensible response to dire conditions. The analytic task is to explain how reactions vary in social space not to settle whether actions are or are not deviant. The key questions are why some conduct is considered to be deviant, why actions are judged as one sort of norm violation rather than another, and what difference these definitions make in the response to people who violate norms.

In this work, I treat the normative aspect of action as something to be explained rather than as a given quality of behavior (Black, 1984a). Acts are not inherently deviant, but their deviant quality arises from the social context of the action. Whether victims and offenders are combatants in wartime, participants in a street brawl, or spouses is an inherent aspect of how actions are evaluated.[4] Physical violence between playmates, for example, is typically judged to be an entirely different kind of action than physical violence between unrelated adults. The former is typically defined as inconsequential, whereas the latter may result in severe sanctions. The "deviantness" of conduct is not independent of

[4]The focus on explaining normative evaluations rather than using these evaluations to predict social reactions does not mean that what actors do has no significance apart from observers' evaluations. Indeed, some actions such as radar-detected violations of traffic speed limits occur independently of the social characteristics of the actor and the observer. The extent to which the conduct in question shapes social control independently of the evaluation process varies according to the nature of the behavior in question. When the conduct is distinct from social evaluation, it can be held constant or treated as an independent variable for purposes of explanation (Gottfredson & Hindelang, 1979). Because the purpose of this work is to explain the normative component of social life, I focus on evaluations as something to be explained rather than something that themselves predict social control practices.

the identity of the participants, but normative evaluations are largely shaped by the relational characteristics of victims and offenders.

Explanations of Social Control

Although concepts form the building blocks for theory, they only become useful if they can explain and predict empirical phenomena. Explanation occurs when variation in phenomena is deducible from the general propositions that comprise the theory. Likewise, prediction refers to the deduction of future observations of phenomena from the propositions of the theory. A good theory explains a broad range of behavior in a testable, parsimonious, and systematic fashion.

A theory may attempt a total explanation of a phenomenon or provide a more limited perspective. Here, I make no effort to provide a complete explanation of social control systems. My interest lies in how social control varies within the dimensions of *social* space. All social relationships have moral attributes that define the obligations parties hold to each other (Firth, 1963). These obligations vary according to the role relationships of the parties involved. Social control efforts occur in the context of the patterns of relationships that link people in specific times and places.

The social structural grounding of social control does not mean that motivations or other nonsocial factors are unimportant or unpredictive of control efforts. Rather, my goal is to produce a structural rather than a motivational explanation of social control. My explanations are couched in terms of the social relationships between people rather than their mental or physical states (Cooney, 1986). This approach does not contradict psychological, economic, or biological theories but strives to develop a purely social theory. This one-sided approach inevitably oversimplifies a far more complex reality but has the potential to clearly focus upon the social structural elements of social control and ultimately to construct a social theory of this phenomenon.

This work uses several aspects of social life to predict the nature and type of social control. The most central is the structural patterns of relationships between individuals. Various styles and forms of social control are embedded in concrete social relationships and correspond to the social contexts in which they operate (Gluckman, 1967). Different individuals are more or less close to one another as indicated by the strength of the bonds between them, their investment in the relationship, and their frequency of contact. Some relationships are uniplex ones where only a sole tie such as a work, neighborhood, or organizational bond links individuals. Others are multiplex bonds marked by many family, work, or leisure ties (Gluckman, 1967). Individuals themselves are more or less integrated or marginal to central social institutions. Socially integrated people are embedded in familial, economic, religious, and organizational institutions whereas marginal people lack these connections.

I frequently use the following terms to explain how social control varies in social space:

- *Relational distance:* the degree of intimacy between people as indicated by factors such as the number and type of interactions between them, the intensity and length of their relationship, and the nature of their ties. Distance ranges from the most intimate ties between family, kin, and close friends to ties among acquaintances and colleagues to transactions between strangers.
- *Uniplex relationships:* social relationships marked by a single limited type of exchange. These might include those between a customer and a merchant; a physician and a patient; or a teacher and a student.
- *Multiplex relationships:* social relationships that feature more than one type of exchange. Examples include community members who patronize each others' businesses, attend the same churches, and engage in common leisure activities; colleagues at the workplace who are also friends; or kin who jointly engage in productive, leisure, or religious activities.
- *Crosscutting ties:* people who have social relationships to both parties in a dispute. If A and B are disputants, and C is A's brother-in-law and B's employer, C would be a crosscutting tie between A and B.
- *Social network:* the pattern of structural ties of an individual or in a social field.
- *Social integration:* the presence of many ties to family, kin, work, educational, religious, and informal organizations.
- *Marginality:* the absence of ties to family, kin, work, educational, religious, and informal organizations.

Different groups feature different types of relational space. Some are marked by many crosscutting links between members whereas others are comprised of relatively isolated individuals; some have members who share similar social, cultural, ethnic, and economic characteristics, others are marked by heterogeneity of members' traits; in some entities most interactions occur between people who share many ties but in others, most relationships are transacted between otherwise unrelated individuals.

I primarily draw on a distinction between individualistic and holistic groups:

- *Individualistic groups:* groups that are organized around the principle that individuals are the key units of social structure and feature values promoting autonomy and self-realization.
- *Holistic groups:* groups that are organized around communal obligations that value group cohesion rather than individual independence.

Hierarchy is another dimension of social life that predicts social control. It refers to the relative possession of valued resources by individuals and groups. Individuals have higher or lower ranking positions that indicate their prestige and power within the hierarchical systems of the group. Societies are also more or less stratified depending on the relative distribution of resources between different social groups. The measurement of hierarchy depends on indigenous definitions of ranking so the sorts of resources that confer status differ across groups. Although wealth forms the most common basis of hierarchy, a wide variety of economic, physical, experiential, political, or organizational factors may also enhance power in dispute situations.

I use the following terms to refer to aspects of hierarchy:

- *Rank:* an individual's position in the prestige hierarchies of a group.
- *Dominant:* an individual with superior power in a relationship.
- *Dependent:* an individual with inferior power in a relationship.
- *Stratification:* the distribution of valued resources in a social group.

Organization is another social property that influences social control efforts. Organizations are supraindividual bodies with structural roles, divisions of labor, and corporate identities. Societies differ widely in the extent to which individuals or organizations form the basic units of social structure. Individuals, as well, vary in the extent of their participation in groups and the degree to which they act in organizational roles. I use the following definition in this work:

- *Organization:* the degree to which a collectivity possesses structured roles, common purpose, and a capacity for collective action.

Social control efforts are exerted in social space between persons who differ in characteristics such as ethnicity, social status, organizational memberships, gender, or age. Each social attribute varies according to its grounding in the major dimensions of social life. For example, age reflects a variety of social statuses such as social integration, status, and organization, as well as cultural assumptions regarding age itself. Youths, for example, are typically less integrated, powerful, and organized than members of other age groups. Youths who are tightly integrated into conventional roles in families and schools may be treated leniently by forces of social control whereas adolescents who live on the streets, challenge adult authority, move in groups, and disdain respectable aspirations and dress may be harshly sanctioned. The coexistence of age with other statuses accounts for the behavior of social control between age statuses.

Gender provides another example of how social characteristics are grounded in social relationships. On the one hand, gender *per se*—the process of constituting social judgments on perceived differences between the sexes—pervades the response to normative violations. On the other hand, men and women have different positions in the relational, hierarchical, and organizational structures of societies. The placement in these structures in addition to gender *per se* predicts the variation in social control. Hence, gender is not a unitary phenomenon but penetrates a number of different social statuses in complex ways.

The impact of any social characteristic varies not only by its grounding in social structure but also on the relational context of a conflict situation. For example, a black who victimizes a white may be treated differently than one who offends another black (e.g., LaFree, 1980; Radelet, 1981). Not the ethnicity of the offender in itself but the relationship between the victim and offender shapes the social control response.

The following concepts refer to the ways that social control differs according to the social relationship between the parties involved in the control effort:

- *Inward social control:* social control applied by a marginal person to an integrated person. It usually responds to *outward deviance* committed by integrated people against marginal ones.
- *Outward social control:* social control applied by an integrated person to a marginal person. It usually responds to *inward deviance* committed by marginal people against integrated ones.
- *Insider social control:* social control between integrated people.
- *Outsider social control:* social control between marginal people.
- *Downward social control:* social control that a dominant party applies to a dependent party. It usually responds to *upward deviance* committed by dependents against dominants.
- *Upward social control:* social control that a dependent party applies

to a dominant party. It usually responds to *downward deviance* committed by dominants against dependents.

The generalizations that I develop do not follow the pure scientific method. They do not precisely state how a change in one aspect of social space produces a defined change in some aspect of social control. Although the ideals of scientific theory represent useful goals, they are rarely achievable in the actual practice of social science. Rather, I more generally relate properties of social life to properties of social control systems. As such, this work is preliminary to more detailed specifications of how social control varies in social space.

SOURCES OF DATA

This work utilizes a broad range and scope of empirical material to develop empirical generalizations about the behavior of social control. These generalizations are not particular to specific historical periods but predict social control processes in many diverse settings. Although studies of the contemporary United States dominate, particularly in the sections about legal control, they are used to illustrate more general social processes. All generalizations are stated in a way that empirical tests can falsify.

One valuable source of data stems from detailed and intensive observational examinations of dispute processes that anthropologists have conducted. Anthropological accounts typically view social control as inseparable from the interpersonal networks within which disputes arise. Grievances, disputes, personality disorders, and misfortunes all are analyzed within the context of social relations. Anthropologists such as Evans-Pritchard (1940), Gluckman (1967), Colson (1974), and Koch (1974) have developed sophisticated theories of the social structural basis of social control that can be applied to modern as well as premodern societies. They focus on informal as well as formal processes in dispute negotiation, examine bargaining and compromise in addition to rules and obedience, and explore not only criminal matters but also a rich variety of normative violations. These works also correct the ethnocentric bias of much sociological work and form the basis for comparative generalizations.

Historians have also produced numerous empirical studies of control processes in many varied times and places. They have conducted many excellent studies of various legal and criminal justice agencies. In the United States and England, studies examine the police (e.g.

Monkkonen, 1981; Phillips, 1977), courts (Beattie, 1986), juries (Green, 1985) and mental institutions (Grob, 1973, 1983; Tomes, 1984). Along with anthropological work, historical research adds a comparative dimension that helps avoid ethnocentric biases.[5] Yet, because social control is practiced in myriad ways across times and places does not mean that it cannot also manifest regularities across social space.

Another major source for this work are the many studies produced by the law and society movement. This movement was inspired by legal realism, which arose in the early part of the twentieth century (e.g. Frank, 1930; Holmes, 1897; Pound, 1942). Legal realists claimed that legal rules are insufficient predictors of case outcomes. Adequate explanations of the actual workings of the legal system must include personality, social, economic, and political factors. The law and society movement was initially marked by a preoccupation with the operation of the criminal justice system and the criminal law in the contemporary United States (Skolnick, 1965). Subsequently, it has produced many rich empirical and cross-cultural studies of many types of law and nonlegal forms of social control, which form the basis for the generalizations I develop (e.g., Felstiner, 1974; Friedman, 1985; Galanter, 1974; Macaulay, 1966).

The primary theme in law and society studies that law is not simply a matter of rules but must be grounded in concrete social settings guides the present work as well. In *The Behavior of Law*, Black (1976), moving beyond the particular studies of the law and society movement, develops a systematic theory that shows how various dimensions of social life explain variation in law and other types of social control. In *Toward a General Theory of Social Control* (1984b), Black and others develop theories about a number of topics related to various aspects of social control. This book builds on these efforts of Black and his colleagues to encompass a variety of styles and forms of social control in a single systematic perspective.

OVERVIEW

This work focuses on three aspects of social control: style, form, and effectiveness. The style of social control refers to the type of response

[5]One limitation of historical studies stems from their reliance on written source material. This forces historical work to focus on those formal institutions that kept records and to neglect informal control processes that rarely leave recorded residues. Because successful efforts to avert disputes are less likely to be recorded than unsuccessful ones, the historical record may be inherently biased toward dissension and conflict rather than harmony and settlement.

normative violations elicit. Black (1976, pp. 4 - 6) has sketched four major styles of social control: penal, compensatory, conciliatory, and therapeutic. These styles differ in the ends they seek, the way they allocate responsibility for actions, the identities they provide deviants, and the focus of their sanctions. Deviance may be regarded as morally outrageous offenses that deserve to be punished; signs of illness beyond the control of individuals; delicts to be forgiven once an apology or payment is forthcoming; or matters to be settled between the parties involved. The key question explored here is the varying social conditions under which these different styles come into play. The following four chapters examine how the location of a dispute in social space is related to the resulting style of social control.

Chapters 5 through 8 consider the form of social control. Form refers to the mechanisms people use to respond to deviance. People with grievances have a range of options: to do nothing; use self-help to obtain redress; negotiate a solution with the offender; or seek adjudicated solutions. I consider the conditions under which people use these various forms of social control. When are people likely to avoid conflicts, resolve them themselves, or seek extralegal or legal third-party assistance? What are the circumstances that lead these various forms to be developed? What factors shape the responses of control agents to cases that enter their domains?

The third emphasis in this book is the effectiveness of social control. Effectiveness refers to the extent to which social control efforts achieve the goals of controllers. The same dimensions of social space that predict the styles and forms of social control also shape how effective control efforts will be. The structure of social life influences the ability of control agents to acquire cases, apply sanctions and rewards, or prevent deviance from arising at all.

In the concluding chapter, I examine some recent developments in social control. Societies marked by fragmented, atomized, and noncohesive relationships face fundamental dilemmas in exerting effective social control. I consider some basic changes in modern social structures and speculate on what their impact on social control systems will be.

This book builds upon and contributes toward the burgeoning study of one of the most exciting topics in social science: the study of social control. The normative aspect of social order is at the core of the sociological enterprise. Understanding the multifaceted ways in which societies define and respond to deviant conduct helps to show both how social order is possible and how new forms of social organization arise.

I

Styles of Social Control

A wide variety of actions can activate social control processes. These include slights to honor, challenges to authority, interpersonal conflicts, insults, violent actions, or property damage. When people feel they have suffered some wrong, they are likely to seek redress. What sort of response they make depends on how they characterize what kind of harm has occurred, who inflicted the injury, and who should be held responsible for damages.

Injuries that lead to social control are never perceived as unique or isolated occurrences. Rather, responders typify them as instances of general categories. These typifications render action intelligible by placing perceptions into common cultural frameworks (Lempert & Sanders, 1986; Schutz, 1967). They provide answers to questions such as: What sort of action has occurred? What type of deviant has caused the harm? Who is responsible for damages? What solution should be sought? In this section, I examine several of the most common frameworks that organize social control practices.

People characterize and respond to normative violations according to their definition of the sort of harm they have suffered. Depending upon how the harm is defined, control efforts may strive to have offenders render compensation, suffer punishment, seek treatment, or negotiate a settlement. In determining what type of harm has occurred, victims are concerned with several aspects of the injury. The first is the issue of responsibility for the wrong: What sort of liability exists for remedying damages? The second regards the identity of the offender: Who should be held responsible for the injury? The next is the goal of the control effort: What do victims seek when they try to redress injuries? The final question has to do with the nature of sanctions imposed: What sort of obligation does the offender have to the victim? I examine each of these aspects in turn.

Liability refers to the nature of offenders' responsibility for deviant actions. It extends along a continuum that focuses on motivations and capacities at one end to behavioral damage without reference to subjective intentions at the other. At one extreme, the objective consequences of behavior are of no concern, and the assessment of liability wholly depends on the subjective mental state of actors. In the purest case of subjective liability, evil thoughts are viewed as equally blameworthy as evil actions (e.g., Tentler, 1977). This is reflected in Jesus' statement that "Whosoever looketh on a woman to lust after her hath committed adultery with her already in his heart" (Matthew 5: 28). The allocation of subjective responsibility involves assessing motivations, intentions, and emotional states. Two questions, in particular, are at the core of appraising subjective liability: Did actors intend to cause harm, and did they have the capacity to avoid harm (Hart, 1968)? Intention refers to whether people meant to cause harm. Capacity indicates whether they were able to choose an alternative course of action.

At the opposite extreme, the intentions and capacities of actors are irrelevant, and the occurrence of harm itself is the only consideration in determining liability (Koch, 1984). Offenses of this sort make no reference to the mental state of offenders. The control system responds to the connection between the act and the harmful outcome that resulted from the act, regardless of the mental state that produced the harm (Hart, 1968, Chapter 9). Pure cases of subjective or objective liability are rare. Most social control efforts lie between these extremes and take into consideration both harmful consequences and the state of mind that produced the harm.

A second aspect in the typification of social control styles involves identifying the responsible party. This may be the particular person committing the act, another party who is responsible for the offender, or a group or organization. In some cases, offenders alone are responsible for making amends for harm. This is typically the case in Western legal systems. In other cases, liability is vicarious, and a collectivity is held responsible for the actions of its individual members. For example, in many tribal societies a homicide renders the clan of the offender responsible for the harm. The identity of the individual who caused the harm is irrelevant, and responsibility for redress falls to the group. Settlement occurs when the group gives up one of its members, who need not be the individual who caused the harm, to the group that has lost a member (Beattie, 1964). In contemporary societies, the actions of individuals who act in organizational roles may render the organization, rather than the individual, liable for damages. The identity of liable parties ranges from the individual offender to the collectivity responsible for the offender's conduct.

The goal of social control efforts is a third dimension of style. Controllers may have many ends in mind such as the punishment of offenders, redress for victims, reconciliation of offenders and victims, or the deterrence of future harmful acts. These goals do not vary along a single continuum. One important dimension, however, is the degree to which the control effort focuses on changing offenders alone or the damaged relationship between victims and offenders.

Controllers may concentrate on sanctioning offenders themselves, whether through punishment, treatment, or incapacitation. The emphasis is on the rule or behavioral standard that offenders have violated and their reasons for violating it. Most modern laws, for example, focus on rule violations themselves without reference to the relationship between offenders and their victims.

In many systems of social control, however, controllers emphasize the relationship that exists between grievants. The offense is considered in the context of the obligations that the parties owe each other. The goal is to repair the damage in the ruptured relationship. This repair may take many forms. In some cases it might mean reconciling offenders with their victims. In others, it may lead offenders to compensate victims for their injuries. Alternatively, control efforts strive to reintegrate offenders into the community. In each of these cases, the focus of the control effect is the relational ties of offenders to their victims or communities rather than on individual acts. A continuum runs from control efforts that try to protect impersonal rules and change particular offenders to those that aim to restore disturbed relationships and obligations.

A final dimension of social control systems lies in the nature of their sanctions. Sanctions vary from those controllers impose on offending parties to those voluntarily accepted by the relevant parties. Coercive styles of social control rest on force and apply sanctions regardless of the wishes of offenders. Persuasive styles of social control, in contrast, rely on voluntary compliance of the parties involved in the control effort. Controllers must persuade offenders to cooperate through appeals to self-interest or moral principles. Many control efforts are neither purely coercive nor purely persuasive but some combination of the two.

The assessment of liability, identification of the responsible party, goal of the control effort, and nature of the sanctions do not exhaust the possible dimensions of social control styles. Because each of these dimensions is a variable, their interrelationships create an abundance of

TABLE 1. Elements of Major Styles of Social Control

	Penal	Compensatory	Conciliatory	Therapeutic
Harm	Value	Material	Relational	Personality
Liability	Individual	Group	Shared	None
Goal	Retribution	Settlement	Reconciliation	Normality
Solution	Punishment	Payment	Negotiation	Treatment

potential social control styles. Although no control effort is likely to illustrate a perfect combination of all elements, these four dimensions tend to cohere in distinct clusters. Following Black (1976, pp. 4-5), I call these the penal, compensatory, conciliatory, and therapeutic styles.

Table 1 summarizes the major characteristics of the four styles of social control. It is adapted and modified from Black (1976, p. 5). This table represents the paradigmatic aspects of each dimension of the four styles. Penal styles involve the punishment of offenders; compensation involves the payment of a debt from offenders to their victims; conciliation features the negotiation of a joint solution to a grievance; and therapy provides treatment to individuals with personality problems.

In many cases, social control efforts contain aspects of various styles. For example, the involuntary commitment of the mentally ill intersects with penal and therapeutic styles; divorce mediation may involve both compensatory and conciliatory efforts; police intervention in family violence often mixes penal and conciliatory efforts; family therapy for mental illness has elements of both therapy and conciliation; or court judgments may mandate both punishment and compensation. Although there are many variants of these styles of social control, for ease of explanation I treat each independently. The following chapters elaborate the social conditions that predict when each style will respond to normative violations.

2

The Penal Style

INTRODUCTION

Elements of the Penal Style

Penal control is one paradigmatic style of social control. Indeed, this style is often equated with the notion of social control itself (Murashin, 1976). The central aspect of the penal style is to inflict pain or other unpleasant consequences on offenders who have committed blameworthy acts (Hart, 1968, Chapter 1). Penal control is a moralistic style that aims to punish offenders who have broken some legal or extralegal standard of behavior.[1]

Penal liability typically depends not only on outward nonconforming acts but also on certain states of mind. Violations that stem from intention and choice most commonly elicit penal control. Punishment is usually imposed only on offenders who intended to commit some wrongful action and who could have avoided committing that action (Lempert & Sanders, 1986). The importance of intention and capacity in allocating guilt is not unique to legal systems but pervades social interaction. In the famous phrase of Oliver Wendell Holmes (1881, p. 3), "Even a dog distinguishes between being stumbled over and being

[1]In contemporary social control systems, the penal style forms the basis of the criminal law and a large part of civil law as well as much social control that occurs within informal networks. Although criminal and civil law are typically seen as distinct systems (e.g., Durkheim, 1893), they share many common characteristics. Both examine the intentions of offenders, morally condemn offenses, and impose punishments on the guilty. Usually, however, civil courts are concerned with assessing damages and criminal courts with punishments. In addition, there are major procedural distinctions between them: In civil law citizens bring complaints and pursue cases, standards of evidence are lower, and sanctions are less severe (Blum-West & Carter, 1983).

kicked." The presence of these mental elements often overrides the extent of harm that actions have caused. A light slap struck in anger during a fight between playmates may be cause for retaliation and further pain whereas one, even if debilitating, that results from an accident or mistake is unlikely to lead to a penal response.

The emphasis on intention and choice leads the penal style to be more oriented to the actions of offenders than to the pain of victims. In modern legal systems, for example, victims and their families get no compensation for their injuries. The punishment of the offender rather than recompense for the victim is paramount. The concern with uncovering motivational factors in penal liability typically occurs at the expense of examining the consequences of actions to victims.

The importance of moral guilt also underlies the fundamental goal of penal systems: to extract retribution from offenders. Penal styles are moralistic systems of social control. Not only are offenders punished for doing something morally wrong, but the justification for punishment also lies in its moral correctness (Hart, 1968, Chapter 9). Offenders have deliberately violated a moral rule, so punishment ought to subject them to pain and suffering. The primary aim of penal systems is to uphold a moral code and exact retribution from offenders, although considerations such as deterrence, incapacitation, or rehabilitation may be coexisting goals (Durkheim, 1893).

Because penal sanctions aim to punish offenders, the penal style is inevitably coercive, rather than persuasive. Individuals rarely bring pain upon themselves willingly. Rather, coercive force must impose suffering upon offenders. Voluntariness and persuasiveness have little place in penal styles of control, which are grounded on the mandatory application of sanctions.

Nature of Harm

The sorts of violations that elicit penal responses vary widely in different groups: incest, witchcraft, or religious blasphemy in tribal societies, property offenses in capitalist societies, or capitalist tendencies in communist societies. What these otherwise widely divergent actions share is that they offend strong and enduring social sentiments (Durkheim, 1893). The violation of core values predicts the sorts of groups, situations, and social roles that are most likely to feature penal control.

All collectivities, whether families, businesses, communities, or states, have certain core values. These are the most deeply held and widely shared beliefs regarding right and wrong. They embody the most profound and important aspects of group life. Violations of community values activate penal styles of social control. Normative violations that strike at core values create demands for vengeance that are not satisfied until redressed through punishment. Whenever actions are directed against the central values of the collectivity, other styles of social control such as compensation, conciliation, or therapy will be seen as inadequate responses to moral outrage, and punishment-oriented social control should result.[2]

The extent to which core values penetrate social life varies widely. Violations against moral values that are seen as constitutive of group life itself are especially likely to elicit penal styles of control (Bergeson, 1984). Actions that violate collective norms elicit harsher sanctions than those that violate individual rights.

At one extreme, lie tribal societies where basic ties of loyalty lie to kin and clan groups rather than to the tribe itself. When no institutional authority is responsible for upholding collective order, harms are only considered wrongs against aggrieved individuals and their kin, not against the community. In such settings, few actions are defined as crimes against the whole collectivity, as opposed to harms against particular units. In most tribal societies, only a handful of offenses, usually including incest, sorcery, witchcraft, religious blasphemy, the violation of taboos, and repeated recidivism are felt to endanger the welfare of the entire community (Beattie, 1964). Offenses such as murder, rape, or theft are considered to harm only particular victims and their kin groups. Because such actions do not offend core group values, they typically evoke compensatory or conciliatory settlements.

At the other extreme lie groups organized on a holistic basis where each individual is strongly tied to the group. Deviance in such settings

[2]In certain respects, this section evokes Durkheim's (1893) association of repressive law with mechanical solidarity and restitutive law with organic solidarity. In societies bound by mechanical solidarity, the conditions of life are alike for all members who consequently develop a strong and consensual group morality that can only be avenged through punishment. In societies based on organic solidarity, a high division of labor leads to a differential distribution of moral sentiments and to restitutive systems of justice. Empirical research has not supported Durkheim's association of tribal societies with repressive control and more developed societies with restitutive control (Schwartz & Miller, 1964; Spitzer, 1975; Wimberly, 1973). However, when Durkheim's thesis is viewed as having a structural, rather than an evolutionary, basis, it may have greater validity (cf. Turkel, 1979). Societies with strong core values, rather than tribal societies, develop repressive styles of punishment whereas those lacking deep and consensual collective sentiments feature restitutive styles. Durkheim properly associated collective offenses and penal responses but incorrectly believed that tribal societies featured many collective offenses.

elicits feelings of indignation, harm, and the desire for revenge. Societies marked by strong and unified central authorities feature more penal control than more pluralistic societies (Bergeson, 1984; Grabowsky, 1984; Spitzer, 1975). Hence, highly authoritarian families, relative to more democratic ones, react with more intensity against normative violations (Swanson, 1971). Totalitarian states feature the greatest extent of penal control (Gross, 1984). When the collective conscience penetrates deeply into everyday affairs, what seem to be trivial delicts may be viewed as offenses against the collectivity itself that are subject to harsh punishment. In totalitarian states, the smallest delict such as improper forms of greeting, inadequate attention at one's job, the theft of tools from a factory, or insufficient enthusiasm for the leader can bring harsh penal responses because they threaten the control of centralized authorities that permeates group life (Bergeson, 1984; Salas, 1979).

Not only certain group structures but also certain situations lead to a heightened sense of threat to group life. When the very basis of a social unit is threatened, the degree of penal control expands. Small groups that face a threat to their corporate structure react to deviants with more punishment-oriented responses than others (Lauderdale, 1976). Within families, the occurrence of adultery, which strikes at the basis of the family unit, is most likely to lead to the use of force between spouses (Greenblat, 1983). In situations such as wars, revolutions, or natural disasters when the basic existence of a group is in jeopardy, actions that previously met with mild disapproval become subject to harsh penal control (Black, 1976, pp. 86-92).

All groups also react to challenges to collective authority through punishment-oriented responses. In the development of legal systems in Western Europe, offenses against the prerogatives of authority such as counterfeiting, smuggling, or speaking out against the government typically evoked harsh punishments (Ruggiero, 1980 pp. 132-33; Spierenburg, 1984). The paradigmatic offense against sovereign authority is treason. The core of treasonous acts is that they betray the sovereign power of the collectivity, whether of a king, lord, master, or nation (Hanawalt, 1979). An offense against legitimate authority can only be met through punishment rather than some weaker response. Hence, all nations punish, rather than use alternative styles against, offenders who commit treason, sedition, or espionage.

Likewise, offenders who victimize individuals whose roles embody collective authority evoke harsh punishment. Deviance against representatives of the collectivity such as theft of a ruler's property, the assassination of a leader, or the killing of a policeman or a judge are always treated with extreme severity.[3] For example, in the eighteenth century, people who attempted regicide were subject to the worst possible punishments: ". . . tortured for days—and for long after death transpired—first with horses to draw and quarter his body, then by hacking off the remaining limbs, then by piercing the corpse with heated metals, and so on" (Katz, 1988, p. 35). In the contemporary United States, the planned killing of a policeman is considered to be the most severe type of crime often leading to sentences of death or life imprisonment (Cooney, 1988; Rossi, Waite, Bose & Berk, 1974). Likewise, attacks against teachers or principals in schools will generate more intense outrage than those against students.

The same considerations indicate why the disrespectful demeanor of suspects is an important predictor of coercive police responses, apart from any possible crime the suspect may have committed (Black & Reiss, 1970; Piliavin & Briar, 1964). Disrespect to police is a form of petty treason that nearly inevitably leads to arrests. Similarly, there is greater tolerance for the use of parental force against children who question the authority of parents than for the social control of other kinds of violations children commit (Ruane, 1986). In medieval England, the defense of family sovereignty reached the extreme that women who killed their husbands were viewed as having committed an act of treason that evoked an aggravated form of capital punishment (Hanawalt, 1979, p. 44). Similarly, slaves who revolt against their masters face extremely harsh penalties, often death (Friedman, 1985, p. 220; Patterson, 1982).

Disrespect toward representatives of the collectivity indicate profound assaults on the basis of sovereignty. Nonpenal responses are not sufficient to remedy the harm the group has suffered. In all forms of social space, whether families (Ruane, 1986), classrooms (McCarthy & Hoge, 1987), work organizations (Grabowsky, 1984), or nation-states (Bergeson, 1984), assaults against authority evoke penal responses.

Penal control flourishes against actions that threaten core values,

[3]The counterpart to the punishment-oriented reaction to offenses perpetuated against corporate officials is the lenient reaction to offenses committed by government officials in their corporate roles (Cooney, 1988, Chapter 5). For example, in England, beginning in the thirteenth century, church officers who committed murders were immune from receiving the death penalty under a doctrine called benefit of clergy. This doctrine expanded greatly over the centuries to cover many more types of persons and crimes (see Beattie, 1986). In early modern legal systems, police had explicit guarantees that they would go free if they killed someone who attacked them (Spierenburg, 1984, p. 128). In this country, killings by police officers are treated with extreme leniency in contrast to the killing of a police officer (Cooney, 1988). For example, one study indicates that only three of 1,500 such incidents resulted in criminal punishment (Kobler, 1975, p. 164).

sovereign authority, or the basis of the group itself. In such situations, moralistic responses to deviance are necessary to uphold the moral order. Whatever the social group, whether a family or a business, a street gang or a church, the logic of group life demands that offenders who assault the constitutive aspects of group life receive penal responses.

PREDICTORS OF THE PENAL STYLE

What conditions predict that punishment rather than redress for victims, restoration of social harmony, or the treatment of sick offenders is the goal of social control efforts? The relational distance between disputants, the distance between each disputant and social control agents, and the nature of ties in the social group shape the likelihood of penal responses.

Relational Distance

The penal style is the most moralistic style of social control. It is invoked after a challenge to moral values. Morality, however, is not constant but varies in intensity according to the social relationships between the parties involved in the conflict. The relational distance between victims and offenders predicts the use of penal styles of social control.

The closer the relational distance between contesting parties, as indicated by factors such as intimacy, common social and cultural characteristics, shared interests, and common linkages to third parties, the less the likelihood of a penal response to grievances (Black, 1976, p. 47; Cooney, 1988, p. 62): *Penal control is directly related to the relational distance between offenders and victims.* Conflicts that arise between intimates or persons with overlapping group memberships rarely feature penal control. Harm that occurs among intimates is considered to be less deserving of punishment than that arising between parties at a greater distance. The logic of social control dictates that nonpenal responses are preferable ways to handle disputes among intimates. In contrast, the penal style flourishes in conflicts between persons at a great relational distance.

Violence that occurs within families is less likely to result in penal sanctioning than that among strangers. For example, in the Micronesian Island of Yap, if a man kills one of his brothers, a surviving brother cannot punish the offender because it would compound the evil (Schneider, 1957, p. 794). Likewise, men who abuse their wives, girlfriends, or children are less likely to be punished than those who attack strangers, although they may enter therapy or reconcile with their victims. In many preindustrial societies, husbands have almost complete license to beat or rape their wives without fear of punishment from outside bodies (e.g., Chagnon, 1977). In modern societies, police and other responders are still likely to attempt to reconcile intimates involved in violence but arrest strangers who engage in physical violence (Black, 1980; Smith, 1987). Correspondingly, parents who harm their own children are unlikely to face criminal sanctions. Even in extreme cases such as infanticide, therapeutic rather than penal responses are often forthcoming (e.g., Brumberg, 1984; Donovan, 1981; Showalter, 1985). Indeed, the criminal law rarely intrudes into domestic settings for any sort of violation.

Grievances between members of the same community are also likely to be handled in a relatively nonmoralistic manner. Disputes among insiders are managed through conciliatory responses that aim to dampen confrontation and deescalate conflict (Todd, 1978; Yngvesson, 1978). When challenges to honor would otherwise demand a retaliatory response, overlapping memberships between disputants can inhibit resort to violence (Evans-Pritchard, 1940).

As social distance increases between disputants, the chance of penal control grows. When marginals have disputes with insiders or vice versa, conflicts rarely result in harmonious resolution but enter coercive systems of adjudication. For example, newcomers to communities are more likely to initiate lawsuits in situations that established community residents would negotiate (Todd, 1978; see also Engel, 1984; Greenhouse, 1986). Marginals do not have access to mechanisms of social control that could lead to compromise solutions so become more likely to use punishment oriented alternatives. One result of this is that murder rates in the modern world are by far the highest among marginal victims and offenders who lack alternative means of dispute resolution for interpersonal conflicts (Black, 1983; Lundsgaarde, 1977; Sampson, 1986).

Disputants who do not share kin, marital, nor residential ties have neither the interest in nor the means to make conciliatory settlements. Crosscutting ties and potential meditating agents are lacking when conflicts arise. Quarrels have the potential to create partisan and mutually hostile factions that try to extract retribution for grievances (Evans-Pritchard, 1940). Therefore, disputes between members of different social groups are especially likely to lead to coercive retaliation. For example, the use of revenge as a response to homicide in tribal groups increases dramatically with growing distance between killers and their victims but is very rarely used as a response to murder among intimates (Cooney, 1988, Chapter 2).

Distance of Social Control Agents from Disputants

Not only the distance between offenders and victims but also the social distance between control agents and each party predicts the use of penal styles. Offenses that intimates commit do not engender the same degree of moral outrage in social control agents as those of more distant parties. Morality intensifies as the distance of the control agent from the offender grows. The degree of moral outrage is also high when control agents and victims are intimates but declines with growing distance between the control agent and the victim. Therefore, the likelihood of penal responses varies directly with the relational distance between control agents and each disputant.

Offenders

The social distance between offenders and social control agents is related to the use of penal styles: *Penal social control is directly related to the relational distance between offenders and social control agents.* Morality is most intense when persons at great social distance to responders commit offenses but diminishes as the distance between offenders and control agents declines.

Penal styles of social control flourish against offenders at great social distance from control agents. In most traditional settings, offenses of strangers are held more worthy of punishment than delicts of ingroup members. In medieval cities, for instance, courts would strive to reconcile offenders and victims who were citizens of the same city but harshly punish foreigners who committed the same offense (Blanshed, 1982). Certain people, such as prostitutes, sodomites, heretics, or ruffians were so distant from the conventional social system that they could not possibly enter remedial control systems, and their delicts could only be handled through punishment. Likewise, members of an Atlantic fishing village respond to the lies, trespasses, or thefts of outsiders through removal from the community or punishment (Yngvesson, 1978). When integrated residents of the community commit the same offenses, the typical response is to either deny a problem exists or to engage in settlement-oriented behavior.

When legal systems were developed in early modern Europe, repressive control was reserved for individuals such as vagrants, slaves, migrants, or gypsies who were not integrated into the conventional social order (Spierenburg, 1984). Early nation states found it difficult to establish systems of penal control because local officials would not arrest their friends and acquaintances, and juries composed of community members would not convict their neighbors (e.g. Green, 1988; Wrightson, 1980). The establishment of punishment oriented legal systems had to await the development of greater social distance between police, magistrates, and juries, on the one hand, and offenders, on the other hand.

In modern societies as well, the most marginal members of communities such as vagrants, migrants, and the homeless are most likely of all to receive punishment-oriented responses (Black, 1976). Within work organizations, deviants who are marginal members are more vulnerable to penal responses, whereas more integrated members who commit the same actions are less likely to be punished (Grabowsky, 1984). Even within families, step-children, who are more distant than natural children from the parent who applies the punishment, are more likely to suffer violent forms of punishment than natural children (Grabowsky, 1984, p. 175).

Whenever control agents and those they are supposed to regulate share common ties, the basis for penal control is undermined, and adversarial relationships are difficult to maintain. The leaders of modern nation-states recognize this principle when they call upon ethnically distant troops to quell disturbances among their population, fearing that soldiers who share linguistic, cultural, and social bonds with demonstrators will not be willing to use sufficient force. Or, the personnel of regulatory agencies in the United States commonly resign their positions to take jobs in the firms they once regulated. The result may be trading of inside information between control agents and their former colleagues rather than the application of universalistic rules (e.g., Braithwaite, 1989, Chapter 9).

Whatever the situation, the actions of persons at a great relational distance from controllers are more likely to be defined as morally wrong and dealt with through penal sanctions. Conversely, intimacy between controllers and deviants diminishes the moral intensity that underlies punishment.

Victims

The social distance between victims and social control agents is also related to the use of penal styles: *Penal control is inversely related to the relational distance between victims and social control agents.* Morality is greatest when persons at a close social distance to responders have been victimized but declines with growing distance between victims and control agents.

Hold constant the identity of offenders and the chance of a penal response grows with declining distance between social control agents and victims. People are most likely to pursue vengeance when their intimates have been victimized. Parents are most likely to seek punishment if their own children have been harmed; community residents to demand arrests when insiders rather than outsiders are victimized; ethnics to retaliate when one of their kind has been injured.

In preindustrial societies, only victims who were members of the ingroup were protected by group sanctions whereas outsiders who were victimized could not expect any sort of redress (Furer-Haimendorf, 1967, p. 212). Within legal systems as well, the victimizations of insiders bring more vigorous responses compared to those of outsiders that are pursued less intensely. Hence, when whites dominate legal systems of social control, injuries to whites are most likely to generate arrests, prosecution, and vigorous punishment (e.g., LaFree, 1980; Radelet, 1981). Conversely, victims at a great distance from control agents, such as prostitutes, drug addicts, alcoholics, or the homeless, are least likely to see their offenders punished (e.g. Stanko, 1981-1982).

Morality, and the resulting penal response, varies within the social space between victim and control agent. Penal control flourishes when victims are close but offenders distant from control agents. It diminishes when control agents are distant from victims but intimate with offenders.

Group Ties

The logic of imposing penal styles of social control in relationships also indicates the sorts of groups in which this style will flourish and those in which it atrophies. Social control is not imposed between isolated individuals. Rather, disputants live in a field of social ties to allies, enemies, and bystanders (Rieder, 1984). It is not simply the distance between disputants and control agents but also the nature of the connections between the social networks of disputants that predicts the style of social control. The social fields most conducive to penal action are ones where few cross-linkages between contesting parties exist that can damper a moralistic response: *Penal control is inversely related to the presence of crosslinkages between groups.*

The moral intensity that penal responses involve lead to the disruption of established relationships and to retaliation. Disputants must calculate the cost that different social control responses will have not only with the other party but also within networks of social relationships. When disputes arise in social fields marked by crosscutting kin, economic, or political ties, not only are disputants likely to share mutual ties, but these ties are themselves likely to share links. The relatives, friends, or workmates of one party to a dispute are likely to know the relatives, friends, or workmates of the other disputant.

Crosscutting ties decrease the likelihood of penal social control because many persons find it in their interest to mediate peaceful settlements rather than be drawn into vengeful feuds (Evans-Pritchard, 1940). Third parties with links to both disputants want to settle conflicts without alienating either party. The presence of cross-linkages in the networks of disputants dampens moral outrage and increases the likelihood that the social networks of each disputant will intervene to prevent a coercive response. Settings that feature crosscutting loyalties will tend to push people away from using penal responses and toward efforts aimed at restoring peaceable relationships (Colson, 1953).

In contrast, punishment-oriented responses are most likely to occur when few bonds exist between group members. When disputes arise between loosely tied individuals, neither party is part of a network with an interest in harmoniously resolving the dispute. In the absence of pressures toward settlement, grievances are more likely to escalate into violent confrontations.

This process is illustrated by the response to harm among the Jalemo tribe of Western New Guinea and the Bedouins in Cyrenaica (Libya). Jalemo norms demand that kinsmen of parties who have been injured or killed seek vengeance from the group of the offender (Koch, 1974). No official third- party authorities are present who might resolve disputes more amicably. Intervention oriented toward resolving disputes through conciliatory or compensatory mechanisms is effective to the extent that the relatives of disputants live in the same area and themselves have common interests. When the kin of the parties in conflict share ties, they work to prevent coercive retaliation and to arrange a conciliatory settlement. Otherwise, the dispute may escalate into warfare between the contesting groups.

Among the Bedouins, as well, the presence of crosscutting ties dampens punishment-oriented retaliation (Peters, 1967). In this group, the response to a homicide varies directly with the number of ties shared by the groups of the killer and victim. When killings occur across segments of different groups who share intense relationships compensation or, in rare instances, the killing of a comparable group member settled the issue. However, killings between more distant groups did not initiate settlement behavior but led to continuing feud and warfare. Growing distance between groups enhances the chance of penal styles of retaliation.

One of the most elaborate systems of cross-linking ties is found among the Plateau Tonga of East Africa (Colson, 1953). The Tonga feature immensely complex networks of alliances and mutually dependent networks. Each member of a residential area is likely to share affinal, economic, or political ties with the others. When parties come in conflict with each other, they are likely to share a number of mutual allies. Because of this, the group is unlikely to be able to impose punishment on one party to the conflict. In general, tribes where members of different clans live in the same areas will have difficulty mobilizing groups of allies to punish their neighbors because of the multitude of crosscutting ties within them.

Because tribal groups do not hesitate to use penal styles in disputes with different tribes, the lack of penal control within tribal groups does not stem from personality or socialization factors. Indeed, the presence of crosscutting ties within tribal societies can lead to less internal violence but to more violence directed at members of different tribes (Ross, 1985).[4] If tribal groups do not have crosscutting ties, they are likely to feature much penal control (e.g., Otterbein & Otterbein, 1965). The likelihood of penal control is structurally based in the nature of group ties.

Other social settings that feature elaborate systems of cross-linked ties also inhibit penal control. In feudal Europe, for example, the duty on a murdered man's relatives to take vengeance extended outward to relations seven or eight degrees removed (Bloch, 1961). Therefore, many neighborhoods contained relatives of both murderer and victim. The result was that the immediate kin groups of victims and offenders had many cross-pressures that induced them to reach concilatory or compensatory settlements rather than to make punishment oriented responses. In the modern world, close-knit communities that feature strong ties between members are also more likely to respond to disputes between community members through efforts at conciliation rather than coercive retaliation (Gulliver, 1979).

The conditions conducive to the penal style arise when individuals are freed from enmeshment in cross-linking group ties and continuing relationships. Social life becomes more and more constituted by transactions at high relational distances. Factors such as a growing division of labor, heterogeneity of interests, and geographic mobility lessen dependency on the group and strengthen the position of the individual. The basic unit of society changes from the kin group to the individual (Maine, 1861). At the same time as conciliatory styles become less fea-

[4]In the modern world when there is a virtual absence of crosslinking ties between different groups that inhabit the same territory such as Protestants and Catholics in Northern Island, Sikhs and Hindus in India, Tamils and Ceylonese in Sri Lanka, or Israelis and Palestinians on the West Bank, cycles of retaliatory penal control are still common.

sible, the consequences of penal styles become less disruptive to the group because punishment influences only isolated individuals, not entire groups of kin. Other things equal, social settings marked by weak and noncontinuing ties should feature styles of social control that focus on the accountability of individuals with the aim of punishing offenders (Yngvesson, 1978).

Moral systems emphasizing the moral responsibility of offenders began to emerge in the West in the late eleventh through the early thirteenth centuries (Berman, 1983; Spierenburg, 1984). By the sixteenth century, punishment enforced by central authorities had largely replaced self help carried out by kin and clan groups. Offenses that had been harms to be redressed or restored by private groups became crimes punishable by the collectivity (Beattie, 1986). The number of violations considered as public, rather than private, increased, and sanctioning systems geared at punishment and not redress became dominate.

Correlatively, the notion of individual rather than group responsibility developed. Motives and intentions became of paramount importance in assessing liability. Responsibility for action shifted to the individual, and punishment became a primary means of guaranteeing order. Elaborate systems for determining the responsibility of the individual developed.

These changes toward a penal style of response occurred as individualism became the principle of citizenship in the modern state. Penal forms of repression were especially common in cities, where individualism was most prevalent (Spierenburg, 1984). Growing individualism leads to two contrasting trends. On the one hand, the state in individualistic societies lacks means other than repressive law to maintain order (Turkel, 1979). Growing numbers of violations occur between strangers who lack alternatives to coercion in settling their disputes. Relational distance grows, and the presence of cross-linkages in the disputing field declines. The weakness of kin and local communal groups render conciliatory strategies unfeasible. The penal style is the only suitable strategy for maintaining social order in the absence of strong group ties.

On the other hand, the growing heterogeneity of individualistic societies undercuts the sense of shared morality that provide the foundation for penal control. Common bonds of family, clan, ethnicity, religion, or neighborhood dissolve. Few crimes provoke moral outrage and the desire for collective vengeance. To this extent, individualistic societies lack the shared morality and capacity for moral outrage that underlie penal control. The same conditions that promote the need for penal strategies undermine their effectiveness. When social organization is loose and marked by frequently shifting ties, avoidance and inaction become major alternatives to the penal style (Baumgartner, 1988; Felstiner, 1974). The result may be a continuous crisis in the normative order of modern, individualistic societies that have the need for penal control yet lack the moral authority to impose it.

The relationship between the penal style and the linkages between disputants and others in the social field indicates the importance of viewing social control efforts within their structural contexts. Disputes among intimates rarely result in coercive retaliation, especially when the networks of each disputant are tied to one another. On the other extreme, when disputes emerge at a great relational distance, no constraints to the use of penal force are present, and violent retaliation is common. The nature of bonds both among disputants and between disputants and others determines the style of control that responds to the troubled situation. The presence or absence of social restraints on the use of coercive force is one important predictor of the penal style of social control.

Hierarchy

The degree of inequality in relationships and groups, as well as the extent of relational ties, is related to the imposition of penal control. Inequality refers to the unequal distribution of valued resources between persons that leads one party to dominate the other.

Dominant parties are better able to exert penal control than dependent ones. At the most general level: *Penal control varies directly with inequality.* Penal control should be maximal in a downward direction—when superiors exercise control over dependents (Black, 1976). More powerful parties in an unequal relationship should be better able to exert penal control over dominated ones. By definition, people who dominate have greater potential than those who are dominated to impose their wishes on others and, thus, to exercise penal control. However, upward social control exercised by inferior parties toward dominant ones also often has a penal character (Baumgartner, 1984). Not just domination but also inequality breeds penal styles of social control.

However, the relationship between inequality and penal control is conditioned by several factors. First, individuals with total power over others will have little actual need to impose penal control. The more economic, prestige, and authority resources people possess, the more force they can potentially use but the less they actually need to use (Goode, 1971). Indeed, where power is absolute, overt social control may be minimal. The actual use of penal control may indicate not the presence of inequality but the failure of the powerful to maintain stable systems of dominance.

In addition to the difference between the potential and the actual use of the penal style, unequal relationships vary by the nature of the dependency. When powerful people share a number of ties with their dependents, they should be more reluctant to exert penal styles than when they have weak ties with them. Domination brings not only power over but also responsibility for dependents. Conversely, weaker parties are not only subjects but also are entitled to certain rights. For example, in feudal societies in medieval Europe the "lord was to protect, assist, and support the vassal, while the vassal was to manage the fief. If the lord violated the faith of the vassal, the vassal was entitled to renounce the lord." (Berman, 1983, pp. 532-3). Penal styles should be maximal when unequal relationships are coupled with weak ties between dependents and subordinates but decline as the number of shared ties grows.

Downward Control

Penal control is often associated with downward social control—the social control exerted by superiors over their subordinates. If superiors must sanction subordinates, the penal style will often be inevitable. Peaceful negotiation between unequal disputants implies equality; therefore, it can undermine the power of the superior party. Asking inferiors for compensation, especially when they possess far fewer resources than the victim, often seems inappropriate (Black, 1987). Although treating the offending party as sick can often succeed in dealing with the deviance of the powerless, therapeutic control is only applicable in certain circumstances (see Chapter 5).

Punishments such as beatings, whippings, or spankings are typically administered in a downward direction. When the objects of social control are considered to be completely dependent or inferior, those who punish them may be completely immune from retaliation. For instance, in sixteenth-century England, men who whipped lunatics were exempt from punishment (MacDonald, 1981, p. 196). Likewise, the control of masters over slaves is extremely coercive (Furer-Haimendorf, 1967, pp. 79, 81). Patterson's (1982, p. 193) study of 45 societies shows that only one-fifth treated the killing of a slave as equivalent to that of a free person, whereas nearly two-thirds allowed the master to kill a slave with impunity. A judge in South Carolina in 1847 stated this theme clearly: "[A slave] can invoke neither magna charta nor common law. . . . In the very nature of things, he is subject to despotism. Law as to him is only a compact between his rulers" (quoted in Friedman, 1985, p. 225).

The subordinate status of children relative to their parents is another situation that typically feature high vertical distance. Parents have great authority to control the behavior of their children, whereas children are almost completely dependent on their parents. Therefore, parents often respond to the deviance of children through penal, rather than some alternative style. For instance, among the Arusha tribe in Central Africa: "Adults often deal peremptorily with children . . . who offend them. The owner of a field may cuff the herdsboy who allows animals to stray on his land; or he, often she, will beat a child caught stealing ripe maize cobs from a standing crop" (Gulliver, 1963, p. 217). Up until at least the sixteenth century in Europe, children were subject to almost absolute authority (Spierenburg, 1984, p. 96). In modern middle-class families, coercion is almost exclusively limited to the control of the delicts of small children (Baumgartner, 1988, p. 47).

Yet, the relationship between inequality and penal control is complex. Using force against a subordinate is often viewed as shameful and humiliates the reputation of the powerful person. Such people ought to command enough legitimate authority so they need not use force. Hence, among the Tlingit of Alaska a nobleman "would be shamed if he were caught in an altercation with a slave or a man of low rank" (Oberg, 1934, p. 153). Men who harm women and children are often viewed as unmanly and lacking in legitimate authority. Although men usually have the right to discipline wives and children, they are not expected to use violence and are seen as reprehensible if they administer regular or public beatings (Loizos, 1978, p. 194). For example, among the Albanians:

> Killing a woman save when taken in adultery or incorrigible pilfering was the most disgraceful thing an Albanian could do. Only one who came from a "a low class family" would do it, he never again had any luck with his fields and he could not hope to have his crime pardoned, but must wash away his crime with his blood" (Hasluck, 1954: 237).

The use of penal styles against dependents may indicate weakness and humiliate dominants.

In addition, some dependent statuses are so subordinate that those who occupy them do not possess the intention and capacity that are necessary for penal liability. In such cases dependency may deflect, rather than attract, punishment. The very fact of their dominated position explains why in some circumstances the penal style is rarely invoked against many dependent populations.

Indeed, the very control that superiors possess over their dependent may render the superior rather than the subordinate liable to third-party social control. This has traditionally been true for women. In many settings, male controllers are punished for the deviance of their female dependents. Until the modern period, the law did not view women as autonomous, responsible persons. Women's actions were defined in relationship to their fathers, husbands, or brothers. In many tribal societies, women cannot institute jural proceedings but must use their fathers or brothers before marriage and their husbands or sons after betrothal (Gulliver, 1963, p. 142). These men were the parties accountable for a woman's behavior. In seventeenth-century England as well:

> In most felonious acts by a married woman to which her husband could be shown to be privy or at which he was present, the wife could not be held entirely culpable. If indicted, she might be acquitted or receive a lesser sentence than he for the same crime. In Normandy and Brittany the husband might have to answer for her crimes in court. . . . The full weight of the law fell only on the ruling male (Davis, 1975, p. 146).

In the law of the United States during the colonial period and up to about 1820, married women had no legal personality separate and distinct from their husbands (Nelson, 1975, p. 103). Married women were deemed incapable of committing crimes at this time.

For women, the *lack*, rather than the presence, of dependency is usually related to the imposition of third-party penal control. Those dependents who repudiate their dominated status become liable to harsh punishment. Female runaways, incorrigibles, prostitutes, or vagrants are not subject to dependent relationships in families. Yet they suffer as much or more legal punishment than their male counterparts (Rafter, 1984). Penal control is an especially likely reaction toward female sexual deviance that involves the repudiation of male control. Women's sphere of respectability has traditionally been sexual conduct. Females who are promiscuous, engage in premarital sexual activity, or commit adultery are typically far more likely than males who engage in these behaviors to face punishment oriented responses. In the case of children, as well, youth who have freed themselves from adult control make themselves more liable to suffer punishment-oriented responses (Stables, 1987).

In settings where women or children come to have growing equality and less men and adults, gender and age differences in the imposition of the penal style decline or disappear. On the one hand, the penal responsibility of women and children for offenses grows. On the other hand, the liability of male offenders also increases. As the dependence of women on men and of children on parents declines, the vulnerability to punishment of their victimizers increases.

The relationship between downward social control and the penal style is thus complex. The power to punish dependents may be an aspect of the rights of superior parties yet it humiliates them if they exercise this right. Dependents may be subject to harsh repression within relationships yet immune to liability for delicts outside of these relationships.

Nevertheless, the actual or potential imposition of penal control typically characterizes downward social control.

Upward Control

The penal style is sometimes associated with upward social control: the response of inferiors to the deviance of their superiors (Baumgartner, 1984). The status of dependency inherently breeds hostility and the desire to punish those who hold power. This is especially true in close relationships of dependency that involve frequent contacts such as between masters and servants, students and teachers, or husbands and wives (Thompson, 1975, p. 307).

Although dependency breeds intense desire for revenge, overt efforts at upward penal control will lead to harsh retaliation. Dependents are always severely restricted from using force against superiors. A young man of the Kalauna tribe in Papua New Guinea succinctly states the difficulties faced by the powerless in sanctioning the deviance of their superiors: "I cannot be angry. There are only myself and my younger brother" (Young, 1971, p. 214). Offended parties must be in some position of strength before they can wield coercive sanctions. When, as with the Kalauna, this depends on their position in a collective vengeance group, someone who cannot forge alliances is unable to exert penal social control.

In addition to their inability to wield coercive sanctions, dependents often cannot use persuasive strategies of control that rely on the cooperation of the superior adversary (Baumgartner, 1984). Their dependency renders the powerless unable to negotiate on an equal footing, extract compensation from superiors, or urge those above them to seek therapy. The lack of adequate social control alternatives is a marked feature of dependency.

Situations of dependency lead to two typical strategies of penal control. The first way the dominated can sanction their adversaries is through *covert* penal styles. Dependents who lack the opportunity to vent their anger through rebellions, revolutions, and other overt actions may exert vengeance through anonymous mechanisms such as vandalism, property destruction, or arson. Their superiors usually are unaware of the identity of the perpetrator so cannot exact retribution (Baumgartner, 1984). Students may slash the tires of their teachers, servants steal from their masters, or workers sabotage the products of their companies (Baumgartner, 1989, pp. 86—87; Richards, 1979; Thompson, 1975). Many of these punishment-oriented actions of the powerless toward the powerful are labeled as crimes (Black, 1983). From the point of view of the dominated, however, they represent penal styles of social control that aim to punish those responsible for causing harm.

A second style of upward penal control is to *disguise* hostility in nonpenal forms such as tears, madness, prophetic utterances, or religion (Weiner, 1975). In situations where fighting is inappropriate and overt hostility impossible, grievances may be channelled into alternative modes. When the conscious or unconscious intent of these actions is to punish an adversary, these modes reflect penal social control.

In many societies, women and dependent young men use mental illness as a way of punishing husbands or parents through imposing guilt, discomfort, and monetary costs on them. For example, among the Somali and other East African peoples, women are often afflicted by a spirit-possession illness called *zar* that provides "a woman with a grievance against her husband with a means of expression for her hostility without recourse to open quarrelling" (Lewis, 1961, p. 262). Symptoms of mental illness can also be used to make intimate others feel guilty, provide attention, or spend money for therapy (e.g., Baumgartner, 1988, p. 31; Weissman & Paykel, 1984.)

Suicide can be another disguised technique of punishment dependents use when they do not have other ways to sanction superiors (Baumgartner, 1984). It may be the only way powerless people can obtain revenge against those who have tormented them (Jeffreys, 1952). For instance, in the Goodenough Islands in Papua New Guinea, women sometimes obtain revenge through self-injury in order to cause shame, sympathy, and contrition in those who created the harm (Young, 1971, pp. 262-63). A case of suicide among the Kaliai of Papua New Guinea illustrates how powerless people can use suicide to punish those who have wronged them:

> [Agnes'] death enabled her to communicate, in a medium that she knew could not be ignored, a message that must be heard. She could reasonably expect that her action would have certain consequences. First, all the villagers with whom I talked agreed that by singling out Victor and his kin to be notified of her death, she had accused them of being responsible for it. Second, she knew that her kinsmen would consider her to have been murdered, "killed with talk," and that they would hold Victor and his parents criminally responsible. As a result, her kin would demand compensation for her death, and they might possibly take revenge. . . . Finally, Victor and his parents would know that they were responsible for her death and, in addition to their disgrace, they would also bear the financial cost of compensation to her kin as well as the fear that they would be killed. (Counts, 1980, p. 335)

Suicide can give satisfaction and vengeance to an aggrieved person who has no alternative for relief from an intolerable situation or who wants to harass, burden, or ruin others.

Although overt strategies of upward penal control are usually unworkable, dependents find other means of punishing those with power over them. Because dependents lack satisfactory ways to punish the powerful, upward penal control is often anonymous or disguised.

Equality

Control efforts among equals feature a diversity of social control styles. On the one hand, conciliatory or compensatory efforts that restore a balance between disputants are more suited than penal styles to control efforts of equals. In addition, status equals are more likely to share common normative systems and ties to third parties that can dampen penal efforts and promote remedial ones. Therefore, status equality among disputants is often not conducive to penal control.

On the other hand, equality itself can be related to efforts at penal control. Codes of honor often dictate that aggressive retaliation for harm can only move horizontally among status equals (Ayres, 1984). Duels, for example, are prescribed responses for slights to honor only among equals. It would be unseemly for a higher status person to accept a challenge from a lower status one or for a higher status person to challenge someone of lower status to a duel. Likewise, in modern societies the highest rate of aggressive violence occurs between young, unmarried men who share equivalent status positions and who typically avenge slights to their honor through aggressive retaliation (e.g., Luckinbill, 1977). When harms suffered by equals lead to compromise and negotiation or to vengeance is a subject in need of further research.

Groups

Groups as well as relationships are marked by more or less equality in the distribution of valued resources. The penal style of control is related to the degree of stratification in groups: *Penal control is directly related to inequality in groups.*

Tribal societies marked by relatively little inequality rarely feature penal control (Spitzer, 1975). The emergence of disparities in wealth and social rank is accompanied by a wider use of the penal style. The growth of complex systems of social stratification is associated with specialized coercive agencies of social control (Robinson & Scaglion, 1987).

The emergence of police and other coercive agents of social control accompanied a change to a market-based system of social stratification. In contemporary societies, areas marked by greater disparities of wealth feature higher arrest rates than those with greater equality (Horwitz,

1984). In families, as well, greater inequality among members is associated with the use of more penal control (Black, 1976, p. 32).

Yet it may not be so much the level of inequality in a group as the nature and degree of stability in stratification systems that predicts penal control. Stable and multistranded systems of inequality need not rely on penal systems of social control. Encompassing systems of dependency that reach across work, family, and marriage feature conciliatory settlements and little coercive social control (Collier, 1973).

The emergence of a market system in Western societies during the seventeenth through nineteenth centuries destroyed an encompassing system of dependence, and the impersonal ties of the market became the only bond between powerful people and others (Polanyi, 1957). Not an increase in the amount of stratification but a shift in the basis of stratification led to a growth in the use of coercive control. As ties of dominance became less focused on the total person and more centered on the productive process alone, penal styles came to predominate. Coercive means of social control such as police rose when ties of dependency broke down and were replaced by the impersonal and single-stranded ties of the market (Robinson & Scaglion, 1987). When only market ties link the wealthy to the poor, order is maintained through impersonal, punishment oriented social control (Collier, 1973).

Organization

A fundamental element of the penal style is the assessment of responsibility on guilty offenders. Criminal intent cannot be imputed to corporate entities that lack consciousness. This creates a fundamental incongruity between penal social control and organizational offenders. The intentionality and capacity necessary to attribute guilt are usually attributes associated with individuals rather than collectivities. Organizations are rarely the objects of penal control: *Penal control is inverse to the presence of organization.*

When organizational deviance occurs, it is often difficult or impossible to implicate responsible individuals. If particular individuals are identified as creating harm, they often acted in their organizational capacity so can claim they should not be held personally accountable. Organizational roles make it possible for individuals to claim they were following the instructions of superiors (Braithwaite, 1985, p. 17). Superiors, in turn, can claim their instructions were misunderstood or misapplied. Or, superiors can tell subordinates that they want a certain result accomplished without wanting to know how it is accomplished. This protects the corporation from the knowledge necessary to prove a criminal action. Because intended harm and choice underlie penal liability, the penal style is typically associated with the punishment of individuals rather than groups.

When offenses are organizationally rooted, compensatory or conciliatory styles are more likely to emerge (see Chapters 3 and 4). Delicts such as environmental pollution, occupational health and safety violations, or consumer protection rarely result in punitive styles of law enforcement (Braithwaite, 1985). Likewise, organizational defendants who are found guilty in cases of housing or employment discrimination will be more likely to compensate their victims than be subject to repressive sanctions (Mayhew, 1968).

The lack of punishment for organizational defendants is often decried and viewed as an example of the protection of the powerful. However, this tendency more likely stems from the inherent difficulty of implementing the penal style against organizations. Indeed, the use of compensatory styles against organizational defendants is often an easier, more efficient, and more effective way of dealing with organizational defendants (see Chapter 3).

Although organizations are less likely to be the objects of penal control, it is not clear if they are more, less, or equally likely than individuals to exert penal control. On the one hand, civil courts are typically marked by organizations pursuing claims against individual defendants (Abel, 1979; Galanter, 1974; Wanner, 1974). This suggests that organizational victims such as banks, credit agencies, or businesses are quite likely to pursue repressive styles when victimized.

On the other hand, organizational victims may be satisfied with obtaining restitution and are less likely than individuals to desire revenge (Spitzer & Scull, 1977). Organizations tend to adopt purely instrumental conceptions of order maintenance that emphasize efficiency and profit (Shearing & Stenning, 1983). These conceptions are not conducive to the moralistic pursuit of justice that characterizes penal styles. For example, despite signs posted in stores that warn of dire retribution, most shoplifters are released rather than punished (Rojek, 1979). In addition, organizations are more concerned with creating systems of social control that prevent deviance from arising than with punishing deviants once they are caught (Reiss, 1984). Indeed, within organizations, social control agents may be employed more to identify loopholes in security systems than to apprehend individual deviants (Shearing & Stenning, 1983). Hence, the question of whether organizations are likely to pursue or refrain from exercising penal styles is unresolved.

When organizations confront each other as grievants, penal styles are unlikely. The complexity of issues and stakes involved mean that cases involving government agencies, corporations, labor unions, universities, hospitals, civil rights organizations, and the like rarely result in penal sanctions. Rather, compensation or conciliation are more likely outcomes for cases between organizations (Galanter, 1974).

Because of the incompatibility between organizations and penal styles of social control, societies that are comprised of corporate rather than individual actors also feature less penal social control than ones that consist of atomized individuals. Hence, one reason that tribal societies feature little penal control is that disputes typically involve groups rather than individuals (Black, 1987). Questions of intent are minimized, and the payment of damages by one liability group to another is paramount. Conversely, the rise of penal styles is accompanied by the development of individualism as the organizing principle of social life.

As organizations supplant individuals as the major actors controlled by law, the use of penal styles should decline. Indeed, in many areas administrative law already substitutes for criminal law and strict liability for criminal responsibility (Reiss, 1984). Collective rather than individual liability has been resurrected in efforts to control the delicts of corporations (Lilly & Ball, 1982). To the extent that offenders are embedded in organizational matrices, the penal style should not respond to their transgressions. Although organizations in contemporary societies face far more social control over their actions than in the past, this control takes a regulatory or compensatory rather than a penal character. The growing expanse and involvement of organizations in social life is accompanied by the growth of alternatives to penal social control.

Conclusion

The penal style varies along several dimensions of social space. It flourishes with growing relational distance, weak ties, and inequality between disputants and in groups that lack crosscutting ties and social equality among members. It also intensifies when disputes arise between members of different social groups, growing individualization, and impersonal systems of inequality but declines with the presence of organization. Whatever grounding the penal style may have in universal biological and psychological factors, it also rests on a social structural foundation.

Yet the social foundation for the penal style leads to an inherent crisis in modern societies. Growing relational distance and a lack of crosscutting ties between offenders and victims leads to the need for coercive means of control. Yet, when individualism becomes the reigning principle of group life, the sanctions of families, communities, schools, churches, or workplaces cannot work. Individualism undermines the basis for strong and penetrating moral sentiments. In the absence of strong informal sanctions, the formal bureaucratic methods of the state are the only available means of punishment. The long delays, plea bargaining, and distance from the citizenry that are inherent in the punishment process of the state cannot vindicate moral claims. Modernity is marked by a constant need for, yet an ineffectiveness of, penal social control.

3

The Compensatory Style

INTRODUCTION

Elements of Compensation

Compensatory social control involves the payment of a debt from offenders to their victims (Black, 1987). Offenders are obligated to compensate victims for damage or other harm that they have suffered. Once restitution has been provided, the matter is settled.

There are fundamental differences between the compensatory and penal styles. The elements of intention and capacity that are essential aspects of the penal style are of lesser importance in compensatory systems. Compensatory liability usually features a connection between an act and some harmful outcome rather than some mental state producing the act (Hart, 1968, Chapter 9). Liability accrues from an external relationship between an offense and a responsible party rather from a particular state of mind of an offender. Just as guilt is fundamental to penal liability, damage is critical to compensatory liability. In compensatory systems the fact of injury alone can give rise to liability. Although considerations of motivation are not irrelevant, they are usually subsidiary to repairing the damage from some harmful act.

Because harm, rather than guilt, is essential to compensatory liability, compensatory styles are less moralistic than penal ones. The basic issue is not who is responsible for some injury but who will pay for it (Lempert & Sanders, 1986). Once the harm has been redressed, the matter is settled (Furer-Haimendorf, 1967, pp. 69-70).

Because they deemphasize morality, compensatory systems are poorly suited to avenge senses of justice. Their goal is to restore a normal state of affairs to disturbed situations through redressing injuries of victims. In compensatory systems, damages are not expiatory but are used as a way of restoring the disrupted situation to its normal state (Durkheim, 1893). Hence compensatory styles strive to provide adequate compensation for the suffering of victims rather than achieve justice through punishment. Because compensatory systems are not oriented toward punishing guilty offenders, they are less suited than penal styles for upholding systems of morality.

The settlement of victims' claims is central to compensatory systems. The justification for compensatory systems often is purely utilitarian. Because compensatory systems need not pay close attention to questions of intention, they often provide a more efficient way than penal styles of providing redress to victims and of administering systems of justice. Although the efficiency and security of compensatory styles abandons the moral underpinnings of penal systems, they do effectively redress injuries.

Compensatory styles also differ from penal ones in that sanctions are grounded in the obligations offenders owe to victims, not in the vindication of moral rules. Damages are paid directly to victims or their kin groups, not to an impersonal state. Victims in penal systems, in contrast, receive no direct recompense save the satisfaction of seeing punishment imposed.

The identity of the liable party also differs in compensatory and penal styles. Penal systems typically impose liability for intentional actions of individuals. Compensatory liability, in contrast, is often collective.[1] Liability does not rest solely on the individual who caused the harm but spreads to the group or organization responsible for the individual's actions. A murderer's family may be as responsible as the actual murderer for redressing harm, or a supervisor may be liable for the damages an employee's mistake creates.

The payment of compensation is usually mandated by some binding authority. Offenders do not chose whether or not they will pay damages to their victims. The coercive power of the group stands behind the imposition of compensatory sanctions. Therefore, both compensatory and penal systems rely on coercive rather than consensual sanctions.

[1]Furer-Haimendorf (1967, p. 64) relates an extreme case of this: "In 1945, when I toured the valley of the upper Kamla river, I met the kinsmen and descendants of men involved in hostilities with a British military expedition in 1912. Since then no European or other outsider had visited the area, and the feud had remained unresolved. As I wanted to establish friendly relations with the local tribesmen, and was taken for a kinsman of the only white men ever known to the people, I had no other choice but to pay compensation for their past losses."

The compensatory style of social control thus seeks to undo some harm by settling disputes when an offender pays a debt to a victim (Black, 1976). As with the penal style, compensation is mandatory, so both styles are coercive modes of social control. However, compensatory liability focuses on the consequences of, rather than the motivations behind, harmful conduct. In addition, compensatory payments are made directly from offenders to victims. In contrast, penal styles typically involve punishing deviants for violating rules, and victims receive no benefit. Compensatory settlements are reached when transgressors fulfill obligations to redress their victims, not when guilty individuals are punished.

Nature of Harm

Some sort of *damage* typically activates the compensatory style. The harm leading to compensation rather than punishment is more likely to damage material rather than moral sentiments. For compensation to proceed, a monetarization of some normative issue must occur (Cooney, 1988). Issues that involve intense value concerns are often not amenable to transformation into monetary terms and are therefore unlikely to involve compensation. On the other hand, when the issue in question can be framed as one involving material damages, compensation can more readily proceed.

What constitutes an attack on norms or material loss widely varies across situations and societies. In some contexts, the intentional taking of a human life can only be avenged by penal sanctions because a core value is at stake. In other contexts, homicides may only damage material interests. For example, if a slave is killed, the slave owner may be mollified through compensation and be unconcerned with revenge. Or, in many tribal groups, the relatives of a slain kinsman will be satisfied when they receive a compensatory settlement. In some settings, though, theft may strike more at basic questions of right and wrong than at material loss, so not the stolen property itself but the vindication of the broken norm is at stake. In other settings where theft is defined in solely material terms, restitution rather than punishment constitutes sufficient resolution (e.g., Ruffini, 1978). Whenever harm can be characterized as damaging to material rather than normative interests, compensatory styles are likely to emerge.

In addition, there is an affinity between the harm that organizations cause with compensatory responses. Although it is difficult to prove that organizations committed some crime that involve intention, it is far easier to show what harm resulted from an organizational action. Hence, compensatory systems are highly suitable to redress the damages that organizations cause.

PREDICTORS OF THE COMPENSATORY STYLE

Compensatory styles are grounded in particular social structural contexts. When grievances arise at intermediate relational distance, when higher status offenders cause harm to lower status victims, and when a number of persons collectively are responsible for the conduct of any particular individual, compensatory control is likely to occur.

Relational Distance

The determination of compensatory liability does not occur in a social vacuum. Rather, the relationship between the parties involved influences whether harm translates into the provision of compensation: *Compensation is a curvilinear function of relational distance* (Black, 1987, p. 572; Cooney, 1988: Chapter 3). Compensation is unlikely to occur between either extremely close or extremely distant parties. Conflicts where disputants are close enough to have some obligations to each other but distant enough so they are not enmeshed in intimate relationships are most likely to result in compensatory outcomes.

Compensation rarely takes place among intimates because monetary payments imply an impersonality that is foreign to the nature of intimacy. In modern societies, close relatives typically cannot sue one another for damages such as those suffered at home or in automobiles.[2] Children, for example, are unable to sue their parents when their basic needs have been neglected (Lieberman, 1981: 165). Despite the fact that 30 to 40% of violent crimes involve persons who have intimate ties, people are only eligible to participate in victim compensation programs if no personal relationship exists between the offender and victim (Ziegenhagen, 1976, p. 273).

There often exists a deeply rooted norm against demanding compensation from one's neighbors as well as from family members. For

[2]This situation may be changing as even individuals within households become more distant from each other and their relationships become more contractually grounded (see Lieberman, 1981).

example, a study of dispute resolution among cattle ranchers in a California county finds that

> Shasta County landowners regard a monetary settlement as an arms length transaction that symbolizes an unneighborly relationship. Should your goat happen to eat your neighbor's tomatoes, the neighborly thing for you to do would be to help replant the tomatoes; a transfer of money would be too cold and too impersonal. (Ellickson, 1986, p. 682)

In another study of compensation in a rural county in Illinois, a woman suffered a skull fracture after she fell in a neighbor's house because of a negligently installed door. She spent 5 days in intensive care and had a permanent loss of her sense of smell and taste. Despite the fact that insurance did not fully compensate even their hospital bills, the woman and her husband did not seek greater compensation from the neighbor reasoning:

> We were thankful she recovered as well as she did. . . . We never considered a lawsuit there at all. I don't know what other people would have done in the case. Possibly that insurance company would have paid the total medical if we would have just, well, I have a brother who is an attorney, could have just wrote them a letter maybe. But, I don't know, we just didn't do it, that's all. (Engel, 1984, p. 560)

In this case, the close relationship between the party responsible for the harm and the victim prevented a compensatory settlement.

Likewise, compensatory systems cannot arise among members of tightly connected groups. When disputants are part of the same liability group, compensation is not feasible because the payers and recipients of compensation would be identical. Among the Bedouins, for example, if one kinsman slays another, a compensatory settlement cannot result because the liability groups of victim and offender are the same (Peters, 1967). The liability of the offender's group would be to itself. Similarly, among the Plateau Tonga, compensation cannot be paid if a man slays his kinsman because an indivisible group would have to divide into payers and recipients of recompense (Colson, 1953). In the extreme cases of intimacy, as when a man kills his wife, compensation would be impossible because the obligation to pay would be owed to the murderer himself (Black, 1987; Howell, 1954, p. 208). Likewise, among the Somali, "where a father kills his son, or a son his father, vengeance is impossible and compensation cannot be paid, for as Somali put it 'Who would pay and who receive damages?'" (Lewis, 1961, p. 257). When compensation is provided in offenses between closely related individuals, it may be smaller than for offenses at greater distances (Evans-Pritchard, 1940, p. 156). Because compensation is often not feasible when disputes arise among members of the same group, alternatives such as conciliation, avoidance, exile, or supernatural sanctioning must be implemented.

Compensatory settlements are also unlikely when social distance is so great that no shared obligations exist between parties. Although intimacy creates obligations that cannot be settled by compensation, great distance rends them completely. Because the compensatory style rests on ties of obligation, it rarely proceeds between completely separate groups. Among the Nuer in Africa, for example, the definition of a distinct tribe is one where no compensation exists between different groups (Evans-Pritchard, 1940). In addition, as groups become larger and more distant from each other, compensation becomes more difficult to arrange.

Compensation is rare between members of separate tribes because there are few social contacts and revenge and feud become more likely ways of settling grievances. Hence, among the Somali of East Africa, disputes between members of different clans will likely lead to retaliation and vengeance, whereas those among members of different lineages of the same clan will be settled through compensation (Lewis, 1961). A study of the social control of homicide in 30 societies shows that compensatory sanctions are most common when killers and their victims are in intermediate social distance but rarer when they are either intimates or strangers (Cooney, 1988, Chapter 2). For example, obligations to pay compensation to each other among Nuer tribesmen in the Sudan depends on the distance between disputing groups (Evans-Pritchard, 1940). When intermarriage led to ties between groups or when disputes arose between different lineage groups in the same village, compensation could usually be easily arranged. Between neighboring villages with some ties between them, it was less easy to arrange compensation, but settlements could usually be reached. However, with growing distance, feuds were more difficult to settle, and compensation would be neither offered nor accepted. Continuing cycles of vengeful feuds became more likely as structural interrelationships between groups declined (Evans-Pritchard, 1940, p. 156). Likewise, among the Jalemo tribe in Western New Guinea, if a man absconds with a husband's wife, the husband must receive a pig as compensation if he has relatives in the village of the absconder but must take penal action if there are no ties between the absconder and the husband (Koch, 1974).

In the contemporary United States, the likelihood of compensatory settlement grows when disputes emerge between people who do not share any intimate ties. For instance in the rural Illinois county mentioned previously, newcomers to the community did not share the reluctance of settled residents to seek compensation for damages from other community members (Engel, 1984).

Another frequent setting for compensation is among parties whose previously intimate relationship has been broken. Divorce, for example, commonly involves the payment of damages from one party to another. Employees who are fired or franchisees who wrongfully lose their licenses also often receive compensatory settlements. In such cases, compensation serves to ratify that a once close relationship has ended as well as to provide damages to the wronged party.

Group Ties

The principle that compensation is unlikely between extremely close or extremely distant individuals also indicates the sorts of group settings most conducive to compensation. Compensation is most likely to occur when there are enough ties between groups to create obligations to redress harm but not enough distance between groups so no obligations exist at all. There must be enough closeness so disputants have obligations toward each other but enough distance for separate liability groups to develop.

Conditions for compensation should be optimal when two groups have some overlapping members who can arrange settlements between contesting groups. Colson's (1953) study of the Plateau Tonga of East Africa show the importance of cross-linkages in promoting compensation in small-scale societies. The Plateau Tonga are highly migratory, so kin and residence ties often do not coincide. Marriage typically leads to an alliance of four groups (the patrilineal and matrilineal groups of the husband and the wife) dispersed in different neighborhoods. Because a quarrel is likely to affect different, yet overlapping, relational systems, a system of crosscutting ties prevents penal retaliation and promotes compensatory settlements.

In many tribal groups, persons with ties to both groups in conflict serve as intermediaries and try to arrange compensation as an alternative to violent revenge (Brown, 1964). Such members both arrange the details of a settlement and dampen demands for revenge on the part of both parties. The presence of people who hold structurally intermediate positions should be inversely related to vengeance cycles between groups but directly related to the payment of compensation.

Compensatory systems of responsibility have a number of positive features for groups whose members are not close intimates but yet must live together in continuing relationships. When groups are organized on a corporate basis, quarrels between individuals quickly become quarrels between groups. Even small matters can endanger the public peace. Systems of compensation can preserve harmony because anyone who suffers harm, regardless of cause, can obtain redress. Grievances will not simmer in settings where growing bitterness could seriously disrupt group life.

For example, among the Bunyoro of East Africa, disputes between fellow villagers are settled when the wrongdoer pays meat and beer to the injured party (Beattie, 1966, p. 171-172). Both parties, as well as settlement agents, consume the payment. The object is not so much to punish the wrongdoer as to reconcile the disputants and restore harmony to the disrupted village. If fault was assessed on offenders or if victims did not obtain redress, grievances would be likely to linger. Compensatory systems effectively provide redress without assessing blame, thus minimizing the resentment of both parties who are involved in continuing social relationships.

Compensatory control is maximal where some ties are present that create obligations and where third parties are present to enforce these obligations. Therefore, compensatory styles are most likely to arise at relational distances where parties have some obligations to each other but are not closely interlocked. The compensatory style flourishes at intermediate distances between individuals and groups: At the closest distance conciliation predominates and at the greatest distance penal styles.

Hierarchy

The direction of an offense in vertical space is also related to the likelihood of the compensatory style: *Upward cases are more compensatory than downward cases* (Black, 1987, p. 572). Although penal styles are typically directed at offenders of lower rank than victims, compensatory styles often feature offenders of higher status than their victims. Compensation should be more frequent when a higher ranking party offends a lower ranking one.

Downward Cases

Compensation is unlikely when a lower status offender harms a higher status victim. Such victims have fewer resources available to provide redress. This is especially true because in most groups upper status persons receive more compensation than lower status ones when injured. For example, among the Yurok Indians of North America: "For killing a man of social standing the indemnity was fifteen strings of dentalium, with perhaps a red obsidian, and a woodpecker scalp headband, besides handing over a daughter. A common man was worth only ten strings of dentalium" (Redfield, 1967, p. 10). Or, among a rural Albanian tribe: "The formula of 'one for one' was disregarded only in a few cases. In

Lume . . . 'two for one' was the rule when a man killed his social superior; nothing less would content his victim's injured pride" (Hasluck, 1954, p. 392). Likewise, among the Lombards in Western Europe: "For the murder of a free man or free woman by a free person, compensation of 1200 shillings was required, whereas the price for the death of a household servant was only 50 solidi, and for a slave 20" (Berman, 1983, p. 54). In India, the murder of a low caste person was considered one-twelfth as sinful as the killing of a high caste Brahman (Furer-Haimendorf, 1967, p. 157).

In addition to a lack of monetary resources, lower status offenders also do not possess the social credit necessary to fulfill the obligations at the root of compensatory liability. Compensation rests on a principle of equivalence in determining settlement. The loss to the victim is matched by at least a corresponding loss to the offender. If a clan has lost a young man, they may wait until the son of the killer is the same age as the victim before he is murdered (Redfield, 1967, p. 12). With the Berbers of North Africa, if a man kills a woman of another group, not the murderer but a woman of the murderer's family must be killed (Beattie, 1966, p. 175). The object of compensation is to restore a disrupted balance between groups. As long as a similar *type* of person is substituted for the victim, the preexisting situation is restored. A lower status person, however, is not only monetarily but also socially unequal to a higher status one. It thus may be demeaning for a higher status individual to accept payment from a lower ranking one (Black, 1987). Hence, higher ranking victims refuse compensation from lower ranking offenders but demand that they be punished instead.

Upward Cases

In contrast to downward cases, compensation is a natural strategy in upward cases of social control when higher status persons offend lower status ones. Higher ranking offenders have a greater ability than inferiors to make payment. Hence the nature of compensation inherently provides well-off individuals an advantage over the poor, even though they may have to pay more damages when they create harm as well as receive more when they are victimized (Bloch, 1961, p. 328; Furer-Haimendorf, 1967, p. 157). Among the Tlingit Indians in Southeastern Alaska if a man of low rank stole from another clan, the injured clan could kill him, whereas if the thief was of high rank, his own clan would make reparation by paying goods to the offended clan (Oberg, 1934, p. 149). In early modern Seville, wealthy offenders could purchase pardons from persons who they harmed by making payments to them and thus be immune from legal justice. The poor, however, were unable to purchase pardons and were therefore punished more stringently (Perry, 1980). Among the Lombards in Western Europe, an unfree person who killed a free person was executed whereas a free person who murdered could fulfill his obligation by compensating the kin of the victim (Berman, 1983, pp. 54-55).

Another reason compensatory settlements are associated with higher class offenders lies in the relatively unstigmatizing nature of compensatory control. Because compensation transforms deviance into a material rather than a moral issue, it does not reflect on the fundamental character of the offender. Compensatory offenses reflect specific harmful incidents rather than moral wrongs that imply a damaged reputation. A criminal label, on the other hand, stigmatizes an offender and undermines the reputation that is essential to the maintenance of higher social status (Aubert & Messinger, 1958). Compensatory settlements that do not harm reputation are more suitable to the character of higher ranking persons.

In some circumstances, the greater resources of the wealthy allow them the capability to monetarize a delict that would otherwise disgrace them. Fines became a widespread means of dealing with the offenses of upper class defendants in England because imprisonment was viewed as incompatible with the status of gentlemen (Beattie, 1986, pp. 88-89). In Sicily, although poor girls must be completely chaste to be marriageable, the sexual delicts of unmarried rich girls can be overcome by a large dowry (Loizos, 1978, p. 193).

The nature of compensation renders it especially suitable for upward cases of social control but difficult to implement in downward cases. When offenders are of lower status than their victims, penal control should flourish, whereas compensation should prevail when offenders are of higher rank than victims.

Organization

The presence of compensatory styles is also related to the nature of organizations: *Compensation is related to organization* (Black, 1987). Just as individual liability is central to penal styles, collective liability is paradigmatic in compensatory styles. An essential feature of compensatory liability is to spread and equalize risk among group members (Posner, 1980). All members of the group are liable for providing recompense to someone who has been victimized by one of the group's members. This leads to a system that can efficiently spread risks across many people and minimize costs to any particular person. The distributive nature of compensatory liability renders it particularly suitable for dealing with the delicts of organizations and collectivities (Reiss, 1984).

Another reason compensatory liability is amenable to the delicts of groups is that it does not require proof of intention. Because it is often difficult or impossible to prove the intent of groups, compensatory styles provide an efficient way of dealing with the violations of collectivities. Whenever an organization, rather than an individual, bears liability for an offense, the likelihood of a compensatory response increases.

Tribal societies should provide fertile settings for compensatory control. In tribal groups, marriage creates dense ties and obligations between different kinship groups, not only the spouses. All rights, privileges, and obligations are determined by kinship relations (Evans-Pritchard, 1940). Property, for example, is held by groups rather than individuals.

As we would expect from the nature of social organization, the collective nature of liability, neglect of motivation, and concern with redress for harm that are at the heart of compensation are typical features of social control in tribal and other premodern societies. The kin group in tribal societies has both the responsibility to pay compensation and the liability to suffer vengeance (Koch, 1974). Wrongs suffered by individuals are considered to be wrongs against the kinship group; claims for redress are exerted by the kin group; and liability is shared by the group (e.g., Lewis, 1959; Redfield, 1967). Concepts of individual responsibility in tribal groups are weak, and lineage segments act corporately to either exact vengeance or pay damages (Barkun, 1968, p. 20). Tremendous shame accrues to those who fail to avenge a slain relative (Evans-Pritchard, 1940). Especially when land and goods are held in common and there is a community of interest, the unit of responsibility will be the clan, kin, or family group rather than the individual. In these groups families act as "mutual insurance companies" (Posner, 1980) who are liable for the wrongdoing of any of their members. Particular offenders are no more liable to the vengeance of the injured parties than are other members of their kin group (Furer-Haimendorf, 1967, p. 110).

Tribal societies are unconcerned with notions of individual guilt and display little regard for inner motivations and intentions that are at the basis of penal control (Weber, 1925, p. 51). In such settings, the concept of liability does not distinguish between intent, negligence, inadvertence, or accident, but the obligation to provide restitution and indemnity arises out of the consequences of conduct (Koch, 1984). If harm occurs, tribal social control responds only to the damage some event has caused and neglects the motivation behind it. This leads tribal groups to feature systems of strict liability based on causation of harm, not on judgment of the intentions leading to the harm (Falk-Moore, 1972).

Although the compensatory style is particularly common in tribal groups, it also appears in many other premodern settings. Compensatory sanctions paid by the kin of the offender and received by the kin of the victim typified the law of all European peoples prior to the twelfth century as well as Greek, Roman, and Hebrew civilizations (Berman, 1983, p. 55). Compensation served not as a fine but as an indemnity for a killing or as restitution for stolen or damaged property (Spierenburg, 1984, pp. 2-3).

In medieval Europe, each individual was tied to corporate groups of kin and allied servants. The honor or dishonor of one member of the kin group affected all. Vengeance as a sacred duty imposed on the group of the wronged individual (Bloch, 1961). Because the corporate structure of these societies meant that relatives and servants automatically became involved in quarrels, the public peace could be endangered by the smallest incident between neighbors. The need for community peace, stimulated by the Church and state, led to the development of compensatory systems in place of vendettas.

Liability in medieval European societies also emphasized the consequences of harmful actions rather than intentions and motives, compensatory remedies for harm, and collective rather than individual responsibility. The payment for the wrong, when accompanied by the appropriate gestures of apology, put an end to the offender's obligation as well as to the victim's group obligation to seek revenge (Blanshed, 1982; Bloch, 1961).

Compensatory systems persisted into the early modern period. When the state is not powerful enough to punish offenders, compensation may provide an alternative way of maintaining order. Before effective police forces developed, corporate liability based on community responsibility was the only method that could allow commerce to proceed. For example, English communities had corporate liability for crimes that occurred within them and were responsible for indemnifying individuals who were robbed while traveling through their boundaries (Rock, 1983). Many peasant cultures in areas where effective policing by nation-states has not penetrated still rely on compensation to punish transgressions such as the theft of livestock or murder (Hasluck, 1954; Ruffini, 1978).

Compensation declines with individualism. When societies are based on mobility, heterogeneity, and atomistic relationships, groups lack the necessary cohesion and solidarity to back collective liability systems. They do not have the stability of membership that promotes obligations. Whereas most people were once enmeshed in groups with authority over them, now only young children are totally subject to the authority of others.[3] With the breakdown of cohesive groups, collective liability loses its grounding in social organization, and the structural conditions for compensation decline.

Groups that lack a structural basis for corporate liability should not feature compensation. Members of hunting and gathering groups, for example, may flexibly leave the group and associate with other groups, so each band has an ever-changing composition (Koch, 1984). In such settings, liability is more likely to be individual than collective, and compensation is not likely to be used to settle grievances.

In the West, the greatest development of individual systems of responsibility occurred with the growth of laissez-faire capitalism in nineteenth century Great Britain and the United States. Duty for harm could only be assessed on individuals who intended to commit harm or who broke some contractual duty (Lieberman, 1981). As autonomous self-seeking individuals became central to social organization, liability came to rest on individual intentions rather than on the consequences of injurious conduct. In most cases, redress could only be obtained when victims could prove their harm resulted from intentional wrongdoing, although people were still liable to pay for harm caused by their servants or employees (Levi, 1949). The penal style of social control flourished under these conditions.

Yet, in hindsight, the nineteenth-century emphasis on individual responsibility for creating harm may diverge from conventional ways of assessing liability (Lieberman, 1981). Compensatory systems that are based on objective harm rather than personal responsibility have once again emerged in contemporary societies. There has been a movement from emphasizing personal responsibility to relying on objective standards of harm (Lilly & Ball, 1982). Systems based on strict liability or negligence, which do not rely on guilty intent, expand and become predominant ways of determining fault. Injury from defective products, automobile accidents, environmental disasters, or damages suffered from corporate health and safety violations now are all likely to be settled through compensatory systems. The embeddedness of individuals in social groups has not increased over the course of the twentieth century. What, then, is responsible for the growing trend toward compensatory social control in modern societies?

Several trends have led to the rebirth of compensatory systems. The first is the growth of organizations in modern society. Between 1917 and

[3]Compensation between parents still persists within neighborhoods as a typical response for delicts of children such as vandalism, mischief, or property damage (Baumgartner, 1988).

1969, corporations grew fivefold (Coleman, 1982). The structure of these organizations is comprised of positions rather than persons, who move freely between positions in organizations. Individuals are now dependent on organizations in many or most aspects of their lives. They not only work in them but also place their children in day care centers, shop in chain stores, live in condominiums controlled by developers or homeowners associations, are cured in hospitals, and play in recreational leagues. Because so many transactions occur between individuals and organizations, many disputes, accidents, and grievances arise in this context. As organizations replace the extended family in the compensation of misfortune, one sort of collective liability is substituted for another (Black, 1987, 1989a).

When organizations supplant individuals as the actors controlled by law it is difficult to assess penal responsibility because it is hard to prove organizational intent to violate rules (Reiss, 1984).[4] Organizational subordinates can claim that they were following explicit or implicit instructions from their bosses. Superiors, in contrast, can claim that their employees misunderstood or failed to follow their instructions (Braithwaite, 1985). In addition, with growing division of labor, it is often not clear who is at fault for many misfortunes. Harms often do not result from anyone's intentions but create a hugh amount of damage that must be redressed.

Most modern regulations aimed at corporations therefore emphasize compensatory damages rather than criminal penalties. Although penal sanctions such as corporal punishment or imprisonment are not applicable to corporations, corporate entities do own property and are involved in economic activity (Lederman, 1985). The monetarization of corporate deviance therefore suits the logic of organizations.

Although criminal cases are rarely brought against groups, groups are often sued to obtain compensation (Black, 1987). Compensation is most likely when a grievant who is an individual sues an organizational defendant. The compensatory style can more efficiently obtain damages for victims because they need not prove that an organization was criminally responsible for harm. For example, there are about 11,000 deaths in occupational settings annually in the United States (Hoskin, 1986). These deaths, and the many more injuries that occur in these settings, are typically handled through workmen's compensation and only very

[4]Although there has been a growing trend to hold corporations criminally liable for certain actions, these crimes are usually limited to those committed within the scope of employment with the intention of benefitting the corporation (Bernard, 1984, pp. 8-12).

rarely lead to any sort of penal sanctions. All offenses by corporations are more likely to result in compensatory rather than penal restitution.

A second reason for the reemergence of the compensatory style lies in the changing nature of damages in modern societies. The proliferation of mechanized technology has drastically raised the number of harms and the degree of damage they create. Industrial processes produce large amounts of waste in the air, water, and ground that may result in hundreds of thousands of deaths each year (Reiman, 1979). Many harms such as polluted air, contaminated water, or toxic chemical waste are distributed across many individuals who may not even be aware they are being injured (Lieberman, 1981). It is difficult or impossible to link corporate activities with harm caused to any particular individual. In addition, modern societies that rely on mass goods produced by many suppliers often find it impossible to determine precisely responsibility for harm (Levi, 1949). Some alternative means to assessing individual responsibility must be found to provide redress for a large number of victims.

Insurance becomes a dominate compensatory system to redress the increased scope of harm in modern societies. It provides a modern counterpart to collective liability in tribal groups (Koch, 1984). For both individuals and organizations, the potential disaster of being held accountable for negligence is replaced by a system of compensation based upon pooled risk. When damages occur, offenders are protected by a collective liability system (Ross, 1970). The critical question is not who is responsible but who will pay for damages (Lempert & Sanders, 1986). Victims similarly benefit from the knowledge that they will obtain redress for the harm they have suffered. In extreme cases, such as New Zealand, tort liability has been abolished completely and replaced by a no-fault system for all injuries (Lieberman, 1981). The moralistic nature that forms the basis for penal control is inverted, and both safe and negligent individuals suffer similar costs and receive similar rewards for their injuries.

In contemporary societies, automobile accidents are the most common elicitors of compensatory settlements. Injuries suffered in automobile accidents can best be conceived as occurring not between the individuals directly involved but between the corporate bearers of liability who stand behind them—insurance companies. Payment is usually made regardless of fault. If the driver is sued, the parties most interested in the outcome are not defendants but their insurance companies who must pay any damages (Ross, 1970). Despite the great relational distance that typically holds between individual parties involved in automobile accidents that would otherwise predict penal outcomes, the presence of collective liability leads to compensatory solutions.

A final reason for the rise of compensatory control in modern societies lies in the greater efficiency of this system compared to the penal style. Especially with organizational offenders, individual responsibility is difficult to prove. Compensatory systems, compared to penal ones, provide fewer safeguards, feature lower standards of proof to assess damages, and can be less time consuming (Frank, 1983). When large numbers of people are victimized, as with faulty products, environmental disasters, or airline crashes, compensatory settlements are efficient means of providing redress for severe harms that might go unrewarded in a system solely based on the punishment of individual wrongdoing. There may thus be an inherent affinity between large size and the compensatory style.

CONCLUSION

Compensation is grounded in particular social structures. Groups marked by little interdependence between members such as hunting and gathering bands or groups where autonomous individuals are the bearers of rights and duties rarely resort to compensatory styles. Compensation thrives at intermediate social distances, when groups are involved, and in cases of upward social control. When group life is based upon membership in different family, kin, or clan groups or in more impersonal organizations, compensation is likely to be a prominent style of social control. As organizations come to dominate more and more aspects of modern life, the use of compensatory styles of social control should continue to expand, and the scope of individual responsibility correspondingly diminish.

The compensatory style thrives in settings marked by corporate liability (Black, 1987). These occur both among clan-based tribal societies and organizationally based modern societies. Yet, there are key differences between compensation in holistic and individualistic settings. In the former, there exists a greater emphasis on the repair of disrupted relationships. As a member of the Arusha tribe in east Africa put it: "A court makes a man pay a fine, but who knows where the money goes? Perhaps the magistrate eats it; perhaps the Government. But an Arusha fine is not money; it is beer, and we all drink it together. We are friends then. Is that not so? Is that not right?" (Gulliver, 1963, pp. 285-286). Where group membership, conformity, and harmony are emphasized, apologies that indicate regret for the harm caused and willingness to restore positive relationships are central aspects of compensation

(Wagatsuma & Rosett, 1986). Hence, compensation in holistic settings emphasizes relational repair and restoration of group harmony.

In individualistic settings, the payment of damages itself is the central aspect of compensation. Victims are less concerned with receiving apologies because there are no relational ties involved that need repair. In such settings, the assertion of individual rights and payment of monetary recompense rather than reconciliation is paramount. Restitution is severed from moral responsibility, and compensation becomes solely a cost of doing business (Stables, 1986). Although the form of compensation is similar in holistic and individualistic societies, its substance changes when the entities involved have few or no binding ties between them.[5]

The compensatory style has both advantages and disadvantages. It provides efficient redress for victims and repairs the damages they suffered. It serves to avoid feuds and lingering resentment in communities. It ensures that offenders will not suffer vengeance and stigmatization. On the other hand, because compensation is not a moralistic style of social control, it can weaken the normative system of social groups. Offenders who have caused harm intentionally and unintentionally are treated alike. The cost of losses accrues to both innocent and guilty members of liability groups. Whether or not the advantages of the compensatory style outweigh the disadvantages depends on a number of factors, including the nature of the harm suffered, the relationship between the parties involved, and the moral system of the society in question.

[5]There have been attempts in modern societies to institute compensatory systems where individual offenders make payments or perform services for victims. These programs are usually short-lived and ineffective because they lack the grounding in collective responsibility that has been the historical basis for compensatory systems (see Stables, 1986).

4

The Conciliatory Style

INTRODUCTION

Elements of Conciliation

Conciliation is a third ideal type of social control. The parties involved in conciliatory control work together or with the aid of third parties to negotiate a mutually agreeable outcome. Solutions are obtained through mutual bargaining between the parties involved, not coerced through imposed sanctions.

The conciliatory style focuses on the relationship between contending parties rather than the actions of individual deviants. Its overriding goal is to reconcile the parties in conflict. Rendering one party responsible for harm would defeat the purpose of conciliation. Therefore, conciliatory styles typically avoid imposing total liability on either party to the dispute. Disputants are not singled out as offenders or victims but liability is jointly shared or no liability is assessed. A tale from the Sufi Islamic tradition in the Middle East illustrates this aspect of the conciliatory style:

> One of the stories told of the Mulla Nasrudin depicts him as a magistrate hearing his first case. The plaintiff argues so persuasively that Nasrudin exclaims, "I believe you are right." The clerk of the court begs him to restrain himself, since the defendant is yet to be heard. Listening to the defendant's argument, Nasrudin is again so carried away that he cries out, "I believe you are right." The clerk of the court cannot allow this. "Your honor," he says, "they cannot both be right." "I believe your are right," Nasrudin replies. (Berman, 1983, p. 78)

There is no identified deviant in the conciliatory style. Instead, the relationship between disputants itself is often seen as the fundamental problem. Whatever difficulty has occurred is an obstacle to be overcome by joint efforts. In this regard, the conciliatory style differs from both the penal and compensatory styles, which determine winning and losing parties. There are no winners or losers in conciliation, but both parties share equal credit or blame for the outcome (Nader, 1969).

The goal of conciliatory styles is to restore harmony to a ruptured relationship. Harmony can usually be achieved only if contending parties work together to achieve a satisfactory solution. Therefore, conciliatory goals are only accomplished when the decision is acceptable to both conflicting parties.

Because both parties in the conciliatory effort must agree on an outcome, conciliation is a persuasive style of social control. Typically, outcomes reflect compromises between the claims of the parties to the dispute. Imposed solutions would likely leave one party less satisfied than the other, defeating the aim of reconciliation. Parties must accept voluntary solutions through either moral suasion or self-interest.

The conciliatory style differs in all respects from the penal style. Disputants are not held accountable for moral transgressions but reconcile with each other. The goal of the control process is harmony, not punishment. To this end, persuasion, rather than coercion, brings disputing parties together. Because of these differences, the social structural conditions facilitating conciliation diverge from those promoting the penal style.

Conciliatory styles are more similar to compensatory ones. Like compensation, conciliation is grounded in obligations parties have to each other. In both, the major concern is to repair some harm that has arisen, rather than to avenge some value. Hence the conditions that predict conciliation should be closer to those in which compensation arises than those where penal styles flourish. Yet, unlike the one-sided nature of compensatory liability, blame is shared or not allocated at all in conciliatory styles. In addition although compensation is a coercive style where offenders have no choice but to pay victims, conciliation results in mutually agreeable outcomes.

Nature of Harm

Relational damage predicts conciliatory control. When harm primarily affects the relational ties between the parties involved, conciliation is likely to arise. A rupture in the particular obligations one party has to another, rather than normative or material damage, leads to conciliatory control.

Whenever a dispute involves a fundamental matter of value, conciliation is unlikely to arise because the intense passions generated prevent reconciliation between disputants. Likewise, if material damage is extensive enough, compensation rather than conciliation may be the only effective mode of providing redress. When, however, the parties involved see their reciprocal obligations overriding moral or material issues, conciliatory control is likely to occur. This definition of a problem arises when the relational obligations between disputants are strong enough to warrant some effort at repair.

The shared nature of liability in conciliation also implies that both parties participated in and contributed toward the trouble at hand. An incident where one party commits, and the other party suffers, all the harm is unlikely to lead to a conciliatory outcome. For example, an unprovoked attack by one person on another is unlikely to generate conciliation because the victim shares no fault for the offense. In contrast, if the matter at issue emerges within an ongoing chain of provocations and responses, both parties may be more willing to assume some responsibility and reach a compromise solution.

PREDICTORS OF CONCILIATION

Relational Distance

Two related aspects of social relationships predict conciliatory styles of social control. The first is whether social relationships involve many ties or only a single tie. The second is whether one or both disputants wish to continue their relationship in the future.[1] *Conciliation is related to the presence of multiple and lasting ties between conflicting parties.*

When disputes arise among people who share many ties, each disputant must calculate the extent to which enmity will disrupt entire networks of relationships. To the extent that the relationship involves multiple interests, parties will be more likely to settle amiably, thus preserving their wider network of ties. When, in contrast, parties who do not share common bonds become involved in disputes, they are con-

[1]Although relational continuance often overlaps with the multiplexity of ties, this need not be the case. For example, retailers who must obtain goods from one supplier have a single tie that they have a strong interest in maintaining. Likewise, tenants may have a strong interest in preserving a uniplex relationship with their landlords. Conversely, residents of total institutions such as prisons, nursing homes, boarding schools, and the like may have multiplex relationships with each other and their keepers that they have little interest in maintaining.

cerned neither with preserving their relationship nor with alienating members of their wider networks. Hence disputants who are not tightly bound together face fewer potential sanctions from their informal networks if they pursue hostilities than those who are more tightly intertwined.

Another element of relationships that affects the possibility of conciliation is the degree to which relationships between contesting parties are likely to continue in the future. Disputants must judge whether the continuance of their relationship or the pursuit of a grievance is most important to them. If continuance is desirable or unavoidable, the chance of a conciliatory outcome is enhanced, and social control efforts strive to reconcile the parties in conflict. Because both sides in a continuing relationship must continue to live together, an unbalanced outcome to a dispute can disturb relational harmony. Because conciliatory styles do not feature a winner and a loser but provide balanced outcomes, they are most suitable for preserving relationships (Nader, 1969). The logic of conciliation is based upon continuing and interlocking networks of interaction.

Finally, the probability of conciliatory control varies according to the embeddedness of disputants in social groups. Relationships and groups that are marked by multiplex and continuing ties feature much conciliation. Integrated members with kinship, religious, work, and organizational ties to traditional social institutions have a stake in maintaining their reputations and social positions. In contrast, marginal individuals who lack social ties and reputational stakes are less concerned with protecting their position in their communities so are less likely to engage in conciliation.

The association between conciliation and multiplex and continuing relational ties implies that the probability of conciliatory outcomes decreases as disputes move from kin to friends and neighbors to strangers (Black, 1976, p. 47). Therefore, *conciliation is inverse to the relational distance between disputants.*

Conciliation should be an especially prominent style of resolution when disputes arise within intimate social space. Conciliatory settlements abound in groups that feature strongly bonded relationship that people cannot escape. Gluckman's classic study of dispute settlement among the Lozi of Northern Rhodesia indicates that

> most Lozi relationships are multiplex, enduring through the lives of individuals and even generations. Each of these relationships is part of an intricate network of similar relationships. Inevitably, therefore, many of the disputes which are investigated by Lozi kutas arise not in ephemeral relationships involving single interests, but in relationships which embrace many interests,

> which depend on similar related relationships, and which may endure into the future. . . . The Lozi disapprove of any irremediable breaking of relationships. For them it is a supreme value that villages should remain united, kinfolk and families and kinship groups should not separate, lord and underling should remain associated. . . . Therefore the court tends to be conciliating; it strives to effect a compromise acceptable to, and accepted by, all the parties. (Gluckman, 1967, pp. 20-21)

Conciliation is particularly necessary when disputes arise among kin. Unlike other social ties, ties between kin cannot be dissolved. The lingering resentment from nonconciliatory efforts would be especially troubling between kin who must continue to live together.

Social control efforts among persons integrated into a common community should also be likely to result in conciliation because disputants share common bonds and face common normative pressures from other people. In addition, neither compensation nor punishment is an acceptable strategy of social control within intimate social space (See Chapters 2 and 3). For example, among the Jalemo of New Guinea, when disputes occur among members of the same men's house, the typical system of corporate liability cannot arise because members cannot be responsible for both providing and receiving compensation or punishment. In such a situation, they must strive to reconcile the two parties instead, or, reconciliation failing, to create avoidance relationships (Koch, 1974).

Among the Tiv of West Africa, when disputes arise among kinsmen, neighbors and other relatives are called in to help settle matters in a communal context called a *moot* (Bohannon, 1957). These moots consider the particular dispute within the overall context of disputants' relationships with each other and the community. Their goal is to insure that past grudges will not linger and that future obligations will be met. This can only be done if the solution provided is mutually acceptable to both parties. When neighbors are also linked by many shared ties, conciliation is similarly a prominent feature of dispute resolution systems (Evans-Pritchard, 1940). Among the Bunyoro of Uganda, disputes between members of the same community are handled through community forums where all residents are invited to participate (Beattie, 1973). Such common forums strive not only to settle the dispute but to reconcile the disputants with each other. Reestablishing good relationships between the parties rather than assessing liability is the central aim in conciliatory settlements between parties who must continue to live together.

Among the Arusha of East Africa, disputes between age-mates are settled through the "friendly acceptable intervention of other age-mates who are concerned both with the reconciliation of their fellows and with the preservation of group unity" (Gulliver, 1963, p. 55). Disputes between members of different age groups, in contrast, typically proceed to resolution at a parish assembly. Or, in an Atlantic fishing village, when offenses arose among integrated members, the typical response was to either deny a problem existed or to engage in settlement oriented behavior (Yngvesson, 1978). Likewise, the insiders of a rural Bavarian village managed disputes through nonconfrontational approaches whereas marginals pursued more aggressive strategies (Todd, 1978).

When disputes arise within close relational space in modern societies, as well, the natural inclination of third parties is to reconcile the disputants. The police, for example, are decreasingly likely to reconcile and increasingly likely to arrest as disputes occur between kin, acquaintances, and strangers (Black, 1971; Smith & Klein, 1984). Legal officials attempt to reconcile and strive to avoid penal resolutions for cases among intimates that enter courts. Forums such as juvenile and family courts that deal with intra-family conflicts feature attempts to reconcile disputants and preserve relationships rather than to punish and assign blame (Pleck, 1987). Or, within professional organizations, the reaction to transgressions of insiders strives toward reconciliation and is rarely punishment oriented (Grabowsky, 1984, pp. 176-177). Whenever disputes arise among classmates, workmates, or participants in common endeavors, attempts at conciliation are likely to precede the use of more repressive styles of social control.

Conciliation, however, is unlikely when intimates do not expect or want their relationships to continue. For example, abused wives who are separated or in the process of obtaining a divorce from their husbands are more likely to demand that the police arrest their husbands than to reconcile with them (Berk, Berk, Newton, & Loseke, 1984; Black, 1980, Chapter 5). Disputes are particularly likely to become bitter when once close parties who have become adversaries confront each other. Former spouses seeking redress, siblings fighting over an inheritance, severed employees suing ex-employers, or dealers who have lost their franchises (Macaulay, 1963) may resist all efforts at compromise and demand total vindication of their claims.

The possibility of successful conciliation declines with increasing relational distance. Conciliation is rare when disputes involve parties at a greater distance because "if a dispute arises between two people who are comparative strangers to each other, there is no need for the court to reconcile them, since they are associated by a single contractual or delictual relationship which can be adjusted by a clear decision" (Gluckman, 1967, p. 55). Social control exercised by integrated persons against marginal ones or marginal people against more integrated ones is likely to display a penal orientation (see Chapter 2). Such disputes are more likely to involve efforts at punishment and legal redress and display little effort at harmonious resolution (Baumgartner, 1978; Todd, 1978; Yngvesson, 1978). Even in communities with strong normative pressures toward conciliation, marginal members are likely to pursue confrontational approaches both against insiders and each other (Ellickson, 1986; Engel, 1984; Greenhouse, 1986).

Disputes among marginals have the least probability of conciliation because both disputants lack the reciprocal obligations and community ties that underlie conciliation and neither party is part of a network that has an interest in harmoniously resolving the dispute (Todd, 1978). Because marginals have neither ties to each other nor to potential mediators, their conflicts are far more likely to feature cycles of aggression and retaliation rather than negotiation (see Chapter 2).

The predominance of conciliation in premodern societies and its decline in contemporary societies is due to the changing nature of relational ties in groups rather than to an affinity of tribal culture to conciliation and modern culture to litigiousness. In both settings, conciliation occurs in dense and intimate social space and atrophies with growing relational distance. Although the type of social space conducive to conciliation has diminished, the logic of its use has not changed.

Group Ties

It follows from the nature of social ties giving rise to conciliation that certain types of groups are more likely to feature this style of social control. Social settings marked by tightly interlocked configuration of social bonds inherently push toward conciliation because each relationship is entangled into a number of different overlapping system (Colson, 1953). When both disputants are embedded in social networks that share mutual ties, not only will each disputant face pressures from each other but also from other network members who would suffer from a rupture in the relationship. In contrast, weak, distant, and temporary bonds provide the least likely settings for conciliatory outcomes. Groups that are based on kinship status, that have dense ties within a fixed space, and that feature many cross-linkages should all display much conciliation.

Conciliation should be a prominent style of social control whenever kinship forms the basis of citizenship rights. Unlike marriage or friendship, people cannot choose to abolish blood ties. Where one's status derives from kin relationships, people have no choice but to get along with agnates or become expatriates (Bohannon, 1957). Groups where kin groups collectively share wealth, jointly hold property, arrange marriages, and guide all other important areas of life feature much conciliation.

In addition to kin-based societies, conciliation should predominate within groups that feature strongly bonded ties with fixed residence. Social conditions that make dispersal unfeasible should promote conciliatory styles of control. In such settings, it is especially difficult to terminate relationships or maintain hostilities for long periods of time. For example, in settled agricultural communities that require coordination and fixed residence, disputes must be resolved in the context of continuing relationships (Roberts, 1979). Disputes that linger create a great degree of structural disturbance in groups with interlocking bonds. The assessment of blame on only one of the disputing parties enhances the chances of continuing resentment. Hence such groups resist assessing individual liability and focus on repairing ruptured social relationships. Conversely, when disputants can easily leave the problematic situation, reconciliation becomes less likely. For example, hunting and gatherers feature little conciliation (Roberts, 1979).

Finally, whenever group life is marked by strong cross-linkages, conciliation is likely to be a prominent style of social control. Third parties who know both parties in conflict face pressures either to remain neutral or to reconcile the disputants, rather than to support one party in a conflict. The pressure of multiple affiliations, crosscutting loyalties, and participation in joint spheres of attachment enhance the desire to continue a ruptured relationship and to use conciliatory settlement styles. Hence, a study of the social control of homicide in 30 societies finds that killings within interconnected networks are only half as likely to lead to revenge as those when killers and their victims belong to discrete networks (Cooney, 1988, Chapter 2). In general, crosscutting ties push conflicts toward less drastic means of pursuing grievances than would otherwise occur.

The degree to which conciliation is a likely style of social control varies according to the interlocking interests of the relational networks that are involved. Among the Jalemo of the New Guinea Highlands, when marital disputes arise, kin typically pressure each spouse to reconcile (Koch, 1974). Yet the vigor of their efforts depends on the extent to which the kin network of one spouse has ties with the network of the other spouse. When network ties, as well as the marriage itself, are disrupted, pressures increase for a conciliated settlement. Escalation of the conflict is more likely when no network members show interest in achieving a negotiated compromise. Likewise, conciliation rarely occurs in conflicts between members of different groups that do not share crosscutting ties.

Barton (1919, p. 93) explains in his study of the Ifugao tribe of the Philippines how crosscutting ties promote settlement when disputes arise among kin:

> It is the duty of mutual, equally related relatives and kin to try to arrange peace between opposing kin or relatives. In the event of procedure on the part of one kinsman against another, those who are related to both take sides with him to whom they are more closely related. Besides blood relationship, there is marriage relationship oftentimes to make it a very complex and difficult problem for a man to decide to which opponent his obligation binds him. This is most frequently the case among the remoter kin. A man who finds himself in such a position, and who knows that on whichever side he may array himself will be severely criticized by the other, becomes a strong advocate of compromise and peaceful settlement. Hence quarrels between residents of the same valleys typically end through conciliation whereas those between individuals who live further away often escalate into feuds.

Disputants who live in the same physical space face pressure as well from parties who also know their adversaries. Persons with links to both disputing parties are optimally placed to arrange conciliatory outcomes. Among the Murngin in Australia, individuals who have ties to two feuding clan groups have divided loyalties. They attempt to arrange reconciliation ceremonies between the warring clans (Warner, 1958, p. 156). Or, among the Shavante Indians in Brazil, minority members of groups with ties to other villages served as negotiators in attempts to bring fighting and warfare to a halt (Maybury-Lewis, 1967, p. 212). In rural Albania, when friends request a disputant to compromise, he must listen or risk quarreling with his friends as well as his adversary (Hasluck, 1954, p. 405). The presence of many cross-linking relationships in a group assures the presence of many potential conciliators with linkages to both disputing parties.

Whenever groups feature dense networks of interaction between people who share many binding ties, conciliation is prevalent. Hence conciliatory styles typify many preindustrial communities as well as tribal groups. Most traditional societies display a strong inclination toward compromise in disputes among settled residents. This is illustrated in the maxim of eighteenth-century rural Frenchmen that "a bad agreement is better than a good lawsuit" (Castan, 1983, p. 224). For example, in Lebanese villages, situations of conflict begin with individuals but come to involve family groups (Rothenberger, 1978; Witty, 1980). There is a strong preference to settle grievances peaceably because of the necessity to maintain ongoing relationships. Resolution is successful to the extent that the families concerned share economic and political alliances.

In the Colonial period in the United States, when disputes arose within tightly linked communities, conciliation predominated (Auerbach,

1983). Indeed, it still thrives in those pockets of close knit communities that remain in this country. For instance, tightly-knit Chinese (Doo, 1973) and Hasidic Jewish communities (*Columbia Journal of Law and Social Problems*, 1970) turn to conciliatory forums to resolve disputes that arise among their members.

Conciliatory styles also still flourish in societies that feature strong cross-linked groups. Dispute settlement in Japanese society features a strongly conciliatory nature (Kawashima, 1963). The embeddedness of Japanese in interlocked groups leads to the presence of many potential mediators. When disputes arise in Japan between groups who have no cross-links, a conciliatory settlement becomes less likely (Kawashima, 1963). If the appropriate social conditions are present, the logic of social relationships leads to a conciliatory style of resolving disputes.

In most settings in modern societies, however, the conditions conducive to conciliation are absent. Cohesive and stable communities with many cross-linked individuals rarely exist. Even when disputants live in the same neighborhood, they are often not integrated into a unitary social structure (Merry, 1982). Where no overlapping ties or interests exist, there is little hope for conciliatory solutions to disputes. In such socially fragmented situations, coercion, exit, or simply avoiding the other disputant become more common responses than conciliation to grievances.

Hierarchy

Conciliation is premised on a fundamental equality between disputants. Shared liability implies that neither party is superior to the other. In addition, the joint nature of conciliatory liability implies that both parties have the capacity and autonomy necessary for a shared resolution. Only parties who are sufficiently close to one another in not only horizontal but also vertical space should be capable of the mutuality and reciprocity at the heart of conciliatory social control. This indicates that *conciliation varies inversely with inequality*. The logic of conciliation only applies when there is a relatively egalitarian relationship between disputing parties. In this respect, conciliation differs both with the penal style, which is typically applied between unequal parties, and with the compensatory style, which often moves upwardly.

Because conciliation entails a mutually agreeable settlement, it is most likely to occur where contesting parties and their networks are relatively equal in power. When there is great inequality, the more powerful party or group is able to dictate terms of an outcome, vitiating the nature of a conciliatory outcome. Because coercion cannot be applied in conciliation, a more powerful party will rarely have an incentive to bargain with a less powerful one. A powerful party who is not satisfied with an outcome may simply refuse to comply with it. This usually means that a mutually acceptable solution is only possible if the less powerful party gives up more to satisfy the more powerful one.

When disputes arise between unequal parties, people who arrange compromises usually have a greater incentive to side with the stronger party. For example, among the Shavante Indians of Brazil:

> A case of [theft] that involves members of factions between which there is already bad blood can lead to serious consequences. The chief tries to talk out the matter and restore harmony. If he is unsuccessful then the community as a whole takes measures primarily intended to restore peace rather than to restore property. So if the accused are stronger than the plaintiffs the easiest way to restore harmony is to side with the former. (Maybury-Lewis, 1967, pp. 183-184).

Or, among the Konyak Naga villagers in India:

> Where guilt and innocence are beyond doubt the judges often evince remarkable impartiality, but where the balance of rights and wrongs is unclear and the councilors strive for a compromise solution, the influence of a powerful clan may well be decisive. For a judgement which disgruntles a large and powerful group does not contribute to village harmony, and it is this harmony more than an abstract notion of justice which the judges consider the principal aim of their endeavors (Furer-Haimendorf, 1967, p. 92).

Social harmony is more easily achieved when the more powerful party is satisfied.

In legal forums, as well, disputes between grievants who are status equals result in more compromise outcomes whereas status inequality leads to more one-sided outcomes. For example, in the seventeenth-century New Haven Colony, three-quarters of court cases resulted in the declaration of a winner and loser and only one-quarter in a compromise solution. These compromises disproportionately occurred between plaintiffs and defendants of equal status (Baumgartner, 1978). In the courts of medieval Bologna, as well, equality led to compromise and inequality to one-sided solutions (Blanshed, 1982). Modern court decisions reproduce the logic that equates equality with conciliation and inequality with one-sided outcomes (Galanter, 1974).

The same dynamics indicate why conciliatory outcomes are most likely to occur in small-scale groups marked by relative equality and why increasing group stratification leads to more punishment-oriented settlements (Schwartz & Miller, 1964; Spitzer, 1975). Other things equal, highly stratified social settings do not provide conducive social space for conciliatory resolutions of disputes.

Organization

The same factors that predict conciliation between individuals also predict when organizations in conflict are likely to reach conciliatory solutions. Conciliation between organizations is most likely when organizational relationships involve persisting and multistranded ties and continuing relationships. An organization that is dependent on another is most likely to comply voluntarily when the latter requests cooperation (Braitwaite, 1989, pp. 135-136). In addition, when organizations possess a relative equality of resources, compromise is often in the mutual interest of the parties. For example, when disputes arise between governments and defense suppliers or between major industries and strong unions, conciliation is a likely outcome (Macaulay, 1966). The welfare of each party depends on maintaining a working relationship with the other, and neither can afford to break the tie completely. Similarly, businesses that depend on repeated purchases from consumers will have a greater incentive to reconcile with complaining customers than ones that do not expect repeat business (Ross & Littlefield, 1978). On the other hand, if disputes occur between a government with a choice of many suppliers or between a business with a monopoly and disorganized customers, it is often easier for the organization to either discontinue the relationship or pursue a penal strategy (Hirshman, 1970).

There may also be a greater tendency for disputes that involve organizations to reach conciliatory outcomes than those between individuals. Whereas ties between individuals may be fleeting, organizations are by their nature less transient. The inability of organizations to leave a conflict situation may make them more likely to negotiate solutions. Organizations also are likely to derive mutual benefits from their association and be less likely to desire vengeance when wronged (Reiss, 1984). This facilitates the bargaining relationships that are at the heart of the conciliatory style. In addition, cross-linkages are often present between members of the disputing organizations, so potential mediators are likely to be present who can facilitate settlements. Because so many disputes in modern life involve organizations, more conciliation occurs than the nature of social relationships between individuals alone would predict. As the importance of organizations expands, the use of conciliatory control should also grow.

Conclusion

Conciliation occurs in different social space than do penal and compensatory control. It arises among parties at closer relational distances than compensation or punishment. The penal style emerges at the greatest social distance when disputants share few or no ties in common. Compensation is most likely to occur at intermediate social distances when there are some links of obligation between parties. Conciliation, in contrast, is more common where closer ties exist between members of linked kin, peer, neighborhood, or family groups. In these settings, compensation seems too impersonal a style of dispute resolution whereas punishment threatens the continuance of relationships.

The direction of conciliation also differs from compensatory and penal styles. Penal control moves across great distances of intimacy and power but atrophies in close and equal relationships. Compensation is more likely to be paid by higher to lower status and from more to less organized parties. Conciliation, on the other hand, flourishes among integrated and equal members of tightly knit communities.

Conciliatory control thus emerges when enmeshed and relatively equal persons and groups find themselves enmeshed in disputes but atrophies with individualization, social distance, and inequality. The paucity of settings that would allow the conciliatory style to take root in modern societies explains the relative absence of mutually agreed upon and harmonious outcomes for many disputes in the contemporary world. As transient, impersonal, and distinct ties become characteristic features of social life, the conditions for conciliatory control are undermined.

Two aspects of modern life, however, do promote conciliation (see also Chapter 7). The first is the growth and prominence of relationships between organizations that are likely to produce conciliatory solutions. The presence of organizations reproduces at a different level in modern societies the conditions that typify preindustrial groups. Conciliation becomes a prominent means of settling organizational conflicts that emerge in modern life (Galanter, 1974).

Lawyers provide a second means of transforming the disputes of modern life into a form that renders them more accessible to conciliatory outcomes. Although the mobilization of a lawyer in a dispute situation represents a penal rather than a conciliatory strategy, once lawyers have become involved they may render conciliation more likely (Black, 1989). Lawyers bring into play their own networks of ties in disputes between parties who otherwise would have no basis for negotiation. Attorneys for disputants often share many ties themselves, are involved in mutually overlapping networks, and share a common legal culture (Macaulay, 1979). The cross-linkages between attorneys substitute for the absence of ties between disputants to create the social space necessary to negotiate conciliatory outcomes. Lawyers become the modern equivalent of mediators in tribal groups, creating the conditions for conciliation in an unexpected location. In this way, the growth of the legal profession can lead not just to greater litigiousness but to more conciliatory outcomes. In cases where the nature of ties between disputants are too weak to bring about conciliation, those between attorneys may successfully lead to compromise.

The emergence of organizations and lawyers produces new settings for conciliation in the modern world. Paradoxically, compromise now settles disputes between otherwise weakly linked parties because of the growth of a legal profession ostensibly oriented toward litigiousness and advocacy but in practice often working to arrange mutually agreeable outcomes.

5

The Therapeutic Style

INTRODUCTION

Elements of Therapy

Therapeutic social control changes the personalities of impaired individuals. Their behaviors seem strange, wayward, out of sorts, or incomprehensible to themselves or others. The providers of therapeutic control strive to return patients to normality through manipulating symbolic systems. Patients must cooperate with therapists for successful healing efforts to result. The intended outcome is not an order directed at an adversary, the fulfillment of an obligation, or the repair of a damaged relationship, but a change in a disordered personality.

The allocation of responsibility in therapeutic styles differs from other styles. People who enter therapeutic systems are not seen as morally wrong but as victims of an illness process beyond their control. In such cases the attribution of responsibility seems unwarranted. Rather, their behavior is often viewed as symptomatic of an underlying illness condition to be remedied by diagnosis and treatment.

One goal of therapeutic control is to allow afflicted individuals and those around them to make sense of their disordered behavior. Incomprehensible and disturbing actions must be rendered explicable within cultural frameworks of meaning. Another goal is to return disrupted personalities and relationships to normality. Therapeutic processes aim to change personalities rather than uphold moral standards.

Because the problems of disordered individuals are perceived to lie in their personalities, the techniques of therapeutic styles are geared toward changing inner states. Therapies rely on manipulating symbols that are meaningful to people undergoing change. Because the symbolic reorganization of the personality is impossible if participants do not believe in the efficacy of the therapeutic technique, therapists must mobilize the expectations and trust of those they attempt to heal (Frank, 1973). Therefore, therapeutic agents are often associated with medical and religious roles because medical and religious healers occupy positions that mobilize symbolic commitments (Parsons, 1942).

Because therapeutic control must rely on symbolic commitments it needs the willing consent and participation of disordered people. Although punishment or compensation can be mandated, personality transformations can only occur when patients and therapists cooperate to bring about change. Therefore, therapy must be a voluntary style of social control.

Therapy is a distinctive style of social control. Individuals are not held responsible for their actions, and controllers do not pass moral judgments. The afflicted bear no liability because their intentions and capacities to exercise free will seem impaired. They are seen as possessed by symptoms beyond their control that render them the victims rather than the agents of their behaviors. Persons in healing roles assume responsibility for treatment and strive to return clients to normality through manipulating symbolic systems.

Nature of Harm

Disruptions to personalities activate therapeutic control systems. When some sort of damage is perceived to result from disordered personalities rather than from deliberate rule breaking, accident, or negligence, therapy is a likely response. Whether harm is characterized as stemming from damaged personalities rather than some other source is highly variable. A number of factors influence this characterization.

The damage that activates therapeutic control does not result from deliberate rule breaking. Therapeutic control typically results when the motivations behind deviant actions seem senseless, incoherent, or unintelligible to observers (Horwitz, 1982, Chapter 2). In contrast, deviant actions that stem from recognizable motives such as insult, greed, or quarrels, activate penal, compensatory, or conciliatory styles. When observers cannot fathom why persons engage in actions that seem to have no rational basis such as exhibitionism, child molestation, or kleptomania they often regard therapy as an appropriate response. People who enter therapy lack the rational intent and ability to control their actions that might otherwise render them blameworthy and liable to punishment.

In all societies, bizarre behavior and motiveless violence are subject to therapeutic control. For instance, among the Laotians, psychotic people are seen as having no control over their behavior so are not held responsible for their actions. Witches, however, are viewed as responsible for their delicts because they deliberately seek to harm others (Westemeyer, 1973). Therefore, Laotian witches are punished rather than treated. Likewise, among the Konyak Nagas in India, arson that stems from intention or carelessness is punished by exile. However, a person known to be insane who sets a house on fire is neither banished nor punished (Furer-Haimendorf, 1967). In Western societies, people who commit otherwise criminal acts who either lack criminal intent or the capacity to control their actions because of mental illness are not liable to punishment.

Typical behaviors that enter therapeutic systems also have a special relationship to the element of capacity. Unlike persons who are liable to punishment because they chose their actions, mentally ill people seem to become disordered in spite of themselves (Aubert & Messinger, 1958). Because their actions do not enhance their self-interest, it seems that the mentally ill lack the capacity to alter their behavior. This explains why harm that results from negligence or accident does not give rise to therapy: those who act negligently or accidentally presumably were capable of rational behavior. In contrast, the absence of reason seems behind the actions of those who are subject to therapy. Not only do actors not benefit from their actions but what they do seems to harm their self-interest (Feinberg, 1970).

The harm giving rise to the therapeutic style stems from a defect in the personality system. Punishment is inappropriate since actors lack elements of intention, capacity, or both. Compensation presumes some personal gain or culpability while conciliation presupposes conscious bargaining and negotiation between equally capable people. When wayward behavior seems to arise from a fundamental personality defect, therapy becomes a likely style of social control.

Predictors of Therapy

Relational Distance[1]

The probability of a therapeutic response is related to the social distance between the agents and objects of therapy: *Therapeutic control is*

[1]The prediction of who uses therapeutic styles diverges from explaining the use of other styles in one important respect. Because the entry into therapy is often self-initiated, the agent and object of therapy are identical. Therefore, the factors that predict who enters therapy also predict who initiates therapy.

inverse to the relational distance between persons. Therapeutic control flourishes when problems arise between persons at the closest relational distance: husbands and wives, parents and children, or boyfriends and girlfriends. When these problems are perceived to lie in one of the parties rather than in their relationship, therapy becomes the social control method of choice. As the relational distance between parties grows, comparable actions are more likely to be defined in modes designed to discredit, rather than to help, the objects of control.

The sorts of problems that eventually lead people to enter therapy often arise within intimate interpersonal space. For example, in sixteenth-century England, typical problems evoking a therapeutic response included people who attacked members of their own families, children who challenged elders, wives who rebelled against husbands, or husbands who neglected their families (Macdonald, 1981). Similar attacks and rebellions against persons at a greater distance would have elicited a penal reaction. Or, in contemporary Barbados, quarrels with family members, within villages, and disputes with those of similar class standing typify the precipitants to therapy (Fisher, 1985). In contrast, more distant members are rarely involved. Although family members are typically involved in getting intimates to enter psychotherapy, efforts to impose psychotherapy on friends, neighbors, or more distant parties are rare (Baumgartner, 1988, p. 84; Horwitz, 1982).

Actions that would be crimes if they occurred among strangers often lead to therapeutic responses if intimates are involved. The likelihood that persons who commit incest, child abuse, wife beating, or spouse murdering will be referred to psychiatric therapy is far higher than when similar crimes occur between strangers. Infanticides, for instance, often result in successful pleas of insanity (e.g. Brumberg, 1984; Donovan, 1981; Showalter, 1985).

Even within families, the greater the intimacy between spouses the greater the likelihood of a therapeutic response. Spouses in close, affectionate marital relationships respond to strange behaviors with more sympathy, sensitivity, and persuasiveness. More distant spouses are more likely to react through rejection and negative labels indicative of contempt or moral dereliction rather than of psychological illness (Clausen, 1983).

Growing social and cultural distance between people who apply labels and those who are labeled leads to more punishment-oriented responses (Horwitz, 1982, pp. 47-51). All else constant, when responses move toward less integrated and more marginal and culturally distant members, they are more likely to have a penal than a therapeutic character. Consider, for instance, the reaction to a case of attempted homicide between members of different Somali clans who were living in England:

> A twenty-four-year-old Dulbahante seaman shot a man of the Habar Tol Ja'lo [clan] in the back in Bute Street on the 8th of February. . . . At his trial, the accused alleged that he was being victimized and was stated to have delusions that an organization had been formed to intimidate him. A Medical Officer gave evidence to the effect that he suffered from paranoiac schizophrenia. . . . In spite, however, of the medical evidence the case was regarded in Somaliland as simply another manifestation of Dulbehante and Habar Tol Ja'lo hostility. What was significant, was that a man of the Dulbehante had tried to kill a man of the Habar Tol Ja'lo. (Lewis, 1961, pp. 254-255)

Whenever deviance crosses great social distances, a penal, rather than a therapeutic, response is likely.

Throughout Western history, integrated members of communities have been treated sympathetically whereas socially marginal disordered individuals were either expelled from communities or incarcerated in isolated institutions (Fox, 1978; Rosen, 1968; Rothman, 1971). The character of mental hospitals themselves changed from therapeutic to custodial over the course of the nineteenth century as their population came to consist of marginal, foreign born, and culturally distant individuals (Grob, 1973). The great distance that emerged between controllers and patients predicted the decline of therapeutic and the rise of custodial responses. In modern societies, employed, married, higher status, and integrated members of society enter psychiatric treatment voluntarily whereas involuntary commitments are disproportionately reserved for marginal members of society such as the unemployed, unmarried, divorced, or powerless (Linksy, 1970; Mandersheid & Barrett, 1987, p. 93).

Therapeutic control, then, thrives in the most intimate social spaces. The sympathetic exploration of the personality is maximal in social control that arises among intimates. When, however, disturbances are created by strangers, motivations are less relevant, and punishment-oriented responses are more forthcoming. Therapy is also likely when social control is directed at insiders but rarer when control efforts move outwardly toward marginals.

Gender

The use of therapeutic social control varies by gender: *Women are more likely than men to provide therapy* (Horwitz, 1982, p. 75). Women not only initiate therapeutic help seeking more often for themselves but also play a more active part in therapeutic help seeking for their male and female intimates. In a wide variety of cultures, wives of disordered husbands respond sympathetically and with efforts at initiating therapy, whereas men ignore or react with anger to the problems of their wives (Horwitz, 1982, pp. 76-77; Rogler and Hollingshead, 1965; Safilios-Rothschild, 1968; Scheper-Hughes, 1979).

In modern American, as well, wives are more prone than husbands to recognize the psychiatric problems of spouses, respond sympathetically and provide support, and participate actively in the help-seeking process (Clausen, Pfeffer, & Huffine, 1982; Ginsberg & Brown, 1982; Horwitz, 1977b). For example, one study shows that wives are twice as likely as husbands to play a major role in their spouses' entry into psychiatric treatment (Clausen *et al.*, 1982). In contrast, males react to the psychiatric problems of others with neglect or more punishment-oriented responses. In many times and places, the responsibility of women for the upkeep of the moral order of intimate social groups extends to their prominent role as agents of therapeutic control.

Social Status

Therapy is a unique style of social control not only because of its location in gendered social space but also because of its status character. Higher status people are more likely to react therapeutically to the delicts of both themselves and other people: *Therapeutic control is directly related to social status* (Horwitz, 1982, p. 64). Controlling for the presence of personality problems, people of high social-class standing and educational attainment who maintain humanistic cultural orientations are most likely to respond to deviance therapeutically.

Therapeutic responses are more likely to be rendered to higher than to lower status persons (Horwitz, 1987). In the nineteenth century in both the United States and Europe, the treatment of mental disorder as a psychological disorder amenable to psychotherapy was mostly confined to the upper classes (Dain, 1964, Chapter 2; Ellenberger, 1970). Likewise, throughout the developing world, only members of the middle and upper classes are likely to apply therapeutic labels and bring to psychiatric attention cases other than the most severe psychoses (see Horwitz, 1982, p. 67). In the contemporary United States, although a consistent finding of epidemiological surveys is that rates of mental illness vary inversely with socioeconomic status (Link & Dohrenwend, 1980), rates of entry into therapy vary directly with social class. Upper-class people define their problems through illness frameworks, are treated sympathetically, seek help for a wide range of emotional and interpersonal disturbances, and enter treatment near the emergence of psychological disorders through self-referrals or referrals from family or friends (Goldberg & Huxley, 1980; Hollingshead & Redlich, 1958; Kadushin, 1969). Although few higher class patients ever enter public mental institutions, those who do are likely to receive psychotherapy whereas lower-class patients are ignored or treated repressively (Hollingshead and Redlich, 1958; Link & Milcarek, 1980).

In contrast, lower-class persons are likely to interpret mental problems as symptomatic of physical problems or negative personality traits such as laziness or drunkenness and are unlikely to initiate voluntary therapeutic help seeking. Their problems come to the attention of the mental health system through referrals from social agencies or formal agents of social control rather than self-referrals or referrals from intimates (Goldberg & Huxley, 1980; Hollingshead & Redlich, 1958).

Studies that separate the components of social class differences generally find that education is more important than income in accounting for therapeutic help seeking (Gurin, Veroff, & Field, 1960; Veroff, Kulka, & Douvan, 1981). In particular, participation in liberal and humanistic culture facilitates contact with mental health professions (Greenley & Mechanic, 1978; Kadushin, 1969; Marmor, 1975). People in humanistic professions such as teaching, social work, psychology, or the arts are far more likely than others to react therapeutically to the problems of themselves and others (Horwitz, 1982, p. 71).

Similarly, ethnic groups such as Jews who are marked by high levels of introspection, cosmopolitan orientations, and participation in reference groups supportive of psychotherapy have far higher rates of therapeutic utilization than other ethnic groups (Srole *et al.*, 1962; Veroff *et al.*, 1981). In contrast, members of Chinese or Hispanic ethnic groups who have little congruence with psychiatric culture resist help seeking from mental health professionals (Garrison, 1977; Lin, Tardiff, Donetz, & Goresky, 1978).

Why should certain groups such as women, Jews, or higher status people respond to personality problems more therapeutically than others? One reason lies in the nature of conflict management therapeutic control entails. Avoidance as a style of conflict management predominates among higher social classes (Baumgartner, 1988). Problems that are defined therapeutically are located within personalities, rather than relationships. This definition allows people who enter therapy to avoid direct confrontations with intimate others. In addition, therapists are of equivalent social status and share a common culture with patients of higher class standing, so provide more acceptable outlets of conflict management than would mobilizing the police or other control agents of lower status than the grievant (Baumgartner, 1988). Another reason lies in the introspective orientation toward inner feelings among these groups compared to the attention toward external and formal rules that predominates among lower status groups (e.g., Bernstein, 1964; Kohn, 1959; Mechanic & Hansell, 1987). This orientation allows the upper classes to interpret therapeutic help for personality problems as a valuable resource rather than a stigma to be avoided.

In past decades, these cultural differences resulted in highly divergent rates of treatment across social classes (Hollingshead & Redlich, 1958). Now, however, a concern with psychological adjustment and attitudes favorable to psychiatry may be more broadly distributed across American culture than previously (Veroff *et al.*, 1981). The result is that therapeutic help seeking is being transformed from the concern of a small, psychiatrically sophisticated elite group to a process utilized by many segments of the population (Stern, 1977).

Group Ties

The personality and interactional problems to which therapeutic styles of control respond are found in all social groups. Regardless of whether biological, psychological, or social factors cause symptoms, signs of mental disorder are universally recognized and treated (Horwitz, 1982, Chapter 2). Therefore, the fundamental difference between social groups does not lie in whether therapeutic systems arise at all but in what style these systems feature: *The style of therapeutic control reflects the degree of group bondedness* (Horwitz, 1984).

Tightly bonded groups develop communal styles of therapeutic control that share many similarities with conciliatory systems of social control. Communal styles of therapy emerge in groups that grip each member in a tight network of social relationships and bind them to communal purposes. These styles deemphasize the exploration of the personality and deal with problems of normality through strengthening the ties of individuals to the group. They strive to reconcile afflicted individuals with their intimates and restore them to their roles in the community. In contrast, individualistic societies generate individualistic styles of therapy that emphasize subjective motivations and promote individual autonomy. Individualistic therapies arise when people are freed from group ties. They strive to enhance the autonomy of afflicted individuals. In both cases, the social control of the personality corresponds to the nature of the social relationships in the group.

Communal Therapies

In tribal groups, the treatment of mental illness ignores the inner motivations and unique experiences of the ill member (Kaplan & Johnson, 1964, p. 227; Murphy, 1964, p. 79; Prince, 1964, p. 115). Mental symptoms are divorced from the character and uniqueness of the individual and are transformed into elements of a social category rather than of a personal state. These groups respond to mental problems by anchoring the ill person's experiences in the communal symbolism of the group and not in the idiosyncratic experiences of personal life. For example, when the illnesses of Taiwanese are explained by the statement "your soul has been away from the body and has not returned yet" (Tseng, 1976, p. 166) all Taiwanese so inflicted will be given the same explanation, regardless of the details of their illnesses. Or, demonic possession in Ceylon is defined in religious terms that are rooted in group experience and articulated through common cultural categories (Obeysekere, 1970). In such systems, the unique aspects of the patient's personality are not scrutinized because the explanation involves a ritualized symbolic system common to all sick members of the group.

The treatment of mental illness in tribal groups has many similarities to conciliatory styles of social control. In these groups, the community is mobilized to participate in the actual therapeutic process. Therapy is carried out in the presence of family and community members. For example, when confession is used as a treatment for illness, it usually occurs within a public setting (LaBarre, 1964). Cures commonly occur when the individual is placed at the center of group attention during collective activities such as feasts and dances (Frank, 1973, pp. 58-66; Geertz, 1973, pp. 104-105; Murphy, 1964, p. 80).

The Pueblo Indians of North America sometimes respond to illness by ritually adopting the sufferer into a new clan group (J. R. Fox, 1964). Among the Plains Indians of North America, a disturbed individual takes peyote within a collective setting, confesses his sins, and is integrated into the group through collective discussion (Kiev, 1972, p. 112). Group participation in healing ceremonies among the Navaho is involved to the extent that "when hot pokers were applied to the patient's body, the others would receive the same treatment" (Kiev, 1964, pp. 25-26). The healing process in tribal groups is one in which kin and tribe are intensely involved, serving to reconcile the afflicted individual with the wider community.

The nature of social bonds in tribal groups dictates the communal response to illness. In closely knit groups, social dissension or withdrawal presents a severe threat to the solidarity of the entire group. Affected persons must continue to have relationships with those around them. The group response emphasizes the affirmation of the bonds between afflicted individuals and the group and their reintegration into the collectivity. All aspects of the control process stress the similarity of the individual to the group, the values of the collectivity, and the promotion of conformity to group norms. The response to illness not only in tribal societies but in all tightly knit groups such as religious communes, homogeneous ethnic communities in modern societies, and small towns displays these features (see Horwitz, 1982, pp. 158-165).

Individualistic Therapies

Therapeutic control in modern, individualistic societies *inverts* the essential aspects of communal therapies (see Levi-Strauss, 1964). Symbols drawn from self-experience are used to interpret personality problems, not ritualized and communal symbols such as taboo violation, demonic possession, bewitchment, soul loss, or spirit intrusion that do not correspond to a personal state of mind. Cure occurs through self-exploration and consequent self-awareness, not through conformity to the normative order of the group. The individual personality is not submerged into collective ritual but is of paramount concern in the therapeutic process. Finally, therapy itself is an oasis from the social world, rather than a communal affair that mobilizes the energies of the community.

Individualistic styles of therapy develop and thrive in heterogeneous societies where social bonding between members is weak. For example, the first prominent individualistic therapeutic style, psychoanalysis, emerged in Vienna, an urban center of European culture at the turn of the twentieth century, and possibly the most cosmopolitan city of the time (Janik & Toulmin, 1973). Many different ethnic minorities, including the Jews, comprised its heterogeneous population. Freud himself was an urban intellectual alienated from the culture of his forefathers and a member of a marginal Jewish ethnic group. It is fitting that the foremost developer of psychotherapy was someone who, in his own life, had none of the long-standing bonds characteristic of communal social groups. The people who use therapy are also disproportionately drawn from people who lack strong bonding to social groups as well as those who have cosmopolitan and humanistic value systems (Horwitz, 1987).

Although the influence of psychoanalysis is now sharply reduced, it has been replaced by many other even more individualistically oriented therapeutic techniques (Horwitz, 1982, pp. 176-180). The entire social climate of the contemporary United States, the setting where individualistic therapies have flourished to the greatest extent, has itself been called "therapeutic" (Bellah, Madsen, Sullivan, Swidler, & Tipton, 1985). The contemporary United States is also the society where individualism has reached its greatest heights.

The presence of individuated social structures leads not only to a different therapeutic style but also to a growth in the number of problems viewed as liable to therapeutic control. All societies view severe symptoms associated with incomprehensible behaviors as signs of mental disorder to be treated therapeutically (Horwitz, 1982, Chapter 2). In closely knit tribal groups, the definition of mental disorder tends to be limited to a small range of behaviors that modern psychiatrists would call psychoses or organic brain disorders (Horwitz, 1982, p. 79). Indeed, through the end of the nineteenth century, in addition to the psychoses, only a small number of discrete symptoms such as hysteria, phobias, and obsessive-compulsive preoccupations were labeled as mental illness (Leifer, 1969, p. 107).

The breakdown of closely knit social structures and the emergence of less cohesive, industrialized, and urbanized societies is associated with the expansion of the sorts of problems that are liable to therapeutic control. The problems people now bring to therapy have expanded to include various forms of interpersonal disturbances, vague feelings of dissatisfaction, depression, anxiety, and other problems of living (Szasz, 1961). In the contemporary United States:

> People seek treatment because they sleep poorly, or have headaches, or feel apathetic toward loved ones, or because they are dissatisfied with their lives. Patients complain of the boredom and vacuity of their inner freedom, and desire to learn how to fill it by means of strategies that guarantee more direct satisfaction. (Rieff, 1961, p. 334)

In addition, many forms of behavior such as alcohol abuse, drug addiction, or juvenile delinquency that were once punished and now treated therapeutically (Conrad & Schneider, 1980).

Individualistic therapeutic styles flourish to the extent that individuals who lack strong social ties are free to explore the depths of their personalities. When individuals are freed from group ties, they not only define a wide range of problems as suitable for therapy but receive treatments that are suited to an individuated social structure. In psychoanalysis and other forms of individualistic psychotherapies, the cause of problems is located in the personality, symbols are drawn from self-experience, and the goal of treatment is to maximize individual autonomy. In contrast, where individuals are submerged into settings with strong social bonds, the response to their personal afflictions reconciles them with valued others but does not explore the depths of their personalities.

Although the social control of personality problems is found in all social settings, its characteristics reflect the nature of social ties.

Hierarchy

Therapeutic control is often associated with the response to the problems of dependents in interpersonal relationships: *Therapeutic control is related to interpersonal dependency*. Self-definitions of therapeutic need have certain advantages for dependents. In situations where distress cannot be formulated explicitly and directly for fear of alienating the party toward whom the hostility is felt, grievances may be expressed indirectly through personality problems (Ingleby, 1983).[2] Bearers of symptoms can also gain sympathy and relief from adapting the role of victim of an illness (Guarnaccia *et al.*, 1989).

Dominants also obtain benefits from applying therapeutic labels to dependents. When less powerful parties in intimate dyads have grievances against more powerful ones, many common control options are unsuitable for the more powerful party. Conciliation, a common alternative in intimate space, presupposes relative equality between the parties as well as the willingness of the powerful party to engage in negotiation. Compensation is usually an unsuitable outcome for grievances among intimates. The use of penal control is often dishonorable against dependents, especially among higher status people. In contrast, therapeutic responses allow intimates to avoid open confrontation, express sympathy for victims of an illness, and maintain the relational status quo. Through providing individualistic definitions of problems, therapeutic responses protect dominant parties from having to confront directly grievances others may have against them.

One implication of the association of therapeutic control with dependency in intimate social space is the predominance of women as users of therapeutic systems. In most times and places, women have been subordinate to their husbands, fathers, or brothers. One of the most striking aspects of therapeutic control, especially in comparison to other social control styles, is the degree to which women are at least as likely as men to be subject to therapeutic control efforts.

The association of therapeutic systems and female clients holds in a wide variety of times and places. People who enter therapeutic cults in premodern societies are often unmarried women who have been frustrated in love and who have no other means of expressing their outraged

[2]From the point of view of the presumed sufferer, mental symptoms can sometimes be a disguised form of penal social control (see Chapter 2).

feelings, as well as married women who have been neglected or rejected by their husbands (Lewis, 1966; Lambek, 1980; Messing, 1959). In East Africa, Lewis (1966, p. 318; see also Lambek, 1980) comments on the: "widespread use of spirit possession, by means of which women and other depressed categories exert mystical pressures upon their superiors in circumstances of deprivation and frustration when few other sanctions are available to them." The typical patients in Zar therapy in Northern Ethiopia are "married women, who feel neglected in a man's world in which they serve as hewers of wood and haulers of water" (Messing, 1959, p. 320). Therapy provides some relief to less powerful, dependent parties who face situations where the direct expression of hostility and conflict is difficult or impossible. Similarly, in Sri Lanka, women who have conflicts with husbands can symbolically discuss their problems in religious idioms within ritual treatment for demonic possession (Obeysekere, 1970). Seeking help from therapists becomes a strategy for changing a situation through mobilizing a third party who indirectly intervenes and provides relief to the grievant. Gains such as sympathy, attention, and relief from role responsibilities accrue to the patient. Although the structural conflict the treated women face is with their husbands, only the wives enter therapy.

The link of the therapeutic style with female clients also appears in the records of a seventeenth-century physician in England (Macdonald, 1981). Of 2,039 cases where mental disturbance led to consultation, over 60% involved women, most of whom were married. The most common problems were conflicts with husbands, lovers, and parents. Strongly patriarchal values in this society enforced the dependency of women on husbands or parents but limited their ability to remedy disturbing situations in family life. In the vastly different society of modern Korea, a typical client of a folk psychotherapist "had been supporting her family since her husband's business failed. The husband . . . had been chronically unemployed, spending his days lounging at home and his evenings out drinking up her meager earnings. He often beat her, accusing her of hiding money from him. If she complained, he would tell her to get lost" (Harvey, 1976, p. 192). Not the husband, however, but the wife, seeks the assistance of a therapist.

The divergent reaction to psychiatric problems in the contemporary United States still shows clear differences in the style of social control brought to bear on men and women who suffer from psychiatric disorders. There are no consistent gender differences in overall rates of treatment from mental health providers among people who have been identified as psychiatrically disordered in community studies (Fox, 1984; Leaf & Bruce, 1987; Link & Dohrenwend, 1980). Yet substantial differences exist in how men and women react to psychiatric symptoms and seek help for them.

Faced with the presence of personality problems, the response to the symptoms of females is likely to be therapeutic, that to males often displays a penal character. Women seek help voluntarily whereas men are more typically forced into treatment by others (Horwitz, 1977a). Women show greater readiness to define their problems in psychiatric terms; men to resist admitting personal vulnerabilities (Veroff *et al.*, 1981). Given the perception of a psychiatric problem, women more readily think of themselves as in need of help and discuss their difficulties with other people (Horwitz, 1977b; Kessler, Brown, & Broman, 1981). Women typically use voluntary outpatient services or seek help for mental health problems from primary-care physicians whereas men predominate in more coercive inpatient settings (Leaf & Bruce, 1987; Taube & Barrett, 1985). Men are twice as likely as women to be found in public mental hospitals whereas women outnumber men in the presumably more therapeutic settings of private psychiatric hospitals and psychiatric beds in general hospitals (Manderscheid & Barrett, 1987, p. 93). Studies that use hypothetical cases of disordered people also find that the public rejects males more often than females (Phillips, 1964) and defines comparable male and female deviant behavior as criminal and mentally ill, respectively (Phillips & DeFleur, 1982).

The preponderance of women in therapeutic settings across wide cultural and historical settings indicates a structural basis for therapeutic control that is rooted in interpersonal dependency. If this assumption is correct, when men and women share similar structural positions, there should be few gender differences in rates of therapy.

Those men who do enter therapy often share the position of structural dependency that characterizes female patients. For example, among the Valley Tonga in East Africa, women were in inferior positions and dominated spirit possession cults (Lewis, 1966). Among the Plateau Tonga, however, where relative equality existed between the sexes, men and women were equally likely to be found in spirit possession cults. When men did enter possession cults in these groups, they are often young bachelors who have been deprived and frustrated in establishing independent families (Lewis, 1966).

In contemporary societies, rates of therapy are similar for single men and women who share relatively equal positions of dependency. When men do enter psychiatric treatment they are likely to be in subordinate statuses to their parents or wives (Horwitz, 1977a; Tudor *et al.*, 1977) Correspondingly, as equality between the sexes grows, gender differences in entry to therapy decline (Fox, 1984; Leaf & Bruce, 1987).

The reaction to young people who are dependent on parents also illustrates the relationship between dependence and therapeutic control. Misbehaving juveniles have traditionally been considered as deserving of help rather than as evil (Warren & Guttridge, 1984). The delicts of the young are more likely to be treated therapeutically at early ages but elicit penal responses with increasing age (Graham & Rutter, 1977). As dependence declines, the chances of penal reactions grow.

Women in modern societies are becoming full social equals to men. This should attenuate the association between female gender and therapeutic control. Recent studies indeed indicate that the readiness of women and reluctance of men to interpret their problems in therapeutic frameworks and to seek therapeutic help has been more distinct in the past than at present (Fox, 1984; Leaf & Bruce, 1987). The ways in which the sexes respond to psychiatric problems are converging, perhaps because the social space that men and women occupy is now more similar than previously.

Why should women, dependent men, and young people be the typical clients of therapy in a wide variety of times and places? Not gender *per se* but a common position of structural dependence that women share with powerless men, young people, and others who are not able to directly confront those against whom they have grievances accounts for the use of therapeutic control. Defining themselves as victims who suffer from an illness elicits sympathy and pity for afflicted parties. In addition, the lack of autonomy and capacity that are associated with entry into therapy are more congruent with the roles of dependents than of dominants. The result is that dependency and therapeutic control are closely associated when problems arise among intimates.[3]

[3]Little evidence relates therapeutic social control to the degree of inequality in groups. Because therapy rests on persuasion rather than coercion, I would speculate that it is unlikely to occur across wide vertical distances. Therefore, *therapeutic control is inverse to social stratification.* Relatively egalitarian groups should feature more therapy than hierarchical ones. Other things equal, highly stratified societies should respond to deviance through coercion rather than through sympathy for the victims of personality afflictions.

Groups based upon unambiguous authority relationships use commands, threats, or impersonal status appeals to generate conformity whereas less hierarchical groups rely on more person-centered exploration of feeling that can communicate unique experiences of the self (Bernstein, 1964). This implies that settings marked by sharp authority relationships such as working-class families (Bernstein, 1964) or the military (Daniels, 1972) are unlikely to feature much therapeutic control, relative to comparable egalitarian settings. It also appears that totalitarian societies such as Nazi Germany or Stalinist Russia reacted punitively rather than therapeutically to the mentally ill (e.g., Wallace, 1972). The decline of authoritarian rule taking place in the contemporary Soviet Union and Eastern Europe at the beginning of the 1990s, in contrast, should lead to more therapeutic treatment for the mentally ill.

Organization

In every respect, therapeutic styles are inappropriate responses to organizational deviance. The irrational aspect of the deviance to which therapy responds opposes the essentially rational nature of organizations (Weber, 1925). The focus on personality inverts the corporate essence of organization. It is difficult even to imagine how organizations could undergo therapeutic processes.[4] Therefore, *therapeutic control is inverse to the presence of organization.*

Deviance engaged in by more than one person hardly ever results in therapy. A folk saying among the Barbadians—"People drink together but go mad alone"—expresses this process (Fisher, 1985, p. 60). Indeed, the participation of another person in deviant actions is enough to indicate that the act was a rational one inappropriate for a therapeutic response (Goffman, 1971). Whenever deviance is organizationally grounded, even to the extent that more than one individual is involved in an action, a therapeutic response is not likely to be forthcoming.

Conclusion

The therapeutic style is universal. In all settings, the typical elicitors of therapy involve problems that arise in close relational distance. The nature of therapy and the range of problems that elicit therapeutic responses, however, depend on the type of social bonds in the group. Therapeutic control thrives among people whose intimate relationships are characterized by structural dependency. Therapy is the only style of control that disproportionately occurs among women who are otherwise excluded from central social institutions, including social control institutions. In modern societies, it flourishes among people who lack strong bonds to groups and those who share the introspective and individualistic culture of the psychiatric professions. The growth of individualism in modern societies insures that therapy will continue to be a prominent style of social control.

This Part has outlined the social conditions that predict the emergence of four ideal typical styles of social control: the penal, compensatory, conciliatory, and therapeutic. Each embodies different ways of

[4]Family therapy represents a rudimentary modern attempt to treat a corporate unit rather than an individual (e.g., McFarlane, 1983). Whether this treatment will ever become a prominent therapeutic technique is open to question.

constructing harm, defining liability, responding to injuries, and imposing sanctions.

Tightly bonded groups tend to utilize compensatory and conciliatory strategies of control whereas individualization brings about the rise of penal and expansion of therapeutic styles. Highly stratified groups feature penal styles whereas egalitarian groups respond to conflict through conciliation.

The social relationship between disputants also predicts the nature of control responses. As relational distance between disputants increases, therapeutic, conciliatory, compensatory, and penal responses become increasingly likely. Quarrels between parents and children may lead to therapy; between neighbors to conciliation; between different clans to compensation; and between strangers to punishment.

The location of a dispute in vertical space also predicts the style of social control: Downward social control tends to be penal; upward control compensatory. Grievances among marginals or subordinates tend to have a penal character; those among equals to be reconciled. Organizational offenses often lead to compensatory or conciliatory responses; rarely to penal or therapeutic ones. Women tend to provide and accept therapeutic control; men both to give and receive penal responses.

The embeddedness of conflicts in social space influences the style of social control that responds to them. Their grounding in social life also affects the mechanisms that resolve them. The next Part examines how the nature of social relationships shapes the forms of social control.

II

Forms of Social Control

Social life inevitably produces a vast array of conflicts, injuries, injustices, rivalries, discomforts, and irritations. The form of social control refers to the mechanisms that deal with these problematic situations. In most settings, a variety of alternative forums might resolve these troublesome occurrences. Disputants might choose to do nothing at all, avenge the wrong by themselves, negotiate with each other, or take their claims to informal or specially designated social control agents. This chapter considers the factors that determine the sorts of forums people use to resolve their conflicts.

The style and the form of social control are two separate dimensions of control efforts. Each style can proceed through inaction, resort to the extralegal network or the mobilization of official social control agents. Personality problems might be hidden from others, discussed with spouses or friends, or brought to a trained therapist. An abused wife may silently suffer from her husband's violence, withdraw sexual favors, mobilize her kin to punish him, or call the police. Negotiation, as well, can proceed only among the two parties to a dispute, through lawyers representing each party, or within the legal system. Finally, compensation might be pursued directly with the offender, through informal representatives, or in an adjudicative system. A theory of social control predicts when various forms of social control arise.

This Part examines the expansion of social control efforts in social space. Expansion refers to the extent that responses to grievances radiate outward beyond disputants themselves into informal and formal networks for resolution. The least response involves *inaction* where an aggrieved party neither mobilizes third parties for help with a conflict nor negotiates with the other disputant. Inaction falls into a number of distinct categories. One is when people tolerate or ignore behavior and do nothing to sanction behavior they define as deviant. Or the victim may choose the route of avoidance and cut off further interaction with the offending party (Felstiner, 1974). Another type of inaction occurs when victims exit from situations without imposing sanctions on offenders.

Social control efforts when respondents move beyond inaction to make some direct response to a grievance can be grouped into unilateral, bilateral, and trilateral forms of social control (Black, 1984a). *Unilateral social control* occurs when victims pursue courses of self-help. Self-help responses involve the imposition of sanctions without bargaining with the other disputant or mobilizing third-party control agents.

Bilateral social control involves both parties to the conflict. The contesting parties may negotiate with each other or enlist supporters to act as advisers, advocates, or surrogate sanctioners (Black & Baumgartner, 1983). In the latter case the control effort moves beyond the disputants themselves but still does not involve third parties unallied with either side to the conflict.

An additional elaboration of social control develops with *trilateral social control*. The form of social control fundamentally shifts as the problem changes from a private grievance to a public problem subject to the rules of some more formalized system (Emerson & Messinger, 1977). Third parties become involved in resolving the conflict. These might be arbitrators whose decision the contending parties have agreed to accept beforehand or adjudicators with the power to enforce their decisions regardless of the wishes of the contesting parties (Nader & Todd, 1978).

Most societies feature a range of forms that can potentially resolve disputes. A theory of social control should predict when troubled situations lead to inaction including tolerance, avoidance, and exit; unilateral efforts at sanctioning undertaken by one party alone; bilateral negotiations between the two sides to a dispute; and, finally, trilateral intervention by authoritative third parties who can impose resolutions.

This section develops several theses regarding the forms of social control. Its central contention is that in several ways *informal* mechanisms predominate in shaping forms of social control. One of the most striking facts about social control in modern societies is how rare the trilateral resolution of disputes actually is. We can conceive of social control as a ladder with very wide rungs at the bottom, where injuries are first perceived, that narrows progressively into very small steps at the top, where official third parties reside. At the bottom of this grievance ladder lies all human experience that is or can be perceived as violating normative expectations and creating some sort of injury (Miller & Sarat, 1980-1981). People typically respond to deviance through toleration, avoidance, exit, or various forms of self-help. The immense number of conflicts, disputes, and grievances in social life narrows into a small proportion that eventually are settled within formal control systems. The majority of grievances, disputes, and offenses never escalate beyond the particular parties involved, so never come to the attention of third-party controllers.

Even in such a supposedly litigious society as the contemporary United States, very few grievances ever enter the legal system. Of all grievances that are uncovered by population surveys, fewer than 1% are ever aired in a court setting (Black, 1984b). The police, for example, are called upon to resolve only a small proportion of potentially criminal matters. More than half of victims of index crimes do not report victimizations to police (Ennis, 1967). Even when the police are mobilized, they typically only make arrests in about 15% of cases (Black, 1972; Smith & Klein, 1984).

An even greater tolerance exists in civil disputes. One survey of consumer grievances found that only 3% of complaints were pressed before legal forums (Ladinsky & Susmilch, 1982). Another study found that people with a potential civil case involving more than $1,000 only contacted lawyers one-tenth of the time (Trubek, Grossman, Felstiner, Kritzer, & Sarat, 1983). Most symptoms of mental illness, as well, never enter formal treatment settings. At any particular time, only about one-tenth of diagnosed cases of mental illness are treated by mental health specialists and only about one-quarter of such cases ever enter such treatment (Link & Dohrenwend, 1980; Shapiro *et al.*, 1984).

In addition to the prevalence of private forms of settlement, the major determinants of which incidents do escalate into the formal system lie in the preferences of the aggrieved parties rather than in the choices of official third parties. Official social control agencies do not generate their own cases but depend on the claims citizens make on them.

Finally, grievants are likely to file legal charges only in cases such as divorce or probate where rules mandate a legal resolution of disputes, or those such as automobile accidents where the social organization of the legal fee system facilitates bringing cases to law. Few of even those grievances that do enter formal systems reach a legal resolution. The master pattern within courts is negotiated outcomes within the shadow of legal rules (Galanter, 1983). Most cases are withdrawn or abandoned before coming to a formal resolution. Informal bargaining rather than imposed decisions settles many other cases. This includes between 90% to 95% of criminal cases and 90% of civil cases (Trubek *et al.*, 1983). The desires and characteristics of the parties involved in the dispute determine which cases are withdrawn, settled, or adjudicated. In each of these respects, formal systems of social control are responsive to the social fields that generate cases.

No theory can encompass all the factors that contribute to the expansion of social control. Individuals differ in their degree of exposure to potential injury, their capacities to prevent injuries from occurring, and the stock of definitions they use to define whether an injury is remediable and another is at fault. Both individual and social characteristics shape each of these factors.

I do not explore all of the factors that influence the use of various forms of social control but focus on several structural variables. The first is the relationship between the parties in conflict. Of particular importance is whether or not they wish to continue their relationship, are indifferent, or wish to end it. The relative status of disputants is another aspect of relationships that affects what form of social control grievants choose. Another prominent determinant of the form of social control is the availability of various forums of resolution. Forms of social control do not exist in isolation, but their use depends on the presence or absence of other sorts of resolution agents. Finally, the distance of the available remedy agents to disputants shapes the response made to conflicts. Disputants typically first mobilize third-party agents at a close distance before invoking agents at a greater distance. The growing elaboration of control efforts varies in predictable ways, depending on relationships between disputants and between disputants and control agents.

This Part shows the conditions under which forms of social control become more or less elaborated. I begin with the conditions that predict inaction as a response to deviant behavior. The following chapter considers unilateral forms when one grievant attempts to impose a solution and bilateral forms when disputants jointly resolve disputes. Chapter 8 examines the social fields conducive to the development and utilization of authoritative trilateral forms of social control. Finally, Chapter 9 studies the factors that shape the responses of legal officials to cases that do enter their domains.

6

Inaction

Social control is minimal when observers impose no sanctions on behavior they feel departs from social norms. In some cases, observers may do nothing; in others, avoid offenders or leave the troubled situation. This chapter explores the social conditions that are conducive to the absence of vigorous social control responses.

TOLERANCE

Tolerance indicates the absence of social control efforts when they might be appropriate. Two conditions define tolerance: First, the responders must perceive that the behavior in question might be deviant and, second, they take no action to sanction offenders. Tolerance of deviance does not necessarily mean that observers are sympathetic to behaviors. This might be the case, as when more highly educated people are more tolerant of homosexuality. On the other hand, wives who tolerate their husbands' violence do not approve of it but, nevertheless, do nothing to sanction it. We make no assumptions about whether or not observers are sympathetic or hostile to the behavior in question.

Relational Distance

The social distance between victims and offenders predicts the degree of tolerance for a potentially deviant action. Not the characteristics of offenders and their victims in themselves but the relationship between them accounts for the degree of tolerance. Stated most generally: *Tolerance for deviance varies inversely to the relational distance between victims and offenders.* Hold constant characteristics of victims, and tolerance is minimal toward offenders who are socially distant from control agents. Correspondingly, when characteristics of offenders are constant, tolerance is minimal when victims are socially close to control agents. Tolerance is greatest when socially akin offenders victimize marginal people and least when the marginal offend the integrated. Tolerance levels are also high for victimizations that occur between people who are at the social margins. When intimates victimize each other, tolerance levels are highly variable.

Outward Deviance

When offenders close in social distance from third parties victimize people at a great distance, high tolerance for deviance exists: *Tolerance is maximal for outward deviance.* When insiders victimize outsiders, morality is quiescent and social control minimal. Instead, potentially deviant actions are often justified, rationalized, or admired. Victims of such offenses have little opportunity to obtain redress.

In many tribal groups, theft from those in a distant lineage is not viewed as a serious delict; but such thieves are often admired (Bohannon, 1957, pp. 124, 128; Evans-Pritchard, 1940). Among various tribal groups in Southeast Asia, the killing of an in-group member is severely sanctioned, but the killing of an outsider is viewed with moral neutrality or approval (Furer-Haimendorf, 1967, p. 109). Similarly, the shepherds in the Sardinian mountains view theft from a more distant person as an approved way of showing one's worth and obtaining wealth. In contrast, taking livestock without permission from a kinsman, friend, or neighbor is wrong (Ruffini, 1978).

The same principle explains the response to adultery in many groups. In African tribes, someone who seduces the wives of distant tribesmen is likely to be envied, although seducing the wive of an age-set mate is viewed as a serious deviant action (Bohannon, 1957). Likewise, killers of members of distant groups often gain honor, prestige, and rewards within their own group (Cooney, 1988, Chapter 4). War heroes, for example, are universally glorified (Lewis, 1976, p. 341). Whenever potential deviance moves from insiders toward outsiders, tolerance should flourish.

Inward Deviance

If morality is minimal when persons at a close distance victimize those far away, it is most intense under the opposite social condition: *Tolerance is minimal for inward deviance.* When outsiders such as strangers, foreigners, immigrants, and other marginals victimize socially integrated persons, the most severe control responses result. In medieval Bologna, for example, foreigners were three times more likely than Bolognese to be convicted and punished for similar offenses (Blanshed, 1982). Marginals who victimize social integrated people are still subject to harsh punishment (Black, 1976, pp. 49-54).

The punishment of sexual deviance illustrates this principle. In the United States, rapes are considered most heinous when black men rape white women (LaFree, 1980). Seriousness ratings of crimes in contemporary society reflect the same phenomenon: Crimes occurring when a stranger is the victimizer are seen as more severe than when a relative, friend, or acquaintance commits the same action. For example, forcible rape of a stranger after breaking into a house is considered to be the fourth most serious of 140 crimes whereas the rape of a neighbor or a former spouse are seen as the twenty-first and sixty-second most severe crimes, respectively (Rossi *et al.*, 1974). The harsher treatment of sexual victimizations between relationally distant people in contemporary society reflects a more general phenomenon: Jews who had intercourse with Christians in medieval Europe (Spierenburg, 1984, p. 124); blacks who fornicated with whites in the Colonial United States (D'Emilio & Freedman, 1988); or Moslems who engage in sexual activities with Hindus in India (Furer-Haimendorf, 1967) are liable to severe punishment. The reaction to sexual deviance illustrates the more general principle that the movement of deviance from outer toward inner social space is not conducive to tolerance.

Outside Deviance

Instances where close offenders prey upon distant victims or distant offenders harm close victims are clear cases of minimal and maximal tolerance. A third possible relational configuration involves actions committed between socially distant offenders. Here, both victim and offender are marginal members of groups. In such cases, *tolerance for deviance between outsiders is high.*

When marginal people prey upon one another, third parties view their deviance as inconsequential and accord it minimal response. Deviance among lower class persons, children, or women is typically ignored (Black, 1983). For example, higher caste Hindus are indifferent to the deviance of socially inferior castes that would arouse indignation if engaged in by a member of their own caste (Furer-Haimendorf, 1967, pp. 173-76). Although violence among the lower class in nineteenth century England was frequently noted, it roused little concern (May, 1978,

p. 143). Indeed, remedy agents for such disputes are often not even available, and no real resolution of the dispute can occur (Rothenberger, 1978). Crime victims who are prostitutes, drug addicts, alcoholics, or other unrespectable people, for instance, are not likely to be able to prosecute their victimizers in the criminal justice system (Williams, 1976).

As societies become extremely individualized and marked by great heterogeneity, more deviance occurs at the social margins. Cities, in particular, allow for the development and growth of a wide variety of deviant subcultures. This leads to a growing degree of tolerance for deviance in such settings (Black, 1989a).

Inside Deviance

The most variance in tolerance for offenses exists when intimates victimize each other: *Tolerance for deviance between insiders is variable.* These offenses are sometimes tolerated but sometimes sanctioned very severely.

On the one hand, tolerance can be a common response to grievances between insiders or intimates. A general principle of social life is that one should not introduce exterior power into private domains (e.g., Jones, 1974, p. 225; Stinchcombe, 1963; Young, 1971: 140-41). Insiders typically share a common normative universe and many common ties. Escalation of a grievance can provoke hostility from other community members. The mobilization of formal control agents against intimates often leads to ostracism, censure, and other negative sanctions (Nader & Todd, 1978). Complaints to legal officials regarding intimates are betrayals of norms regulating intimate relationships. The potential loss of reputation insiders would face from pursuing the elaboration of social control may outweigh the lingering anger from not seeking redress.

Often, actions that would be severe wrongs if perpetuated by outsiders are tolerated or receive mild sanctions within the group. In many groups, the response to perceived victimizations from another insider is to "lump" whatever injuries have occurred (Felstiner, 1974). Among the Jalemo of Western New Guinea, when someone takes crops without permission from a relative, the incident is talked over and settled between the two parties. The same action perpetuated against a nonrelated person often escalates into warfare (Koch, 1974). In a Sunni Moslem village in Lebanon when children have disputes with their parents or siblings, remedy agents of any sort are rarely used, and redress is not possible (Rothenberger, 1978). In a North Atlantic fishing village property taken by an insider is defined as "borrowing" or "not being careful to distinguish what's mine from yours," whereas that taken without permission by outsiders is considered theft (Yngvesson, 1978). Likewise, among the Shavante Indians of Brazil, taking food or objects from fellow clansmen, members of one's own faction, or kinsmen would at most lead to grumbling. Taking property from someone in another faction, in contrast, may precipitate intergroup conflict or warfare (Maybury-Lewis, 1967, pp. 181-182). A woman of the Baiga tribe in India who commits adultery with another Baiga suffers no community sanctions, but one who has intercourse with an outsider is excommunicated (Furer-Haimendorf, 1967, p. 49).

In the contemporary United States, integrated members of communities show a high degree of tolerance for the deviance of insiders. For example, in a rural Illinois county, persons who pursued personal injury claims were perceived as antisocial, greedy, and troublemakers. The injured parties typically absorbed most of their losses themselves rather than pursuing claims against other community members (Engel, 1984). Cattle owners in a rural California county also act according to norms expressing that one should "lump" minor injuries or trespass caused by neighbors' cattle and ignore the formal law that would have entitled them to damages (Ellickson, 1986). Tolerance was not likely, however, when either victims or offenders were marginal members of the communities.

Violent acts among intimates are often defined as less serious than comparable acts committed at greater distances and are less likely to be reported to third party control agents. Victims of even serious violence committed by intimates often go to great lengths to protect their abusers from outside intervention (Finkelhor, 1983). Violence committed in defense of one's honor or family is also viewed as deserving of toleration. Crimes of passion, such as when a husband murders a spouse caught in adultery, are usually accorded a great deal of tolerance. In medieval England, for instance, a husband who killed a man in the act of committing adultery with his wife was typically judged as acting in self-defense, regardless of the actual circumstances of the killing. In the same communities, homicide occurring in defense of a kinsman was excused, even when the slayer was not himself in mortal danger (Green, 1972). In Mediterranean societies, husbands who kill wives who have committed infidelity are frequently acquitted, as are brothers who kill their sisters who have dishonored the family through sexual deviance (Safilios-Rothschild, 1969). Indeed, in these societies, killing to defend the family honor is considered a socially expected and approved behavior rather than a crime. Likewise, citizens of the contemporary United States accord far less severity to the homicide of a spouse's lover than other forms of homicide (Rossi *et al.*, 1974). Similarly, the social control of violent acts between intimates such as child abuse or wife beating still lacks the moral fervor that similar acts between persons at a greater distance would engender.

The behavior of tolerance in social space also explains the societal reaction to persons who have been released from total institutions. Stigmatization grows with growing social distance between an ex-inmate and the reactor. Ex-convicts are often treated sympathetically by family members and celebrated by friends but stigmatized by neighbors and employers who are at a greater social distance from them (Ericson, 1977, p. 20).

The response to mental illness follows the same pattern. Mental symptoms that occur within families are typically normalized and tolerated for long periods whereas the same symptoms that become apparent in more distant settings result in more formal control responses (Clausen & Yarrow, 1955; Horwitz, 1982, Chapter 3). A case in one fishing community on a Scandinavian island illustrates this process. Young adolescent girls complained that a resident kept pestering them to swim naked. The man's kin group claimed that his behavior was "normal, stating simply he is that way, or referring to the fact that [he] had run naked since he was a child in the rocky uninhabited areas of the island" (Yngvesson, 1976, p. 165). On the other hand, more distant community members who were born off the island felt that this man's actions were serious and deserving of sanctions. Similarly, relatives of former mental patients are less likely to stigmatize such individuals than more distant reactors (Phillips, 1964). In many situations, deviance within close relational space is accorded great tolerance.

On the other hand, delicts among insiders are not universally tolerated. Indeed, reprisals for deviance occurring within close social fields illustrate a basic dilemma in exerting social control that all groups face. Socially akin victims must be protected, and their offenders must be punished. It is difficult, however, to do both simultaneously. The result is a high variability in responses to offenses between intimates.

Offenses committed among intimates are often viewed as particularly reprehensible offenses. In many groups, sexual intercourse between close relatives is the most serious offense imaginable (Lewis, 1976). In tribal societies, the violation of the incest taboo is often among the only offenses leading to a community rather than a private response. Murder within the group is also often felt to be a particularly heinous crime. Among the Cheyenne Indians, the murder of a tribesman is considered a grave sin that pollutes the whole group (Hoebel, 1954). In the Mosaic Law of the Hebrews, the response to crimes against neighbors was far more severe than crimes committed against outsiders (Jacoby, 1983, p. 90).

Among the Tiv of West Africa, theft from kin belonging to the minimal lineage system is viewed as among one of the most reprehensible crimes possible (Bohannon, 1957, p. 124). For shepards in the Sardinian mountains, taking livestock without permission was only viewed as wrong when the victim was a kinsman, friend, or neighbor (Ruffini, 1978). Deviance that betrays one's own group is especially reprehensible. In a white ethnic community in Brooklyn, Rieder (1984, p. 137) reports that white homeowners who sold houses to blacks were the targets of particularly violent reprisals by their neighbors: "They do it to the white who sells, not the black who moves in. It's really a form of retaliation. The white who sells is the betrayer of the community."

The dilemma arising when groups must simultaneously punish offenders and avenge victims can cripple social control systems. Indeed, groups sometimes find victimizations at very close social distances impossible to handle. For example, homicide within the closest lineage segment among the Bedouins leads to a complete impasse (Peters, 1967). Because any offense is viewed as an offense against the group, vengeance against the offender exacerbates the loss. Compensation paid from a group to its own members is a contradiction in terms. The result is that such an intragroup homicide "causes an impasse in relationships, which creates chaos among a small group of related people, and produces internal calamity" (Peters, 1967, p. 264).

Among the Lugbara of Uganda in precolonial times, a killing within a lineage was considered to be a sin that could not be humanly punished or avenged. Such crimes were unthinkable, and the killer was avoided as an unnatural human being: "The usual cleansing rites did not apply to such a killer who commits a deed that is unthinkable and that could never be done deliberately" (Middleton, 1965, p. 51). Among the Somali in East Africa:

> Where a father kills his son, or a son his father, vengeance is impossible and compensation cannot be paid, for as Somali put it "Who would pay and who receive damages?". . . . It is particularly between close agnates that the taint of a religious wrong attaches to murder and parricide is viewed with abhorrence although no specific ritual measures are applied to cleanse the culprit. (Lewis, 1961, p. 257)

Similarly, no punishment of fratricide occurred on the island of Yap in Micronesia, but vengeance was left to the ancestral spirits (Schneider, 1957.) The responsibility for sanctioning of intrakin offenses rested with the kin group so no outsider would interfere. Yet because kin would not proceed against each other, sanctions became supernatural ones administered by ancestral ghosts.

In modern societies, as well, killings within families such as infanticides, parricides, or fratricides lead to the use of mental illness, rather than criminal, labels to handle offenders who have committed horrendous crimes but who are too socially close to their victims to be punished (e.g., Brumberg, 1984, p. 248). The case of Francine Hughes, who killed her spouse, James, is illustrative:

> James had frequently beaten her, partly because of his violent opposition to her effort to become independent through education. The day of the killing, Francine's 12-year-old daughter called the police while James was beating Francine, but the police did not arrest him. Francine packed to move out, a decision that had the moral support of her children, and then poured gasoline around the bed in which James had fallen asleep, lit the gas, and drove straight to the sheriff's office to make a hysterical confession. The fact that James was asleep when the fire was set made a finding of self-defense difficult. Instead, the jury found Francine temporarily insane because of James's long-term abuse of her. (There was no indication of a belief in her continuing insanity. Francine was freed soon after the administration of psychological tests) (Katz, 1988, p. 14).

Deviance within a group creates a social puzzle. Deviance is usually defined as actions outsiders perpetuate and insiders are protected from. When insiders are both victims and offenders the social response may be one of great tolerance, great severity, or a failure to come to grips with the deviance at all. The variability in response to deviance perpetuated by one insider on another illustrates a fundamental problem groups face when they protect their moral order.

Hierarchy

The degree of tolerance for deviance varies according to the status relationship between the victim and offender.[1] Social control is most intense when lower status offenders victimize their superiors but is restrained when superiors offend the dominated. Although much tolerance

[1]The degree of tolerance for deviance is typically viewed as dependent upon the status of offenders (e.g., Hay, 1975). Delicts of privileged people are presumably tolerated, whereas offenses of the powerless and socially marginal are seen as subject to harsh repression. Yet the vast literature addressing the relationship of social status and tolerance typically finds little relationship between low social status and severe sanctions. For example, most studies of contemporary legal systems show little or no difference in the severity of punishment accorded offenders of different income groups (e.g., Chiricos & Waldo, 1975; Hagan, 1974). Similarly, most studies show that blacks are not sanctioned more harshly than whites for the same crimes and that whites are sometimes punished more harshly than blacks (Myers & Talarico, 1986; Peterson & Hagan, 1984). This lack of support for the predicted association between the status of offenders and tolerance is not surprising because of the failure to attend to the status relationship between offenders and their victims.

exists for the offenses lower status people perpetuate on each other, tolerance is low when people of higher status victimize each other.

Upward Deviance

The most heinous deviance is committed by the dominated against their superiors. As Durkheim (1899, p. 301) noted "An act which is simply reprehensible when directed against an equal becomes sacrilegious when it concerns someone who is superior to us." Universally, moral indignation rises and tolerance falls with growing status of the victim (Black, 1976, p. 21): *Tolerance for upward deviance is low.*

Among the Tlingit Indians in southeastern Alaska, "if a man of low rank had illicit connections with a girl of high rank, the father of the girl demanded either the man slain or a great deal of property. If the man was of as high a rank as the girl, her father could force them to marry" (Oberg, 1934, p. 149; see also Castan, 1983, p. 255; Furer-Haimendorf, 1967, p. 65). In the colonial United States, black slaves who raped white women could be subject to castration or death whereas white masters were allowed great license in subjecting black women to their sexual demands (D'Emilio & Freedman, 1988). In Albanian mountain villages, a homicide perpetrated by an inferior against a superior was not settled until two of the offender's kin were killed (Hasluck, 1954, p. 129). For centuries in English law, the slaying of a master by a servant and of a husband by his wife were among the most reprehensible of homicides (Green, 1972). Indeed, to protect the honor of the victim, indictments would state that the victim was slain while asleep or taken in ambush, regardless of the actual facts of the situation. Such offenders were burned alive or disemboweled and quartered (Beattie, 1986, p. 79). Among the Zapotec in Mexico beating one's father is accorded a very different response than beating one's wife:

> They were discussing a case at dinner of a son who had to go to jail in Villa Alta because he hit his father. I said, "For that they sent him to jail?" The father said, "Of course," and sounded surprised at my question. I probed further: "But many men beat their wives, and they never go to jail." He answered, "Wives are one thing, fathers another." Then I asked what if a father was in the wrong. The son in the family said, "Fathers are never in the wrong for beating their sons. They always do it for their own good." (Nader, 1964, p. 414)

A husband in a patriarchal family may be free of restraints when he beats his wife but severely punished if he engages in the same behavior with his own father.

Downward Deviance

The great tolerance for offenses of the powerful against those socially beneath them contrasts with the moral indignation toward the deviance of the dominated against their superiors: *Tolerance for downward deviance is high.* Tribal groups illustrate this pattern in its starkest form. Among the Ifugao of the Philippines, whereas the compensation owed by a lower status person increases with the escalating rank of the victim, that owed by a higher status person decreases as the victim's rank declines (Barton, 1919). Or, consider the Nuristan of Afghanistan:

> Whereas the killing of a *bari* or *sewala* [lower status person] could, in theory, be satisfactorily settled by the payment of 120 [goats], the killing of an *atrozan* [higher status person] could not be resolved by paying 240. In the case of *atrozan* the figure of 240 is a base and the amount of restitution required depends upon the rank of the deceased [and] settlement will only be achieved by giving multiples of this, as arranged by the mediators. The killing of a man of high rank is said to require the payment of . . . twelve men or 12 times 240. (Jones, 1974, pp. 99-100)

At the extreme low point of status among the Nuristan, if a man kills his own slave, no penalty at all is assessed (Jones, 1974, p. 100). Similarly, among the Jalemo of New Guinea, the killing of very low status persons such as women and foreigners was unlikely to result in any efforts at punishing offenders (Koch, 1974). In late nineteenth-century Austria, many German-Austrians felt it was impossible to offend a Jew, and no Jew could demand satisfaction for any sort of insult (Clare, 1980, p. 29).

In early Renaissance Venice, the penalty for offenders also depended on the rank of their victims (Ruggiero, 1980). When women were crime victims, the offending behavior was often subject to more tolerance. Rape, for instance, was considered a minor crime because of the low status of women. Penalties for the rape of a woman of lower status woman were much lower than when the victim was of higher rank. Indeed, in this setting, virtually nothing was defined as criminal when the victim was a marginal woman unprotected by a kinship group.

The high tolerance for the deviance of dominants creates a particularly problematic situation for dependents. This is especially true in relationships marked by frequent interaction such as those between children and their parents, wives and husbands in inegalitarian families, or employees in authoritarian work settings. In such cases, victims cannot confront offenders without risking the loss of the relationship itself. Exit behavior may also not be possible. Remedy agents in such situations are either unavailable or will not listen to complaints. Parents are given relative immunity from formal social control and are often able to exert control virtually at will over their children. Similarly, police are typically likely to take little action against the husbands of abused women. Rape victims, for example, may face disgrace if they report victimizations, so many choose silence instead. Hence, in sixteenth-century England, only one in eight women abused by their masters pressed prosecution against them, a similar reporting rate to rape victims in the modern world (Macdonald, 1981). Weak, dependent parties are at the same time vulnerable to being wronged and incapable of avenging the wrong (Rieder, 1984).

The inability of dependents in intimate relationships to pursue confrontational or exit strategies may leave tolerance as the only option available to weaker parties who are dependent upon their victimizers. Powerless people with grievances against more powerful offenders are reluctant to express complaints. Such people often have little choice but to tolerate perceived wrongs because they are less likely to obtain redress from third parties. Hence, dependent wives often do not confront husbands with their complaints; children may suffer their parents offenses in silence; students do not complain about the delicts of their teachers; and employees are not likely to stand up to the slights of their bosses.

Yet, it is not likely that people can endure structured patterns of victimization over long periods of time without taking some sort of remedial action (Baumgartner, 1984). The quiescence of morality in the face of victimizations of low-status people may be a powerful fomenter of lasting, albeit unexpressed, injustice and aggrieved feelings. Forced tolerance may lead the victimized in such situations to displace hostility toward superiors onto themselves through psychiatric symptoms such as depression, anxiety, or guilt or onto minorities such as witches, Jews, or blacks. Such symptoms everywhere predominate among parties who are dependents in hierarchical relationships (see Chapters 2 and 4).

Deviance among the Powerless

When both offender and victim are powerless, social control is minimal: *Tolerance for deviance between powerless people is high.* At the extreme of low social status, all forms of redress may be denied. Among the Kiowa Indians of North America, the lowest orders of society were "utterly declasse and in effect without the law. They were so far beneath contempt and attention that their thefts went unpunished" (Hoebel, 1954, p. 171). Disputes among children typically result in little social control, and remedy agents who deal with such disputes are often completely absent. For example, in seventeenth- and eighteenth-century England, it was expected that disputes between young men would be settled violently, but the resulting injuries would not engage the attention of authorities unless a homicide resulted (Beattie, 1986). In the contemporary United States, as well, as long as fighting remains among peers, police may not interfere when fights arise between competing street gangs (Katz, 1988, p. 121).

In many times and places, offenses that women commit against each other are also accorded a high degree of tolerance. Among the Shavante of central Brazil, for instance, only disputes between men are considered to be worthy of a court hearing before the men's council whereas those of women are seen as "laughable and unworthy of serious attention" (Maybury-Lewis, 1967, p. 179). Similarly, offenses committed by low income people or blacks upon each other are most likely to be ignored by legal authorities and least likely to enter the legal system (Black, 1983). Likewise, offenses against disreputable persons such as prostitutes who claim they have been raped or drug dealers who have been robbed are not treated as serious matters. The high official tolerance accorded to their deviance generates much self help behavior among the powerless (see Chapter 7).

Deviance among the Powerful

When lower status people offend higher status victims, tolerance is low and punishment correspondingly great. However, when victim and offender are both of high status, the social consequences of deviance are also severe. Not only is a member of the dominant group victimized, but another member has violated the normative obligations of that group. Hence we would expect little tolerance for the offenses of the powerful when their victims are other powerful persons: *Tolerance for deviance between powerful people is low.*

Powerful people are sometimes held to higher standards than their social inferiors. The notion of *noblesse oblige* indicates that higher status offenders should be required to set good examples and be held to bear more responsibility than their lower status counterparts (Braithwaite, 1982). For example, in many tribal groups, higher status offenders are required to pay more for their delicts than lower status ones (e.g., Barton, 1919; Furer-Haimendorf, 1967; Koch, 1974).

The low tolerance for delicts of the powerful is primarily due to the high status of their victims. In early Renaissance Venice, nobles had a rate of prosecution for violent crimes that was about five times greater than their presence in the population because their victims were usually other nobles or the state (Ruggiero, 1980). This sometimes led upper status persons to receive harsh penalties for even minor offenses that would have been overlooked if they emerged at any other level of society

(Ruggiero, 1980, p. 69). In this setting, the most severe crimes were those perpetuated by nobles against the commune itself because upper class offenders represented a greater potential threat to the rulers of the commune than powerless ones.

A number of studies of the contemporary criminal justice system also indicate that higher status and white defendants are treated more severely than their lower status and black counterparts for the same offenses (e.g. Bernstein, *et al.*, 1977; Peterson & Hagan, 1984; Wheeler, Weisburd, & Bode, 1982). The severity accorded their crimes stems from the high status of their victims. Contemporary surveys of crime seriousness also show that the offenses of the powerful are considered very severe (Braithwaite, 1989, p. 41). Conversely, the relative leniency of the reactions to lower status people is due to the equally low status of those they offend.

Tolerance grows with the declining status of victims and weakens with its ascent. Yet neither the status of offenders nor their victims in themselves predicts tolerance. Rather, the *relationship* between them predicts the strength of morality. It is most intense when deviance moves upward and weakest in a downward direction. The costs of tolerance may be particularly high for dependent groups. No viable outlets for their hostility may exist when the appropriate targets are beyond their reach (Felstiner, 1974). The result may be that many lower status people direct hostility toward the self or other targets such as witches, minorities, and other outsiders.

Gender

Gender provides an interesting forum for the study of tolerance. All social groups feature norms regarding the gender-related appropriateness of behavior, including deviant behavior. Hence, some component of the degree of tolerance to male and female deviance should be related to gender role expectations themselves. In addition, gender is often viewed as a proxy for social status where women are inferiors and men superiors (e.g., Schur, 1984). To this extent, gender differences in tolerance would be deducible from status differences alone. Finally, much male-female or female-male deviance occurs within intimate social space so would be subject to the principles regarding social distance and tolerance.

Role Appropriateness

Gender differences in tolerance are deducible in part from gender-specific definitions of appropriate behavior. For females, this often involves standards of submissiveness, demureness, and passivity and for males those of dominance, strength, and independence (Spence & Helmreich, 1978). For both sexes, behavior that violates sex role expectations will lead to stricter sanctioning.

For women, tolerance is minimal when standards of appropriate sexuality are violated. Although adultery, fornication, and illegitimacy involve couples, women are more harshly sanctioned than men for these offenses (D'Emilio & Freedman, 1988). Traditionally, girls who become pregnant out of wedlock have brought ruin upon themselves and been subjected to ostracism and rejection (Brumberg, 1984). The prospective father, however, does not suffer the same fate. In many times and places, men who commit adultery are often tolerated by their wives and admired by their peers. A woman who engages in the same behavior risks disgrace, physical punishment, divorce, and loss of her children (D'Emilio & Freedman, 1988, p. 95). Likewise, there are stricter norms of respectability for females than males so girls receive stiffer penalties than boys for "immoral" conduct (Schlossman, 1977). Among young, unmarried couples, females who engage in sex may ruin their reputation whereas their partners may enhance theirs.

The societal reaction to mental disorder also illustrates some attention to the sex appropriateness of behavior. The labeling of mental illness is less likely for females who display "female" symptoms and males who act out in "masculine" ways. In one New York City emergency room, 66% of men but only 43% of women were hospitalized for the presumably more "female" symptoms of neurosis and depression, although no differences were apparent in commitment rates for schizophrenia. In contrast, 50% of women but only 18% of men were committed for "male" symptoms of personality disorder and substance abuse (Rosenfield, 1983). In a large national sample, males were more likely than females to enter psychiatric treatment for depression, anxiety, and emotional problems typically associated with the female role, indicating that gender atypical symptoms of deviance are more likely to receive a severe reaction than gender-appropriate deviance (Fox, 1984).

Among a group of English women, Ginsberg and Brown (1982, p. 88) note that "signs of depressive disorder among women [such as inexplicable crying] tend to be treated lightly by others as normal and expected components of feminine behavior." As long as these women performed their expected roles in maintaining their homes and caring for their children, their psychiatric symptoms were unnoticed. The response of physicians was similar. The doctors normalized symptoms through viewing them as normal accompaniments to women's roles:

> One woman, for example, suffering from sleeplessness, suicidal thoughts, and fears of physically harming her child, told her doctor that she felt agitated, could not relax, and was afraid she would hurt her children. She also told him that she was constantly in tears. His response was, "How can you expect to be calm, you've got four children."(Ginsberg & Brown, 1982, p. 108)

Referrals into psychiatric therapy for children indicate the same pattern (Feinblatt & Gold, 1976). Boys are typically referred for being emotional or passive, whereas girls who enter therapy show signs of defiance or aggression.

Some evidence also indicates that women in contemporary society who commit "male" crimes that involve violent, aggressive, or assaultive behavior will be punished more harshly than men who commit the same crimes (Bernstein *et al.*, 1977). In contrast, fighting, aggression or heavy drinking are more likely to be normalized in males than females.

Males may be less tolerated than females for violating appropriate standards of work. For example, in contemporary Cuba, the law against loafing applies sanctions only to men and excludes women. The Cuban Minister of Labor explains that

> while people are incensed on seeing a lazy man, the problem isn't always viewed the same way when it involves the case of an idle girl who doesn't study work or take care of a house. The same man who becomes indignant over a lazy man may have an eighteen year old daughter who doesn't study or work and is unmarried, yet her not working isn't viewed as something incorrect. The problem isn't viewed the same and really, it isn't the same thing. (Salas, 1979, p. 346)

What sorts of behaviors are viewed as appropriate for each gender vary in different societies. For example, in Irish society, reserved behavior among men is normative. Hence, consistent with the hypothesis, a man who exaggerated the reserved, sexually timid stereotype was seen as queer, whereas his brother who aggressively pursued women was seen as mad (Scheper-Hughes, 1979, p. 98). To some extent, then, the degree of tolerance reflects gender-specific notions of proper behavior.

Presence of Informal Control

A special aspect of the status of women is that, in most times and places, it has derived from their relationship to male kin and affines. The degree of tolerance for female deviance is shaped by the extent of informal social control over women. When this control is strong, female deviance is accorded higher tolerance.

The lenient treatment women receive in formal systems of social control results if there is a high degree of informal control over their behavior. In early modern Seville, for instance, women violators were seen as less threatening than males because they were more constrained by marriage, convents, or social mores (Perry, 1980, p. 67). Women who have strong family ties still receive more lenient treatment when they enter official control systems (Kruttschnitt, 1981).

When, however, women are not subject to male control, there is less tolerance for their behavior. Hence, the witch craze in Europe in the sixteenth century developed as women increasingly entered the job market, postponed marriage, and became less subject to the authority of husbands and fathers (Ben-Yehuda, 1980). Referrals to reformatories in the United States also illustrate the relationship between informal control and gender tolerance. In one New York reformatory between 1894-1931, nearly half of the women were committed for acts of vagrancy, and substantial portions entered for prostitution, waywardness, and intoxication. An unusually high proportion (80% vs. 27% of all women) held jobs, perhaps indicating freedom from familial control (Rafter, 1983). When their actions violated standards of female subordination and sexuality, women were more prone to arrest and commitment. Not surprisingly, in this era, another defining symptom of mental illness for females was uncontrolled sexuality and nymphomania, the epitome of the loss of male control over female sexuality (Showalter, 1985).

The disproportionate incarceration rate of female juveniles for noncriminal offenses such as vagrancy, running away, and incorrigibility in modern society is also due to the particulary low tolerance for females who lack informal familial social control (Chesney-Lind, 1977; Sarri, 1983). In contrast, relative to men, women who are under strong informal controls receive particularly high levels of tolerance for their deviance (Daly, 1987a; Kruttschnitt, 1981).

In addition to the presence of informal control, the degree of tolerance for female deviance toward males is related to its frequent occurrence within intimate contexts. Female deviants typically victimize males who are socially close to them, especially husbands and boyfriends (Cooney, 1988, Chapter 4). Because the intensity of social control is typically least where relational distance between parties is small (Black, 1976, Chapter 3), the close distance involved in family deviance may offset the upward nature of female deviance directed at males. Therefore, women who engage in violence against their husbands and other family members often are treated with leniency. In eighteenth- and nineteenth-century England, women had a better chance than men of pleading insanity, accidental death, or self-defense when they killed their spouses (Beattie, 1986, pp. 85, 95). In the contemporary United States, women convicted of murdering their spouses get lighter sentences than men who do the same (Farrell & Swigert, 1978; Field & Field, 1973). Status and relational distance are sometimes offsetting factors that shape the degree of tolerance for the deviance of women.

Gender Relationships

Tolerance for deviance varies not only by gender appropriateness and the presence of informal control but also by the gender relationship between victim and offender. Do males victimize females, females offend males, or are victim and offender both male or female?

MALE TO FEMALE. Tolerance for males who victimize females is sometimes very high. For example, forcible sexual intercourse with one's wife, female slaves, or lower class women is accorded great tolerance. In one case in early Renaissance Venice, "The noble Daniele Moro got into the home of Maria, a worker's wife, by claiming that he was there in an official capacity as a representative of the commune. He threatened that if she did not open her door she would be arrested. She let him in, he raped her, and he got by with a mild penalty" (Ruggiero, 1980, p. 161). In many times and places, males have been immune from social control when they victimize female family members. Among the Comanche Indians, women "had no demand-rights against their husbands that they be faithful in marriage; they could exact no penalties from them" (Hoebel, 1954, p. 138). In most groups, a wife's infidelity is strongly sanctioned, whereas her husband's adulterous affairs are given little notice (Furer-Haimendorf, 1967). For the Bedouins, whenever a woman is killed, the homicide is viewed as accidental because a man can never intend to kill a woman (Peters, 1967). In such cases, compensation to the degree of one-half of that due if a man had been the victim is paid. In English law, men who were accused of murdering their adulterous spouses or their paramours would usually be successful in pleading self-defense (Green, 1972). In nineteenth century England, neighbors would not intervene when husbands beat their wives (Tomes, 1978).

Yet, males do not have unlimited license to victimize their female dependents. Women are often seen as inappropriate objects of violence and men who assault women are viewed as cowardly (Cooney, 1988, Chapter 4). Only violence men direct against other men is viewed as appropriate role behavior. Indeed, men who victimize women are often treated more severely than women who victimize men (Farrell & Swigert, 1978). In one Washington, DC study, for example, whereas five-sixths of women who killed their husbands were convicted of manslaughter, most husbands were convicted of murder (Field & Field, 1973).

Male deviance against women is only tolerated over women who are their own dependents or in otherwise marginal statuses. When couples are not married, for example, there is less tolerance for male violence toward women and greater willingness of victims and observers to summon the police (Berk *et al.*, 1984; Tomes, 1978). Conversely, the victimizations of married females by men who are not their husbands are subject to less tolerance than those of single women (Myers, 1980). As women come to have growing economic equality with men, standards of behavior equalize between the sexes.

FEMALE TO MALE. Female deviance against males often receives vigorous control responses. In most tribal societies, female sexual delicts are subject to much greater punishment than those of their husbands. Among the Jalemo, a wife always risks harsh punishment by her spouse if she commits adultery, whereas the husband's adultery never leads to marital conflict (Koch, 1974). The only recourse for an adulteress who has been seriously injured by her husband's punishment is go to her kin group. Her relatives, however, often reprimand the woman for jeopardizing their exchange relationship with the husband and his kin group. Among the Comanche, the absence of sanctions for a husband who committed adultery contrasts to the harsh reaction to the adulteress:

> She ran terrible risks. In seven of forty-five Comanche adultery and wife-absconding cases the women were slain by their husbands—one in seven! . . . Of the twenty other adulteresses five were mutilated by their husbands; four had their noses cut off, and one had the soles of her feet slashed so she could not walk. (Hoebel, 1954, p. 139)

Among the Nuristan of Afghanistan, the rule against homicide was not invoked if a husband shoots his wife and her lover because this is a recognized way of resolving adultery cases in this culture (Jones, 1974, p. 212).

Similarly, Blackstone reports that in English law of the fourteenth to seventeenth centuries, wives who killed their husbands were considered to be guilty of the more serious offense of petty treason rather than homicide, a similar situation to when servants killed their masters (Blackstone, 1811). In nineteenth century Britain and France, women could be convicted of adultery on the basis of compromising letters alone and faced up to a 2-year prison sentence if found guilty, although men were only legally liable if they kept their mistresses in conjugal homes and if convicted could only suffer fines (Hartman, 1977, p. 169).

In some cases, however, the dependent status of women can shield them from vigorous control responses. In some tribes, the status of women is so low that the victim of a husband's wrath cannot be the adulterous wife but only her lover. Among the Basoga tribe in Uganda, for instance, not women but only their paramours are punished for adultery. A subcounty chief states that this is because "if someone were to steal your shoes, would you accuse the shoes?" (Fallers, 1969, p. 101). Here, the status of women is so low that social control cannot proceed against them at all. However, their status as valued property means that other males who try to devalue, use, or steal them will be subject to harsh social control.

Same-Sex Deviance

Deviance among females, like that among marginals and other lower status persons, is often accorded great tolerance. Such deviance does not threaten central social institutions or male control. The reaction to female homosexuality illustrates this. Relative to male homosexual behavior, female homosexuality has traditionally received a high degree of tolerance (Trumbad, 1977). In the ancient world, virtually all condemnations of homosexuality referred to the male form (Greenberg, 1988, p. 214). In the United States, Smith-Rosenberg (1985, p. 266) notes:

> While male homosexuality was a well-recognized behavior throughout Western history, condemned in canon and civil law (indeed, a capital offense in English common law), few discussions of lesbianism predate the late nineteenth century. In fact, a category for genteel lesbian deviance originated only in the 1880s and 1890s.

A contemporary commentator summarizes: "By general agreement, lesbians still do not evoke the same hostility as homosexual men" (Greenberg, 1988, p. 391).

In light of the stricter sanctions accorded women for most forms of sexual deviance, what explains the leniency for deviance between females? The leniency toward lesbianism is deducible from the greater tolerance given to all deviance among lower status people. The lesbian does not betray male control in the same way as the promiscuity of daughters or the adultery of wives. The latter flaunt male control of sexuality and degrade the honor of the father or husband. As females become more equal to males, we expect that the greater tolerance for their deviance will decline.

Gender-related deviance among males, in contrast, is usually more harshly sanctioned than that among females. Both males and females show a greater disapproval for cross-gender behavior in boys than in girls (Feinman, 1974). Passivity in men, as well as homosexuality, has usually been subject to sanctions (e.g. Trumbad, 1977). In the Middle Ages, women who dressed as men were not punished, but men who dressed as women were strictly sanctioned (Bullough, 1973). Male homosexuality, in particular, has often been treated harshly. In early modern Seville sodomy among males was not merely treated as a sin but an offense against the political order that was harshly sanctioned (Perry, 1980, p. 72). Challenges to masculinity generate vigorous control responses. Indeed, in the contemporary United States, more homicides arise out of challenges to male honor than any other single cause (Katz, 1988, Chapter 1; Luckinbill, 1977).

Summary

The relationship between gender and tolerance is complex. Each sex has norms of appropriate behavior whose violation leads to sanctioning. Within familial and sexual spheres, there is a general tendency for tolerance toward male and intolerance toward female deviance. However, a number of factors modify this relationship. Male responsibility for females often renders females inappropriate targets of male aggression. In addition, males who victimize women who are dependents of other males can expect harsh retaliation. Further, because male deviance often occurs at greater social distances whereas much female deviance occurs within private spheres, there is often greater tolerance directed toward females. Finally, when gender-related deviance occurs among males, as with homosexuality, a more severe reaction than for the same deviance among females may be forthcoming.

The amount of tolerance also varies by the degree a deviant action departs from gender-appropriate norms. Both sexes will be treated more harshly for behaviors that do not conform to gender specific norms. Yet, these norms, as well as the relative statuses of men and women, are in constant flux. As the norms regarding appropriate male and female behaviors change, so does the quantity of social control directed at each sex. Women now are or have the potential to be economically independent from men, control their own fertility, and leave unhappy unions with men. To the extent that status differences between the sexes are closing, women are becoming more involved in public spheres, and expectations of appropriate gender behavior are loosening, the variance in the tolerance of deviance by gender should decrease as well. Changing gender relationships will undoubtedly lead to a growing equality in the degree of tolerance for the deviance of men and women.

Organization

Little is known about how tolerance varies by whether victims and offenders are individuals or organizations. There seems to be much tolerance for deviance directed against organizations (compare Black, 1989a). People routinely take materials and merchandise from employers, fail to pay for telephone calls from public phones, or make false claims of loss and damage from insurers and large companies but refrain from comparable actions against other individuals. They may regard organizations as more capable than individuals of absorbing deviance and fail to see any damage resulting from their actions (Cullen, 1983, pp. 144-145).

Crimes against the government are also often regarded lightly. In many colonized groups, crimes against the state such as tax default or trade regulations are viewed with tolerance or sympathy (Gulliver, 1963, p. 204). Among Sardinian shepards, "A pious woman, who would rush to confession if she had committed a sin against the Madonna or one of her patron saints, would feel no guilt in connection with tax-fraud" (Brogger, 1968, p. 238). Income tax evasion is still lightly regarded in the contemporary United States (Rossi *et al.*, 1974).

It is difficult to compare the degree of tolerance in the opposite configuration: when organizations victimize individuals. Some organizational offenses that involve deliberate harm such as knowingly selling harmful drugs or contaminated food are regarded as very serious, whereas others such as fraud, price fixing, or overcharging are viewed as routine (Rossi *et al.*, 1974). People also seem more willing to bring civil suits against organizational than individual offenders (Miller & Sarat, 1980-1981). The degree of social control over organizational life also may be increasing at a greater rate in contemporary societies than the sanctioning of crimes between individuals (Coleman, 1982, pp. 88-89). Aspects of the offense involved such as the immediacy of harm, degree of intention involved, and the amount of damage suffered are important but little understood components of the degree of tolerance for organizational delicts.

AVOIDANCE

Avoidance is a second form of inaction that arises when a grievant limits interaction with an offender (Baumgartner, 1984; 1988; Black, 1989b; Felstiner, 1974). As in tolerance, the offended party who engages in avoidance neither remedies the problematic situation nor sanctions the offender. Avoidance is distinguishable from tolerance because the aggrieved party does limit contact with the offender.

Avoidance often arises as a residual category of social control when other forms are unsatisfactory. Among intimates, avoidance occurs when people are unable to leave a troubled situation or sanction the offending party, yet cannot invoke third party assistance.

This configuration often occurs in tribal groups when members of the same lineage are in conflict. No compensation or vengeance is possible between intimates (Koch, 1974; Peters, 1967). Yet, the victimized party is dependent on the group and cannot leave the situation. If hostilities are bitter enough, tolerance may be an unsuitable affront to the honor of the disputants, and conciliation may fail. Among the Jalemo of New Guinea, for instance, when irreconcilable conflicts arise between brothers or between fathers and sons, a mutual shunning of communication develops (Koch, 1974). Among the Chenchu tribe in India, who lack any authoritative means for settling disputes, avoidance among quarreling parties served to avert friction by placing distance between them (Furer-Haimendorf, 1967, pp. 20-23). In such circumstances, avoidance may be the only response available to the aggrieved party.

In modern societies, the fluidity of relationships allows people more freedom to leave conflict situations entirely, so avoidance is usually unnecessary. There are, however, a number of circumstances where avoidance develops in modern life. Spouses who are undergoing a divorce but living in the same household may minimize all interaction. Relatives in conflict may avoid attending the same family gatherings or schedule their appearances at different times. Curtailing interaction with offenders may produce the best solution possible to the troubled situation. Middle- and upper-class families, in particular, have the physical space, independence of possessions, and loose structuring that enhance opportunities for avoidance (Baumgartner, 1988, pp. 60-62).

Another social space conducive to avoidance is relationships among neighbors in contemporary communities (Baumgartner, 1988). Unlike strangers or people who live at great physical distances from each other who come into conflict, neighbors typically cannot exit from problematic situations. Yet, they also often cannot risk the lasting bitterness of mobilizing third party control. The social relationship between neighbors is one where both leaving the situation and invoking third party authority is difficult. Any particular instance of deviance will be considered within the overall context of the relationship and will likely be ignored as long as the overall relationship is not too far out of balance (Ellickson, 1986). In one suburban community in the United States, for example, unruly children, defecating dogs, unsightly property, or noisy parties were typically ignored and formal third-party mechanisms, although available, were unused (Baumgartner, 1988). The loose ties that typically existed between neighbors in this setting as well as the relatively large physical space between them allowed for avoiding undesirable and offensive neighbors.

Avoidance among strangers arises when morality is not strong enough to sustain a vigorous social control response. Extreme atomization of the social order is conducive to avoidance (Black, 1989b). When people have only the most transient ties, moral indignation over deviance is absent. People who are only loosely tied to offenders will feel less loss to honor in conflicts so should have less need to seek revenge (Christie, 1977). The weakness of morality in atomized societies renders avoidance a viable response to deviance.

Contemporary cities in the United States with minimal connectedness and dependency but maximal anonymity and transience feature much avoidance. People step over the bodies of sleeping vagrants, ignore the wails of the mentally ill, and pass by exchanges of illegal drugs. Commuters may plan their routes to avoid these common sights of the modern city (Baumgartner, 1988, p. 126). The heterogeneity, transiency, and impersonality of cities are a prime breeder of avoidance.

Modern suburbs, as well, are prominent loci of avoidance reactions (Baumgartner, 1984; 1988). Middle- and upper-class suburbs have physical and social structures that create only loose and atomized ties between residents. The result is the avoidance of open conflict and use of formal means of social control. For example, in one suburban town in Connecticut, only 6 cases were initiated in criminal courts over a 40-week period (Baumgartner, 1988). The atomization and fragmentation of contemporary suburban life made enmities between residents more difficult to sustain and undermined confrontational responses. People were not involved enough with each other to make even self-help responses, not to mention the mobilization of third party control agents. Suburbanites also lacked ties to networks of supporters who could assist in sanctioning or negotiating. At the same time, residents of suburbs have enough community ties to prevent their exit from conflictual situations. Avoidance becomes a preferred response to conflicts in atomized social space.

Avoidance is a form of inaction that emerges in several diverse social fields. It can arise when intimates in conflict are unable to leave situations or to mobilize third party control agents yet find tolerance a morally inadequate response. Other forms of social control are too uncomfortable to use, so avoidance may be the least costly reaction. Avoidance is likely to emerge among more distant parties where social ties are so weak that deviance does not engender any moral response. As modern life becomes increasingly based on transient and impersonal ties, avoidance should correspondingly emerge as a prominent form of reacting to disputes and deviance (Baumgartner, 1988).

Exit

Exit is a third form of inaction that involves no confrontation between offenders. It occurs when the grievant chooses to leave the conflictual situation, rather than confront the offender or remain in an uncomfortable situation without expressing a grievance. Exit behaviors include moving from a neighborhood to escape unruly neighbors, shopping at a different store after disputing with a merchant, quitting a job after fighting with the boss, finding a new apartment after quarreling with a landlord, divorcing or deserting a spouse, or running away from home after a conflict with parents. In some circumstances, exit becomes the easiest way to deal with problematic situations.

Exit is similar to tolerance and avoidance in that the victim does not confront the offender. It differs from these other forms of inaction because the aggrieved party leaves the conflictual situation. Such behaviors typically arise in different social space than other forms of inaction. Exit commonly occurs when social conditions permit migratory behavior or offer ready alternatives to the relationship between the parties in conflict. When people have no need to continue their relationship with the other party and can readily leave the grievance situation, exit behavior is maximal.

People who exit have the ability to leave a problematic situation. This ability stems from the absence of binding ties to the offending party and to others in the community. Little exit behavior can arise in groups that are marked by the intense dependency of each member on the group. Agricultural groups, for example, are rooted to particular land holdings and cannot take their land with them if conflictual situations arise. Land is often not available elsewhere and people cannot afford to leave the land they own (Furer-Haimendorf, 1967, pp. 37-38; Gulliver, 1963, p. 237; Lewis, 1961, p. 238-239). Hence, exit from a farming community is an extremely costly reaction to a grievance.

In contrast, hunting and gathering societies that have transient and temporary attachments feature exit as a common response to conflict between members. The great dispersion of members and ease of attachment to an alternative band in these groups facilitates exit behavior

(Furer-Haimendorf, 1967, p. 32). Exit is also common in pastoral societies whose members herd animals and are spread thinly across their lands. Disputants can simply drive their animals elsewhere if conflicts arise (Goldschmidt, 1971; Lewis, 1961). Hence, pastoral and foraging societies have fewer vengeance killings than agricultural societies where people are wedded to one location because the ability to move from place to place makes exiting from conflict situations more viable (Cooney, 1988, Chapter 3).

Frontiers are another setting typically marked by mobile populations, great geographic distance, and little availability of third party mediators. These circumstances make leaving conflictual situations a viable option for disputants. Exit is a common solution to conflict in such areas (Reid, 1980).

In addition to the ability to move readily from place to place, a lack of dependency on the other party to the conflict is conducive to exit rather than to tolerance or avoidance. People who are emotionally or economically dependent on a party with whom they fall into conflict are less able to exit from troubled situations. Thus men are more likely than women to exit from unhappy marital or other intimate situations because they are less encumbered by child-care responsibilities or emotional dependency. Men also find it easier than women to exit from troubled situations when they possess occupational skills that are exportable to new situations. On the other hand, as women become more economically independent and less tied to care of children, rates of exit from conflictual marriages should equalize between the sexes.

The ability to readily replace one relationship with another also marks the interaction of customers and businesses. Therefore, exit behavior is a common response of consumers when they develop grievances against businesses (Hirshman, 1970). The relationship with the offending party is one that can usually be easily reproduced by simply bringing one's business to another store. Especially in competitive marketplaces that provide many alternative outlets, exit is a cheap and convenient alternative to pursuing a grievance.

Although individuals can often readily exit from grievances with organizations, organizations face greater difficulties in exiting from situations than individuals. They should have more capital, material, and human investment in particular situations and hence find it difficult to leave grievance situations. Therefore, organizations will be more likely to use other alternatives such as tolerance, negotiation, or litigation to deal with offenders.

In general, fluid and impersonal ties promote exit behavior (Black, 1989b). Whenever individuals are able to pick up and leave situations, exit should flourish as a response to conflicts. The ability to attach oneself to an alternative social group also facilitates exit from a troubled situation. Although such situations are most common in contemporary postindustrial societies, they are by no means unknown in other settings such as hunting and gathering bands or frontiers where movement is the easiest and cheapest way to deal with conflict.

CONCLUSION

Inaction represents a minimum of social control. It arises in several diverse settings. The deviance of intimates against outsiders and dominates against subordinates and between outsiders is accorded much tolerance. Deviance between intimates or equals, however, is problematic and may lead to avoidance, self-help, or negotiation. Individualistic, fragmented, and heterogeneous societies also generate the conditions for all forms of inaction both by increasing social distance and by undercutting shared senses of morality. Tolerance, avoidance, and exit flourish in such settings. As these conditions grow in the modern world, inaction should become an increasingly common response to deviance.

7

Unilateral and Bilateral Social Control

UNILATERAL SOCIAL CONTROL

Unilateral social control is the next stage in the escalation of social control. The essence of tolerance, avoidance and exit is to avoid conflict. In contrast to these forms of inaction, unilateral social control indicates an aggressive and confrontational response. In unilateral responses, the aggrieved party makes a claim for physical, monetary, or symbolic redress to the offender. If these claims are not satisfied, the claimant takes aggressive actions toward the offending party. Unilateral social control often takes the form of vengeance, which is a reciprocal exchange of punishments (Black, 1989a). In contrast to bilateral and trilateral social control, unilateral control involves no negotiation or use of third parties. Its distinguishing characteristic is an assault by one grievant on the other without the invocation of second- or third-party settlement agents.

Unilateral self-help is an inherently risky enterprise. All groups must have some sanctions against unilateral responses because they have the potential to bring never-ending spirals of revenge and retaliation. In addition, people who engage in unilateral social control risk retaliatory action not only against themselves but also against their liability groups. When do people ignore these sanctions and use unilateral responses to perceived injuries?[1]

[1]Because inaction and unilateral social control are associated with different social locations, no linear proposition captures the relationship between social space and the forms of so-

Availability of Third-Party Control

One condition promoting unilateral social control is the availability of authoritative parties of dispute resolution: *Unilateral social control is related to the absence or weakness of third party control.* The use of unilateral strategies is connected to the availability and effectiveness of third party social control. Unilateral control develops to the extent that unofficial or official control agents are weak or unavailable (Black, 1983). When quarrels arise that neither official nor unofficial remedy agents can handle, especially between people with no complex and binding ties, a fierce single-minded sense of right unrestricted by chains of association creates a setting conducive to violent self-help responses (Rieder, 1984).

When authoritative third parties are absent, self-help flourishes. Societies with the least degree of political integration are most likely to use coercive self-help responses in conflict management (Koch & Sodergen, 1976). Societies that lack centralized state authority are particularly vulnerable to self-help responses. In many tribal settings, no third-party mediators are distant enough from both disputants to be accepted as effective dispute resolvers. Among the Jalemo of New Guinea, for example, "the absence of an authority capable of adjudicating disputes creates situations in which even minor disagreements among agnates, such as a quarrel over a few nuts, may result in a war between whole villages" (Koch, 1974, p. 120). In the Goodenough Islands, quarrels between siblings can often become destructive, violent, and prolonged because of the absence of mediators (Young, 1971). Revenge as a response to homicide is especially likely to occur when killings arise between different groups that are not subject to some superordinate political authority (Cooney, 1988, Chapter 5).

The relative absence of authoritative third-party settlement of disputes is not limited to tribal groups. The absence of authoritative governmental control was a feature of Western societies until relatively recent times (Beattie, 1986). Society was a collection of domains managed by a small number of powerful families who were themselves immune from legal regulation. The high rate of interpersonal violence in this period may reflect a social control system dependent upon unilateral forms

---

cial control. For example, Griffiths (1984) postulates that the degree of legalness of social control, ranging from inaction through unilateral, bilateral, and trilateral control, varies inversely with the relational distance between disputing parties. Yet, in some cases, the same conditions that give rise to legal social control—marginality, low status, or relational distance—also are associated with the use of unilateral social control. Despite the methodological advantages of using a continuum of legalness, there is no linear relationship between social space and the choice of forms of social control.

of revenge. Correspondingly, the great decline in interpersonal violence in England between medieval and modern times reflects the emergence of third party mechanisms to resolve disputes (Stone, 1983).

Vengeful self-help still proliferates in settings that lack legitimate state authority. For example, in peasant areas of southern Italy no neutral third parties are present to resolve disputes. Corporate groups are weak, and the basic unit of society is the nuclear family. In the absence of a strong state, public order rests on revenge and the threat of revenge to resolve conflict (Brogger, 1968).

Unilateral forms of self-help are also prominent when third-party forums are ineffective. Third-party forums may be ineffective for many reasons, including physical distance from disputants, the disreputable character of grievants, overloaded case dockets, inefficiency, or perceived prejudice. When such conditions prevail, unilateral forms of self-help should flourish.

Self-help becomes increasingly more common with the growing inefficiency and distance from courts (Bohannon, 1957). Vigilante groups, as well, typically arise when local law enforcement is perceived as inadequate (Little & Sheffield, 1983). In the Colonial period in the United States, vigilante movements arose when the established legal order was viewed as weak, corrupt, or overly slow (Hurst, 1945). In the American West, great geographical distances prevented the establishment of effective formal or informal controls, and vigilante groups arose to fill the gap in social control. Vigilantism was especially likely when the population found public police performance wanting (Friedman, 1985, p. 580; Liebman and Polen, 1978: 337). In nineteenth-century England as well, self-help organizations flourished as the movement of rural people to cities weakened traditional social control while formal legal control was not yet fully established (Little & Sheffield, 1983). The control of crime in developing nations without authoritative court systems also centers on self-help including vigilanteeism by the masses, crowd action against thieves, and the employment of private security guards by the wealthy (Colson, 1974).

Unilateral social control often reemerges in the modern world when legal controls become weak or ineffective. In the contemporary United States, self-help groups arise when legal control is seen as inadequate. The celebrity accorded to the case of Bernard Goetz who shot four black youths he felt were going to rob him illustrates the uncertainty of many citizens in modern society over the ability of formal control agents to protect them (Katz, 1988, pp. 322-23). Relatedly, vigilante groups such as the Guardian Angels who patrol crime-ridden areas or that capture illegal aliens in the Southwestern United States flourish in settings where law or other third-party intervention is seen as ineffective. In contemporary American cities, the ownership of weapons for protection increases when people feel more vulnerable to crime victimization and have low confidence in police protection (Smith & Uchida, 1988). In Detroit, for example, people "purchased more handguns when violent crime and civil disorder reduced confidence in collective security and fewer when these conditions abated" (McDowall & Loftin, 1983, p. 1156). The lack of confidence in formal control leads to weapons ownership as a potential means of unilateral self-help. Within prisons, the loss of the ability of third parties to impose discipline can lead to an increase in reliance on violent self-help perpetrated by ethnically structured groups on each other (Ekland-Olson, 1986). Whenever informal or formal authorities are unable to handle disputes effectively, the use of unilateral social control should be high.

Families are another location where the lack of social control alternatives can lead to much violent self-help. The costs of exiting from family relationships are often high because of strong emotional and economic investments, yet the closeness and intensity of these relationships often make avoidance unfeasible.[2] Third-party adjudicators are usually reluctant to intervene in the affairs of intimates (Black, 1976, Chapter 6). Therefore, grievances often escalate to the point of violent self-help. Two-thirds of murders and manslaughter cases in large American cities involve either family members or acquaintances, often as the culmination of a long series of violent acts and retaliations (Wolfgang, 1958). Rates of homicide are especially high in cities that lack effective social control, as indicated by high rates of divorce and poverty (Williams & Flewelling, 1988).

The importance of third-party redress is particularly apparent in female-perpetuated homicides as forms of self-help. Women are especially likely to kill their male partners when they feel unable to protect themselves from male aggression in alternative ways. Conversely, the presence of alternatives such as shelters for battered women are associated with a decline in rates of female homicides against men (Browne & Williams, 1989). The settings of self-help killings indicate that the weakness of third-party intervention leads to violent self-help, whereas the availability of protective resources reduces such responses to grievances.

Unilateral social control flourishes among people who are unable to use third-party agents of social control (Black, 1983). In the contemporary United States, self-help is frequent among deviants themselves who, because of their disreputable status, cannot invoke the criminal

[2]An exception are middle- and upper-class families with much physical space and little social and economic interdependence (see Baumgartner, 1988).

justice system. Hence, participants in illegal enterprises such as drug dealing, gambling, and other organized crime activities are often involved in violent means of enforcing their claims. For example, homicide as a form of social control is common among drug dealers who have no access to legitimate ways of resolving their disputes.

The exertion of unilateral means of self-help rather than any nonconfrontational form of social control is sometimes the only way an aggrieved person can restore lost honor. *Honor,* the protection of one's reputation, is often an important component of the use of unilateral social control (Black, 1983). When people cannot depend on third-party backing for their claims, their honor becomes an important component of social control systems. People must personally avenge slights to them or face disgrace. This is often the case among members of strong male support groups that are isolated from adult control. These groups, typically comprised of young, unmarried males without jobs, are a prominent source of vengeful self-help in many settings (Horowitz & Schwartz, 1974; Rieder, 1984). When honor is an important trait in reacting to grievances, such as in medieval society (Bloch, 1961), organized crime groups (Reuter, 1984), or on frontiers (Reid, 1980), third-party sanctioning systems are typically weak or unavailable.

Unilateral social control, however, is not an inevitable result of absent or weak formal third-party adjudicators. Weak legal systems may be offset by strong informal third-party dispute resolution systems. For example, modern Japanese society is marked by many effective extralegal sanctioning bodies that are available to resolve grievances. Consequently, despite the weakness of Japanese formal legal institutions, individuals rarely use self-help remedies because of the strength of informal mediation systems (Haley, 1978, 1982). However, when neither formal nor informal resolvers of disputes are present, rates of unilateral self-help should be high.

When state authority establishes itself or increases its effectiveness, unilateral responses recede. There thus appears to be a strong correlation between the absence or inefficiency of third-party authorities and the use of unilateral self-help as an institutional method of conflict resolution (Koch, 1974).

Crosscutting Ties

Social fields that lack strong third party social control are conducive to the emergence of unilateral strategies of social control. In addition, the lack of crosscutting ties between disputants promotes the use of unilateral responses: *Unilateral social control is related to the absence of cross-*

cutting ties between disputants. Disputants who do not share ties to others in the social field do not face normative and structural restraints that might prevent aggressive responses to grievances. They lack mutual ties who might sanction them for using coercive unilateral strategies to settle grievances.

The use of unilateral control poses a particularly difficult problem in tribal societies that lack an ultimate sanctioning authority to guarantee security and order. Retaliation for injuries suffered is both an obligation and a right of injured parties and their kin (Barkun, 1968). Yet, self-help is especially threatening to the well-being of communities that lack an ultimate basis of legitimate force because it can lead to recurring cycles of vengeance and, ultimately, to the thoroughgoing disruption of the community. Because unilateral responses in tribal groups are so potentially disruptive, they are not preferred methods of obtaining redress (Roberts, 1979). When, however, cross-linkages between the networks of disputants do not exist, third-party mediators are difficult to find. Therefore, it is difficult for anyone to impose effective control on disputants, and coercive self-help is a constant threat. Tribal groups must adopt some procedures to quell the possibility of unending spirals of revenge.

Those tribal groups where self-help is common feature weak social structure, few overlapping ties between groups, little emphasis on kinship, and no individual or body with binding authority to adjudicate conflicts (Radcliffe-Brown, 1922). Under such conditions, the lack of normative constraints over the offended party leads vengeful self-help to be a prominent response to grievances. The Eskimo are one group that features these conditions. Eskimo social structure is marked by small, local groups that have weak kinship ties and little contact between different local groups. Social control typically features blood revenge or less drastic but punishment oriented responses such as song duels (Hoebel, 1954). Or, among the Dafla tribe in Northeast India, the lack of authoritative group sanctions leads to patterns of violent self-help, feuds, and raiding (Furer-Haimendorf, 1967, pp. 55-62). The absence of cross-linking ties to groups makes vengeance rather than negotiation a likely response to conflict.

In other tribal settings, each disputant might be integrated into strong clan groups, but these groups have few links to each other. Disputes that arise between members of different clans are far more likely to be disruptive for the entire group and radiate throughout the social structure. They are highly visible; a greater proportion of the group will have ties to the disputants; and more persons can suffer the consequences of social control responses. Such settings should feature much coercive self-help and the continual possibility of feud and retaliatory behavior (Falk-Moore, 1972). Not only will more parties share corporate liability for retaliation, but structural conditions limit the availability of peacemakers. Hence, a study of 30 societies indicates that over 80% of killings between groups resulted in revenge whereas none of the intragroup killings did so (Cooney, 1988, p. 158). Although the absence of crosscutting ties can lead to vengeful means of unilateral control, enmeshment in strong group ties encourages negotiation and mediation.

Hierarchy

The presence of effective third-party control and of cross-linkages between the networks of disputants also have implications for the sorts of relational contexts conducive to self-help. When two higher status parties confront one another, conditions that inhibit the use of self-help should be maximal. Higher status persons both have more ties in the community and more access to legal institutions. Therefore, when third-party remedy systems are well established, the least amount of unilateral self-help should occur when both disputants are higher status and integrated members of the community.[3] A different situation exists when lower status persons have grievances, whether against higher status persons or against their status equals. They face fewer normative constraints over their behavior and have less chance of obtaining redress from third parties. Both conditions heighten the chances that a grievant will use unilateral methods of social control. Thus, parties prohibited from using law, such as juveniles, typically resort to coercive self-help methods such as vandalism, property destruction, or harassment to settle their grievances (Black, 1983).

Coercive unilateral social control flourishes among people on the margins of society who do not have access to third parties who will respond to their grievances. In many societies, unattached young men often resort to violence to avenge wrongs, whereas men with families who are more enmeshed in reciprocal obligations settle disputes through conciliation (Brogger, 1968). In contemporary American society, disproportionately high rates of homicide and assault occur among young, poor, and minority individuals, often as responses to threats to personal honor (Katz, 1988; Luckinbill, 1977; Lunsgaarde, 1977).

[3]Before the development of strong third-party control codes of honor that emphasize violence as a response to personal affronts were especially strong among upper-class males (Ayres, 1984; Bloch, 1961).

Conclusion

Unilateral social control arises when authoritative third parties are absent or weak, when cross-linkages between disputants do not exist, and when marginal people come into conflict. The same weakness of social ties that leads to the use of unilateral forms of social control also contributes to the damaging effects unilateral control creates in social life. All groups must therefore strive to control its use. The degree of success they have is related to the satisfaction people can obtain from bilateral or trilateral forms of social control.

Bilateral Social Control

In bilateral social control, a grievant makes a claim for redress directly to the offender. Some sort of bilateral discussions arise between the contending parties. In some cases, bilateral control proceeds only between the two parties themselves. In other cases, mediators present nonbinding solutions that the parties may accept or reject.[4]

Bilateral control lies between responses where grievants do nothing or use unilateral means to deal with a grievance and where they utilize third parties to decide their claims. It is not mutually exclusive with other forms of social control but often succeeds or precedes unilateral or trilateral control. The failure of both sides to agree jointly to a settlement can lead to the mobilization of third-party control, a resort to self-help, or tolerance of the unwanted condition.

Successful bilateral control entails the agreement of both parties in conflict on a solution. Only when both parties feel that they can gain something from negotiation will they be likely to engage in bilateral control. What social conditions promote the use of bilateral forms of social control?

Crosscutting Ties

Just as the absence of cross-linkages leads to unilateral forms of social control, their presence puts pressure on both parties to work together to settle their disputes: *Bilateral social control is related to the presence of cross-linkages between disputants* (see also Black, 1989b). Cross-linkages

[4]Because mediators must obtain the voluntary cooperation of each disputant (Eckhoff, 1966), mediation is more similar to negotiation than to adjudication where a solution is imposed on the contesting parties regardless of their wishes. Therefore, I consider it closer to bilateral than to trilateral forms of social control.

constrain the use of both unilateral control that can alienate victims from their allies and resort to third-party control from outside the group. The essential conditions for bilateral control—a balancing of claims to promote peaceful reconciliation and a concern for compromise and harmony—should be maximal when groups feature negotiators or mediators who wish to maintain ongoing relationships with both disputants (Gluckman, 1967).

Bilateral rather than unilateral social control predominates when the social field contains crosscutting loyalties to kin and others in the community (Koch, 1984). For successful mediation to occur, mediators must be equidistant from disputing parties. If either party believes that the mediator will favor the other side, they will not agree to a noncoercive solution. The presence of crosscutting ties that link mediators to both disputants can enhance the perception of impartiality (Merry, 1982).

In tribal groups, disputes that might lead to war in the absence of cross-linkages can be averted through negotiation when a mediator with common ties to both disputants is present (Bohannon, 1957). Within most closely knit communities, disputants will face pressures toward settlement from third parties. This situation is especially likely to arise when mediators who share experiences with both disputants are readily available (Felstiner, 1974). Mediators must have enough influence to exert pressure on disputants to agree on a joint solution in the absence of coercive force. This is most likely to occur when the mediator has the respect of both sides to the conflict but is not seen as the partisan of either.

For example, among the Konyak Naga tribe in India, emigrants were used as negotiators when conflicts emerged between their village of residence and their natal villages:

> The last time peace had to be negotiated the village council of Wakching sent one of the Totok men resident in Wakching as go-between, carrying a ceremonial spear, to his ancestral village. On this mission he was safe, because no Totok man could kill a member of a Totok clan—even if resident in another village—without offending against the taboo on violence against a co-villager. (Furer-Haimendorf, 1967, p. 99)

The presence of people who have crosscutting ties to both parties is conducive to bilateral negotiation.

In addition to cross-linkages, certain types of hierarchical social structures are also conducive to the availability of mediators. Hierarchies marked by many ties of dependence are likely to produce members whose structural position puts them in positions of authority over a pool of dependents who are equidistant from them. For much of Western history, the clergy fulfilled this role, whereas in other areas nobles settled many disputes of humble people (Casten, 1983). It follows that bilateral settlements prevail in small, homogeneous communities with influential and respected leaders. Growing population size and heterogeneity weaken the conditions for successful bilateral resolution because they create too great a distance between resolvers and disputants. With heightened distance comes a tendency for authorities to either impose outcomes or ignore the dispute entirely rather than to encourage bilateral settlements (Black & Baumgartner, 1983).

The presence of a common normative universe between disputants is another condition conducive to bilateral dispute resolution. Disputants must consider the implication of pursuing a grievance on their reputations in the community. As one potential litigant in eighteenth-century Granada stated: "My wife has got all the people I most respect in this city to get me to give up this case, and I cannot very well say no, since I have my trade, position and friends to think of" (Casey, 1983, p. 215). Mediation in community forums is most effective in settings where both disputants share common normative constraints but is likely to fail when more distant individuals confront each other (Felstiner 1974). Disputes between residents within ethnic neighborhoods and other closely knit communities often result in bilateral solutions because of common normative constraints and the presence of common ties (Gulliver, 1979).

In one close knit community in rural Illinois, local residents, mindful of community pressures, would not sue or even demand compensation from anyone else. Not only residents but also insurance adjusters knew one another and pursued negotiated, rather than adjudicated, settlements. Persons who pursued personal injury claims were viewed as antisocial, greedy, and trouble making (Engel, 1984). In contrast, when residents became involved in accidents in large cities when they did not know the other party, litigation was far more likely. Those few cases where personal injury cases did enter the court shared common features: "The parties were separated by either geographic or social 'distance' that could not be bridged by any conflict resolution process short of litigation" (Engel, 1984, p. 567).

Bilateral Control in the Modern World

It may seem that modern social life does not feature conditions conducive to second-party control. Not only are disputants unlikely to share common normative constraints, cross-linkages, or ties to mediators, but the availability of legal remedies is also high. Nevertheless, surveys reveal a considerable amount of negotiated settlements (Galanter, 1983; Miller & Sarat, 1980-1981, p. 530). For example, consumer complaints are often resolved through negotiations between sellers and buyers. About 60% of individuals who do press complaints say they were successful in resolving their problem through negotiating with the offending party (Best & Andreasen, 1977; King and McEvoy, 1976). In a study of one chain of appliance stores, most purchasers who perceived defects pressed claims with businesses, and in over 80% of cases, these claims were satisfactorily resolved through bilateral negotiations (Ross & Littlefield, 1978). In one of the most common grievance settings in modern life—traffic accident claims—insurance companies typically resolve 95% of cases with claimants through negotiated settlements. In about three-quarters of these cases, claimants received what they asked for (Ross, 1970). Two major reasons—the presence of organizations and of lawyers—account for the widespread use of bilateral control in modern life.

Organizations

One reason for the unexpectedly high rate of negotiated solutions in the contemporary United States lies in the presence of organizations. Organizations find it difficult to avoid or exit from disputes because they are unable to leave a conflictual situation. Disputing organizations also face many effective nonlegal sanctions that constrain either party from going to law. The use of law may lead organizational reputation to suffer and valued clients to be lost (Macaulay, 1963). In addition, multiplex relationships often exist between members of each organization, further constraining the use of third-party control. Organizations can also afford to hire lawyers who can resolve difficulties through negotiation (Hurst, 1980-81).

The result is that organizations rarely litigate disputes they have with other organizations (Galanter, 1974). When disputes arise between organizations, negotiation or mediation are more likely outcomes than unilateral or trilateral forms of social control. Only when an irreparable split has occurred, such as when a manufacturer terminates a dealer's franchise, is litigation likely among organizations (Macaulay, 1963).

Grievances that individuals have with organizations also often lead to negotiated settlements. Organizations have a number of incentives to bargain with, rather than litigate against, individuals with whom they have fallen into conflict (Ross & Littlefield, 1978). First, their reputation in the community might suffer if an individual grievant is not satisfied. Unhappy customers do not return, so acceding to consumer demands can be good business practice. In addition, the costs of settling an individual claim may be far lower than the costs of pursuing a legal action, especially when the costs of settlement can be passed along to another party such as the manufacturer of a defective product. Small claims individuals make against organizations may be less expensive to settle than to defend in court, particularly when they involve no matters of principle. Especially if any chance exists of a very high recovery, an assessment of costs and benefits leads organizations to settle rather than litigate.[5]

The consumer-dealer relationship may be one setting in modern life where the cost-effectiveness of bilateral solutions to disputes is maximal. The economies of scale that guide large organizations render negotiation rather than litigation a cost-effective form of settling consumer complaints. Likewise, in the criminal justice system, prosecutors find that negotiated settlements with large organizations are often far more efficient than pursuing cases to trial. The inherent difficulties of proving the guilt of organizations and their ability to delay proceedings often means that the public interest is best served by negotiated settlements rather than prosecutions (Braithwaite, 1982, p. 751).

Attorneys

Another reason for the persistence of bilateral forms of control in contemporary society lies in the presence of lawyers (Black, 1984b). Attorneys are typically viewed as promoting litigation, dissension, and conflict. Mobilizing a lawyer does often lead to an escalation of conflict or a break in relationships, especially among parties who share an intimate relationship. Once attorneys are mobilized, however, their role is often the opposite. They regularly serve as negotiators who promote solutions between disputants. They often persuade clients who are interested in the vindication of rights to accept more harmonious bargained solutions.

The role of attorneys in facilitating negotiation is apparent in a number of areas of modern life. One is divorce cases.[6] These often involve

[5]Conversely, organizations will in some circumstances readily use courts to obtain redress from individual defendants (Abel, 1979; Galanter, 1974; Wanner, 1974). Organizations, especially banks and credit agencies, are the most common users of small claims courts, particularly against individual defendants (Yngvesson & Hennessey, 1975). Yet, it is not known whether organizations are especially litigious relative to the number of claims they have.

[6]In contrast to the role of attorneys in dealing with disputes between strangers, their introduction into disputes involving intimates should produce greater social distance and hence a lower chance of a bilateral settlement (Black, 1989a). In divorce cases, however, the desire to end the relationship coupled with the intense hostility that often exists between the parties overrides the once close relationship of disputants. Attorneys, therefore, may mitigate rather than promote hostility between the parties undergoing divorce.

hostile and bitter adversaries who seek vindication of their personal claims and are unwilling to compromise. Although clients typically take an adversarial approach, their lawyers usually strive for compromise and settlement (Sarat & Felstiner, 1986). Attorneys rarely seek court intervention and attempt to minimize conflict through the use of mediative techniques. These can transform an adversarial situation into one where interpersonal resolutions can be created (Griffiths, 1986).

In other situations as well, grievants seek to vindicate their own rights and punish the other party until persuaded to compromise by attorneys. One involves cases when individuals press cases against businesses. Attorneys rarely play an adversarial role in these cases but act more as therapists who allow clients to vent off steam or as mediators between the grievant and the seller (Macaulay, 1979). In general, attorneys adjust claims and seek compromise solutions rather than regard cases as matters of principle.[7]

Even in cases such as automobile accidents where the legal profession is most organized to engage in litigation, bargained bilateral solutions are the most likely outcome. For example, in one large study of accidents, only about a third of claims handled by lawyers resulted in the filing of a suit (Conard, Morgan, Pratt, Voltz, & Bombaugh, 1964). Of these cases, less than 15 percent resulted in a courtroom trial. Bargained solutions are usually a far more efficient and cost-effective way of dealing with accidents for both parties than the pursuit of litigated settlements. The result is that in most instances, lawyers will press cases only when litigation is necessary, as with probate, or in uncontested cases, such as those that involve debt collection (Galanter, 1983).

The role of attorneys is critical not only for facilitating bilateral control but also for altering the location of disputes in social space (Black, 1989a). People usually mobilize attorneys when they dispute with others at a great social distance from themselves. Once people mobilize attorneys, the impact of client social status will largely depend on the characteristics of the attorney rather than the individual (Black, 1989a). Because attorneys typically share ongoing relationships with each other and with court personnel, they create a cross-linked social space that would not exist between their clients alone. Although disputants may have had no previous relationship, attorneys for both sides are often embedded in a common social structure and legal culture and share ties with other attorneys. A normative climate and closer social

[7]When attorneys such as public interest or ACLU lawyers who are interested in general principles, rather than concrete outcomes, become involved in cases, negotiated resolutions should be rarer.

distance between disputants that might facilitate bilateral solutions emerges.

Although the presence of lawyers should typically create a space more amenable for bilateral resolutions to disputes, this should vary according to the position of attorneys and disputants in ongoing networks of social interaction. Attorneys who would pursue a case against a marginal or fly-by-night business with whom they have no ties would hesitate to make an adversarial response if the case involves a local bank or prominent merchant (Macaulay, 1979). When lawyers are integrated into networks with potential adversaries, they should be reluctant to pursue litigated solutions but instead should strive to achieve bilateral solutions. Lawyers should also be very reluctant to litigate against powerful businesses who might be their clients in the future (Macaulay, 1979). In contrast, marginal lawyers who are not tied into strong local networks of interaction are more likely to act in an adversarial manner and press cases to adjudicative solutions.[8]

Conclusion

The presence of organizations and attorneys in modern life creates conditions for bilateral control that would otherwise not be present in societies marked by impersonal relationships, normative conflict, and few cross-linkages. Organizations facilitate negotiations because of their rootedness in communities, desire to maintain relationships with each other and with consumers, and economies of scale. Attorneys have the capacity to transform situations of relational distance, social inequality, and normative dissensus that facilitate adversarial social control responses into situations conducive to settlement and compromise. Unlike their clients, attorneys know that bargained bilateral solutions may provide more reliable, efficient, and profitable outcomes than pressing cases to legal resolutions. They may also realize that if taken to court, judges will press adversaries to adjust their claims in bargained outcomes. Attorneys can expedite negotiation through creating a common culture, cross-linkages, and equality between two otherwise disparate parties. The prevalence of organizations and attorneys produce far more bilateral social control in contemporary society than we would expect from either societal or disputant characteristics alone.

[8]The growing number of women and blacks in the legal systems predicts a growing amount of litigation because they are less likely than white male attorneys to be integrated into traditional legal institutions and culture.

8

Trilateral Forms of Social Control

INTRODUCTION

The last chapter considered forms of social control where grievants do not use authoritative third parties. The intervention of adjudicative third parties marks a critical transformation in the nature of social control. Adjudicators impose authoritative solutions on disputants regardless of their wishes. Matters that once were private become public disputes. A trilateral situation is created where the interests of third parties, as well as those of each disputant, come into play.

In this chapter, I first consider the conditions that lead to the development of adjudicative trilateral institutions. I then examine the conditions that lead disputants to mobilize third-party agents. In the following chapter, I consider the factors affecting the response of third-party controllers at each stage of the legal process.

Three themes run through these chapters. First, the legal system is not autonomous: The emergence, mobilization, and response of legal institutions all depend on the availability and viability of informal social control alternatives. Trilateral institutions emerge when informal control is weak or unavailable; people mobilize law when other alternatives are not viable; and trilateral forums themselves tend to react vigorously only in the absence of other control alternatives (Black, 1976, Chapter 6). Law becomes enmeshed in social life when less formal control systems are unable to manage problematic situations.

Second, most forms of trilateral social control are reactive to the wishes of claimants. People who feel they have been wronged themselves must define the harm as legally relevant and invoke legal authority. Laws remain dormant unless citizens activate them. The norms and interests of laypersons rather than official rules generate legal action.

Even after trilateral authority is mobilized, the official reaction is still largely shaped by the wishes of claimants. The rules of formal law are themselves offense and offender oriented. The preferences and characteristics of victims are, in theory, unimportant. Much work in legal sociology stresses either the autonomous structure of law and legal authority or the nature of offenders and their offenses. Yet, in practice, the fate of cases that enter the domain of law is shaped by the relationship between victims and offenders. In each respect, trilateral control is not autonomous but responsive to the demands of private citizens.

The Emergence of Trilateral Social Control

Unlike unilateral and bilateral control, which are potential options in most social situations, grievants may not have the option of using trilateral parties because they are not available. Trilateral control only arises under certain conditions. Before examining the conditions when third parties are invoked to settle disputes, I first survey when trilateral social control emerges.

Law and Other Social Control

The various forms of social control are not independent of one another but are dependent on the presence and strength of the others. Trilateral institutions emerge with the weakness or breakdown of other types of social control: *Trilateral social control arises when alternative social control is weak or unavailable* (Black, 1976, p. 107). Law appears when other control is unable to resolve social conflict satisfactorily.

Legal control by the state develops when social control provided by the family, clan, church, or community is inadequate:

> The same pattern has appeared in every part of the world, gradually in some societies, quickly, even suddenly in others. In Europe, it happened over centuries. For many Indians of North America, it happened almost overnight, as quickly as they were moved to reservations. . . . In most of Africa, Asia, Latin America, and Oceania, it has come only recently, if at all. (Black, 1976, pp. 108-109)

The scope of the proposition is very broad. Communities with intense face-to-face interaction and strong informal control are unlikely to develop formal third-party forums for resolving disputes. These emerge when individuals or isolated nuclear units form the basis of community structure (Schwartz, 1954). In the developing world, law emerges when members of traditional communities migrate to cities or the authority of senior male members of the group weakens (Colson, 1974; Nader and Metzger, 1963).

In the West, families were once the primary locus of social control. By the sixteenth-century, the responsibility for vengeance had largely been transformed from victims and their relatives to the state (Spierenburg, 1984). Informal controls weakened because of trends including population growth, immigration, geographical mobility, and industrial expansion. Formal institutions such as prisons, reformatories, and mental hospitals arose to handle deviants who once were sanctioned by families and communities (Grob, 1973).

The development of an elaborated legal structure for the control of crime in the United States illustrates this process. Before the early 1800s, there were no special state institutions for the control of criminals or wayward juveniles. Parents, masters, or communities were responsible for errant conduct. In the Colonial period, the public control of crime was left to a nonspecialized constabulary comprised of ordinary citizens (Lane, 1967). The community as a whole or the individual victim, rather than any specialized state agents, was responsible for enforcing the criminal law. The written law itself was little developed, and interpretation of both law and fact was in the hands of juries and not specialized legal agents (Nelson, 1975). Only a rudimentary legal system existed.

Over the course of the nineteenth century, social life became marked by growing heterogeneity, mobility, and urbanization. These trends undermined community surveillance and provided greater individual freedom from traditional family and local controls. The family was decreasingly able to serve as a locus for social control. It could not, as before, absorb vagrant youths as apprentices or servants. Many youths left their families to live in rooming houses in large cities. Specialized police forces developed with the primary function of controlling a "bachelor subculture" of transient young men who faced no informal social control (Lane, 1980, p. 19). Even in the earlier Colonial period, those American colonies that had less effective systems of informal control and a surplus of young unmarried males developed more elaborated legal control systems (Greenberg, 1982).

Not only the police but also specialized institutions such as reformatories and mental hospitals developed to fill the gap vacated by strong family control. As the ability of families to discipline and care for their wayward members weakened, they came to rely on formal control institutions such as juvenile reformatories and mental hospitals. Reformatories emerged as urban lower class families found it increasingly necessary to cast loose their adolescent children. The largest class of entrants into the newly developed institutions were adolescent males, and occasionally females, who either had conflicts with their families or no family ties, and, in addition, were not under the protection of a powerful peer group (Mennel, 1983). The majority of girls who entered the new reform schools were also brought by members of their own families (Brenzel, 1980). Often, their fathers were dead or had deserted the family, leaving it bereft of informal control mechanisms. Immigrants, in particular, believed their children were immersed in strange and incorrigible behaviors and could only be controlled through formal sanctions (Friedman, 1985, p. 600).

The development of mental hospitals in the nineteenth century illustrates the same dynamic. Between 1800 and 1880, commitments increased from 1 for every 6,000 persons to 1 for every 750 persons (Tomes, 1984). The major factor impelling the development of mental institutions was changing notions of family responsibility for the care of the disordered. Families usually commenced the legal process leading to commitment when they became unwilling or unable to provide care (Grob, 1973). Rising expectations of family life, smaller households, and a lesser availability of caretakers in the nuclear family all led to a greater predisposition to commit insane relatives in nineteenth-century families. The mental hospital met a deeply felt need by providing an institutional solution to painful domestic situations (Tomes, 1984). The behaviors that typically resulted in commitment were highly troubling to intimates, although rarely threats to public order or to economic or political elites.

In the modern world, individuals with weak or broken ties in their social networks still are more likely to utilize formal systems of help for personality problems. People who enter therapy lack strong relational ties to others. Among those who are identified as psychiatric cases, people who are socially isolated have more contacts with both the general medical sector (Goldberg & Huxley, 1980) and the mental health specialty sector (Fox, 1984; Leaf *et al.*, 1987; Link & Dohrenwend, 1980). For example, married people are more embedded than unmarried ones in social support networks. Studies consistently show low rates of therapeutic help seeking among the married and high rates among those who are not currently married (Fox, 1984; Link & Dohrenwend, 1980). Other people who lack social support, such as the unemployed, those who live alone, and those with no religion, also utilize medical and mental health services for personal problems more often than those who are embedded in supportive networks of social relationships (Horwitz, 1987).

In contrast, the presence of strong relational networks often impedes seeking therapeutic help. People with large and stable relational networks receive more informal support, remain in the community for longer periods of time, and enter hospitals with more severe disorders than those with weaker networks (Gillis & Keet, 1965; Horwitz, 1977b; Lowenthal, 1964). This may in part explain why members of ethnic groups marked by extended familial networks such as Chinese or Mexicans are low utilizers of therapeutic services (Garrison, 1977; Lin *et al.*, 1978). When people are isolated from strong supportive networks, seeking help from therapeutic professionals may be one way of obtaining such support.

Trilateral controls of all sorts—police, courts, reformatories, and mental hospitals—emerge when family and community controls breakdown. They arise in settings such as large cities that lack networks of kin and neighbors who can contain informally members who create disturbances. Correspondingly, they are disproportionately used by broken and weak families who lack the means to punish or care for a troublesome member or by socially isolated individuals who seek social support.

The corollary of the emergence of trilateral control with the weakness of other social control is that *trilateral social control is unlikely to emerge in the presence of effective negotiation and mediation.* Western history traditionally has been marked by strong systems of dependency between clients and masters. This hierarchical order led to effective mediation because authorities had enough esteem from the population so that their decisions would be respected and obeyed (Castan, 1983). As long as a stable informal system provided effective dispute resolution, there was no need for a legal order. The emergence of capitalist economies marked by solely economic ties between employers and employees undermined the basis of informal dispute resolution and was accompanied by the rise of legal authority.

Contemporary Japanese society also illustrates a situation where a stable, integrated, and hierarchical social structure produces many informal third parties who command trust and obedience. Because of this, Japanese legal institutions are atrophied, and no industrial nation has a weaker legal system than Japan (Haley, 1978, 1982). Only when dealing with persons, such as foreigners, who are outside the society entirely do the Japanese make heavy reliance on legal rules and institutions. In contrast, industrial nations such as the United States that are marked by autonomy, heterogeneity, and mobility do not have the option of using nonlegal and customary norms enforced by informal groups so have much more developed legal systems.

Trilateral and less elaborated systems of social control are thus closely related. Law arises when informal control is weak but is unlikely to emerge when informal control is effective. What social factors predict when informal social control declines and trilateral social control emerges?

Social Distance and Trilateral Social Control

The emergence of trilateral forms of social control is related to growing social distance in societies: *Trilateral social control develops with social distance between disputants and agents of social control.* Social distance arises from many factors including population growth, stratification, urbanization, migration, or heterogeneity. Whatever its cause, distance leads to a vacuum of informal control between disputants and to the development of authoritative third parties that can adjudicate conflicts.

For trilateral forms of social control to emerge, a social field must contain individuals who are in a structural position to serve as authoritative resolvers of disputes. Because trilateral control involves third parties who impose outcomes on disputants, some individual must have enough power to issue binding commands. Such binding power can only arise in groups with hierarchies of esteem, authority, or coercion that lead to enforced solutions. When the centralization of power in a group is so low that no party is in a position to issue authoritative commands, effective forms of third-party control cannot develop.

When groups have little stratification, adjudicators are unlikely to arise. Potential mediators are likely to be equals in power and authority to disputing parties (Roberts, 1979). They must appeal to community harmony because they do not have the power to impose solutions. Tribal groups marked by a minimum of relational distance and inequality among their members are one setting where decentralization prohibits the emergence of authoritative third parties. In societies based on kinship ties, people are obligated to support their kin in disputes. Morality that transcends particular interests cannot take root because any potential settlement agent is likely to be an intimate of one or both of the competing parties. Groups with very strong kin obligations are unlikely to have adjudicators with enough distance and objectivity to be acceptable to both disputing parties. Each party to the dispute believes that a third party will be partisan rather than objective, lessening the likelihood that the intervention will be acceptable to both (Black & Baumgartner, 1983).

In such settings, no party will be distant enough to impose impersonal rules. Instead, resolvers should attempt to mend the damage in interpersonal relationships. Lowie's study of the Plains Indians in the American West shows how this occurs after a homicide in one small-scale group:

> If, for example, a man had been murdered by another, the official peacemakers of the tribe . . . were primarily concerned with pacifying the victim's kin rather than with meting out just punishment. . . . But there was no feeling that any impartial authority seated above the parties to the feud had been outraged and demanded penance or penalty. In juridical terminology, even homicide was a tort, not a crime. (Lowie, 1927, pp. 103-104)

The small degree of relational and hierarchical distance between members of tribal societies does not create the social space for adjudication to arise.

Whenever close interpersonal relationships comprise the social structure, impersonal third-party control is difficult to implement. For instance, among the Somali of East Africa, elders chosen to arbitrate a dispute must be acceptable to both parties and cannot have kinship ties to either party, because these are regarded as prejudicial to a fair judgment (Lewis, 1961, p. 229). In the absence of an authoritative resolvers, bargain and compromise or coercive self-help is inherent in confrontations. The potential damage to social harmony from an adjudicated solution is far greater than the need to enforce the law.

In the West, it was difficult to establish authoritative trilateral control before enough distance was created between control agents and the population they were supposed to police. For example, in preindustrial England:

> If a widow eked out a living by selling ale unlicensed, why should the neighbourhood be troubled with a prosecution which might foment local resentment? The order of the village community could survive occasional drunkenness, erratic church attendance, profane language, neglect of the licensing and apprenticeship laws. It was more likely to be disturbed by the enforcement of the host of penal laws which might excite new conflicts and drain, in fines, its resources. What really mattered was the maintenance of specific, local, personal relationships, not conformity to impersonal law. (Wrightson, 1980, p. 25)

The close relationship between the local constabularies and those they policed prevented effective enforcement. In another case in seventeenth-century England: "Robert Fazakerley of West Derby, Lancashire, when charged with the serving of warrants upon several neighbours conscientiously attempted to do so, but only after first advertising the fact in the hope that they would keep out of his way" (Wrightson, 1980, p. 31).

The growth of social heterogeneity, differentiation, and competing interests leads to greater distance between disputants so creates the social distance necessary for law to develop. Cross-cultural surveys indicate the association of growing social distance with the emergence of adjudication. The sequence of legal evolution follows a path of no legal organization in the simplest societies, followed by mediation, courts, and, finally, police and specialized legal counsel (Wimberly, 1973). This sequence is associated with growing urbanization, population size, industrialization, and social differentiation. One study of 51 societies shows how the simplest societies also feature no third party settlement agents who are available to resolve disputes (Schwartz & Miller, 1964). Growing social complexity leads to the use of non-kin third parties who mediate dispute settlements. As specialization increases and money economies develop, police arise as authoritative third party agents. The final stage of legal complexity that features the presence of specialized legal counsel, as well as mediation and police, occurs in urbanized, fully developed economies with literate populations. Another study of 50 societies similarly finds that foraging, migratory, and low-density groups are marked by dyadic styles of conflict management. Triadic modes of dispute settlement develop in producing, sedentary, and high-density societies (Koch & Sodergren, 1976).

The greatest extension of the state and decay of mediation took place between the seventeenth and nineteenth centuries (Beattie, 1986; Spierenburg, 1984). The emergence of the capitalist economy was accompanied by the undermining of the hierarchical links between clients and fiduciaries that had marked the medieval and early modern periods. With the weakening of traditional hierarchies came the concentration of authority in state bodies.

The anonymity and impersonality of large cities created the social distance necessary for law to develop (Spitzer & Scull, 1977). Formal police forces developed with the expansion of relationships based on impersonal rather than personal ties and growing numbers of rootless and marginal individuals in large urban settings. Growing stratification, combined with the development of an atomized social structure, created enough social distance so third parties could be viewed as nonpartisans who could make authoritative interventions (Black & Baumgartner, 1983).

In the United States, as well, the rise of third-party settlement occurred with growing individualism, social distance, and hierarchy. Wealth and property changed from vehicles anchoring people in their communities to mechanisms of personal advancement (Nelson, 1975, p.

143). Courts developed as merchants, tradesmen, and customers were increasingly unknown to each other and as strangers and outsiders came to enter towns (Auerbach, 1983). As commercial activity multiplied, relationships with unknown parties increased, and transient laborers entered the market system. Growing heterogeneity and the breakdown of the church also accompanied the rise of the courts. Although arbitration and mediation were appropriate for conflicts between neighbors and parishioners, strangers and dissenters had no basis for trust so turned to lawyers and courts. Police forces developed in urban areas during the first half of the nineteenth century as a defense against rootless single men in anonymous urban areas (Lane, 1967). Informal mediation of disputes was no longer workable, and the law correspondingly expanded (Auerbach, 1983).

The development of impersonal systems of stratification also fosters the distance conducive to adjudicated solutions. The growth of organized states and complex systems of stratification are associated with the emergence of specialized legal roles and police functions (Newman, 1983; Robinson & Scaglion, 1987). As the gulf between rich and poor widens, formal, centralized sanctions are more readily imposed on offenders. For example, in England, this occurred over the course of the seventeenth century as local elites who served on juries both became more detached from the poor and more identified with central authority (Green, 1988). Authoritative third-party settlement mechanisms thus increase with the development of stratification systems (Black & Baumgartner, 1983).

Several conditions thus lead from negotiation and mediation to authoritative intervention. Trilateral institutions of all sorts emerge with the weakening of social control in families and communities. Correspondingly, law is unlikely to develop when informal controls are strong. Social distance must be great enough for impartial adjudicators to emerge. Weak ties to informal networks and impersonal systems of social stratification predict the emergence of trilateral systems of social control.

Trilateral institutions develop whenever heterogeneity, mobility, urbanization, or stratification create enough social distance for third parties to emerge as authoritative resolvers of disputes. Informal social control is not workable in social fields that lack close ties between disputants and members of their social networks. Third parties emerge to fill the vacuum created by social distance. Given that trilateral institutions are present and available for use, what factors affect whether or not people will actually invoke them to resolve their disputes?

The Use of Trilateral Social Control

Most cases that enter trilateral forums are initiated at the discretion of private persons. One large victimization survey in the contemporary United States, for example, indicates that police themselves only directly observe 3% of incidents that come to their attention (Reiss, 1971). At the initial stage of entry into the legal system, the grievant has almost full power to decide whether to prosecute offenders, grant clemency, or issue pardons to them. Even a relatively small proportion of serious crimes are reported to the police. For example, victimization surveys in modern societies reveal that about 35% of robberies and aggravated assaults, 42% of burglaries, and 40% of larcenies over $50 are reported to police (Ennis, 1967; Sparks, Genn, & Dodd, 1977, p. 155). Less serious crimes such as larcenies of items worth less than $50 are only reported in about 15% of cases. Given that a range of social control forums are present, what predicts which cases will enter trilateral spheres?

Relational Distance

Few characteristics of individuals predict who uses trilateral forms of control. For instance, income, race, and sex have little impact on the mobilization of the police (Gottfredson & Hindelang, 1979; Skogan, 1976; Sparks *et al.*, 1977). Rather, *the use of trilateral social control is directly related to the relational distance between disputants* (Black, 1976, Chapter 3). The mobilization of legal authorities is enmeshed in the relational field within which disputes arise. Disputants who are close to one another, whether as intimates or members of the same community, rarely mobilize adjudicative agents. However, disputants who are socially distant from each other become more likely to invoke formal control agents.

Intimates

The use of law is discouraged when intimates dispute. Families have a high degree of boundary maintenance and usually hold discretionary control over who can enter them (Stinchcombe, 1963). Intimates are not likely to introduce the power of law into an informal context. Even if they do wish to utilize law, legal forums usually discourage the entry of grievances among intimates, so third party agents will rarely intervene in disputes between family members. Disputes among kin, women, or children often cannot find a hearing in legal forums (Lowy, 1978; Maybury-Lewis, 1967, p. 189; Rothenberger, 1978). Until recently, for example, it was legally impossible for a husband to rape his wife. A woman whose husband forced her to have sexual intercourse with him had no legal recourse whatever. Or, children who feel their parents do not provide them with food, clothing, or shelter will be unlikely to get a court hearing (Lieberman, 1981). Both law and public opinion reflect the incompatibility of "family matters" and legal resolutions.

Dispute resolution within intimate settings normally proceeds informally without the mobilization of third parties. People avoid introducing an exterior power into the private domain of the family, and people do not invoke the law against intimates. In tribal groups, the sense of local solidarity is great enough that persons who bring cases outside of the community to legal authorities are themselves severely punished (Lewis, 1961, pp. 237-238). Instead, disputes between kin are settled by community forums, and only those that involve more distant members are taken to court. For example, the Arusha of East Africa settle disputes between kin by an internal assembly of lineage members, whereas cases between members of a parish who are not kinfolk are brought to a more formal parish assembly comprised of notable members of the community (Gulliver, 1963). Likewise, neighbors, friends, and police have traditionally been unlikely to intervene when husbands beat their wives (Tomes, 1978).

In modern societies, as well, a principle determinant of the reporting of violent crimes is the relationship between victim and offender. The most notable survival of private settlements is still for family matters including wife beating, child abuse, and quarrels between parents and children or between siblings. Within families, even seriously abused victims go to great lengths to protect abusers from outside intervention (Finkelhor, 1983). There is a strong tendency against reporting all crimes when the offender is a close family member (Braithwaite & Biles, 1980). In criminal matters, when victims and offenders are relatives, only 22% of victimizations are reported compared with 58% of those that occur between friends or acquaintances and 75% between strangers (Gove *et al.*, 1985). Assaults (Block, 1974) and rapes (Williams, 1984) between intimates are particularly underreported. Women raped by strangers or acquaintances, relative to those attacked by friends or relatives, are more likely to report the rape to the police (Williams, 1984). When a close relational tie is involved, women are more likely to seek medical than legal help in dealing with the incident (Williams, 1984).

Victims fear that calling the police would both lead to more violence in the future and worsen their relationship with the offender (Berk *et al.*, 1984). When intimates do mobilize the police, they usually do not wish to initiate prosecution of the offender but want to stop an immediate situation such as a beating (Sparks *et al.*, 1977, p. 121). If cases of family violence are reported, wives often settle cases out of court or fail to appear in court (McLeod, 1983).

The reluctance of intimates to invoke the legal process varies by several factors. First, when social control within the family is weak, intimates make more use of legal control. For example, in one Mexican community where the authority of senior males is great and strong extended kin ties form the social structure, husbands and wives in conflict do not appeal to outside courts unless the relationship is being terminated (Nader & Metzger, 1963). Women in another Mexican community with few extended kin ties could not mobilize informal male authority to chastise errant husbands and thus made more use of the courts. In the latter community, courts assumed the control responsibilities once held, but now abandoned, by the extended family.

When the police do intervene in the disputes of intimates, there is usually a vacuum of informal social control (Black, 1980, Chapter 5). For example, most calls for police assistance in situations of family violence stem from disputes between marginals in disorganized settings that lack informal control (Sherman & Berk, 1984). Likewise, the mobilization of formal psychiatric control by parents for their misbehaving children disproportionately occurs in single-parent or step-families (Guttridge & Warren, 1984; Stables & Warren, 1988).

Second, when victims do not want their relationships with offenders to continue, they are more likely to call for police assistance. Thus, wives who have separated or wish to separate from their husbands invoke far more police assistance than others (Black, 1980; Merry, 1979). Similarly, when intimates do not have binding ties, the reluctance to invoke legal authority declines. In nineteenth-century England, when a man beat a women who was not his wife, the victim was more willing to prosecute the offender and neighbors and friends more willing to intervene to stop the abuse (Tomes, 1978). In the contemporary United States, women abused by boyfriends are more likely to invoke police assistance than those who suffer violence from husbands (Berk *et al.*, 1984).

Third, when litigation does not have the hostile connotation it does in the modern world, intimates may bring each other to court. For example, in sixteenth-century Europe, law was often invoked in conflicts between fathers and sons, siblings, or cousins. In this setting, however, litigation did not have the same normative meaning as in modern society and did not indicate a ruptured relationship (Kagan, 1983). Initiating a lawsuit was often viewed as a first step toward instituting a settlement and bringing the dispute to a close. Judges in the courts themselves often had an intimate relationship with disputants, so the legal forum was more mediatory than adjudicatory (Casey, 1983). Finally, the response of the court was usually to promote bargaining and negotiation among disputants, and few cases reached a final, adjudicated resolution (Sharpe, 1983).

Fourth, chronic offenders are always more liable to legal sanctions. This is particularly true in groups with systems of corporate liability when the actions of the offender render the entire network vulnerable to retaliation by the victimized parties (Falk-Moore, 1972; Rieder, 1984). All groups have a breaking point beyond which they cannot tolerate the deviance of intimates and will release them to legal authority.

Finally, there is some evidence that even the most intimate family members are losing their reluctance to bring each other to court. Husbands who beat wives or parents who abuse children are now more likely to be legally accountable (Ferraro, 1989; Sherman & Cohn, 1989). In part, this may reflect a changing definition of intimacy. Family ties are becoming more like contractual agreements between sovereign individuals. Persons who were once defined as intimates outside the reach of the law are now liable to the same rights and duties as other citizens. In addition, as women become less dependent on their husbands, they lose their reluctance to invoke legal authority (Black, 1980, Chapter 5). The rising status of women within the family predicts a growing use of legal authority to protect victimized wives. The result is an increasing role of legal power in matters such as child abuse, violence between spouses, or marital rape.

Disputes among Community Members

When disputes arise among community members, people are usually reluctant to use available third party agents. In most parts of the world, dispute processes within villages strive to maintain ongoing multiplex relationships. Among the Goodenough Islanders in Melanesia, mobilizing formal courts to deal with quarrels with community members leads to an irreparable break in the relationship (Young, 1971). Not only is the relationship with the other disputant damaged, but one's standing in the village is impaired. Among the Jalemo of Western New Guinea, when scuffles occur among age mates or members of the same lineage, observers intervene and plead for cessation because of the need to live together peacefully and in harmony (Koch, 1974). They are resolved within the age set or lineage and only go to a community forum when they occur between different age sets and lineages. Settlement behavior among the Nuristan of Afghanistan also illustrates this principle (Jones, 1974). When a dispute arises between two members of the same lineage segment, agnates will settle it. If the dispute occurs between different lineages but within the same clan, elders from the same clan but from different lineages than the disputants intervene. Only if the disturbance is between members of different clans is there a probability that the Afghan courts will be invoked. If one brings a dispute against a fellow villager to an Afghan governmental forum, it is regarded as a betrayal of group solidarity. If the member persists, he will be ostracized in the village, and no one will have anything to do with him (Jones, 1974, p. 225).

African tribesmen who have grievances first go to the headman with a grievance, then to a parish chief, then to a subcounty chief for an out-of-court settlement, and only as a last resort to a formal court (Fallers, 1969, pp. 313-314). For example, among the Arusha of East Africa, the "public disputation between men of one age-group spoils its reputation, and its external unity in the eyes of other age-groups of the parish. Therefore members of the disputants' age-group make strong efforts to persuade them to accept the intervention and assistance of their fellows, and to prevent the intervention of men of other age-groups" (Gulliver, 1963, p. 184). Arusha courts deal mainly with disputes between men without kin and those who live more than a few miles apart.

In a Sunni Moslem village in Lebanon, the position of the disputant in relation to the opponent determines the choice and course of the dispute-settlement process (Rothenberger, 1978). A strong preference for settling disputes within the village exists because of the necessity for maintaining ongoing relationships and because disputes of individuals tend to escalate into disputes between lineages. Ninety-one percent of 108 cases were settled by mediation and compromise within the village. Those few cases taken out of the village involved factional or political disputes, intervillage disputes, or violent acts. In another Lebanese village, disputants summoned the police in only 28 of 160 cases over a 9-year period. Of these, only 28% featured village members on both sides, whereas 36% involved a village against a nonvillager, and 46% the state against an individual (Rothenberger, 1978).

In preindustrial Japan, disputes between members of the same village were settled through negotiation, whereas those of members of different villages were more likely to be taken to court (Kawashima, 1963). In seventeenth-century England, villagers would not use the law against their fellows but only against marginals, vagrants, or members of other communities (Wrightson, 1980). In colonial America as well, extralegal forums were preferable to the use of law. A law in Boston stated that no one "shall sue one another at lawe" until an arbitration panel had heard the dispute (Auerbach, 1983). Quakers, for example, could not sue one another unless one was disowned by the group, although it was permissible to go to court against people who were not Quakers (Auerbach, 1983). With growing heterogeneity and uniplex ties, however, the courts replaced churches and town meetings, and disputants turned to lawyers rather than ministers or mediators to resolve disputes.

Where homogeneity and multiplex relationships prevail in the modern world, bilateral control is still a preeminent forum for dispute resolution. In Chinatowns, for example, elders use mediation to insure that disputes among community members do not enter legal forums (Doo, 1973). Or, in Hasidic Jewish communities, someone who sues another member in a court of law is viewed as a traitor to the community and treated with contempt (*Columbia Journal of Law and Social Problems*, 1970). Dispute resolution by religious leaders is the preferred mode of settlement.

In modern America, settled residents of traditional communities rarely use law in disputes with their fellow citizens (Ellickson, 1986; Engel, 1984). In one small Georgia town, long-term residents virtually never initiated litigation against each other. Newcomers to the community, however, often used the court to resolve problems both with other newcomers and with settled residents (Greenhouse, 1982). Wherever people are loosely tied together, their reluctance to use law disappears.

Disputes that arise within institutions such as schools, businesses, or governmental agencies where disputants are tied into enduring relationships have traditionally been relatively immune to legal intervention. Courts have been reluctant to penetrate the boundaries of private institutions. Students with complaints against schools, employees who wished to sue employers, or patients with grievances against doctors were unlikely to obtain legal hearings (Lieberman, 1981). When such disputes arise, they tend to be handled by third parties within the institution including school principals, shop stewards, building managers, and administrators (Galanter, 1983). For example, the colleagues of doctors in clinics who engage in deviance first talk to them informally, then mobilize other doctors, and finally use formal committees of colleagues to apply sanctions (Friedson & Rhea, 1972). Within such settings, the costs of mobilizing external control may be high, disputants are likely to share norms, and opportunities for internal sanctioning are present.

In recent years, however, the permeability of most institutions to the law has increased. Courts are more willing to rule on disputes within families, schools, churches, work organizations, professional-patient relationships, or governmental agencies (Lieberman, 1981). Individuals who believe they have suffered harm in such settings can now receive a hearing in legal forums. The increasingly fragmented nature of ties that bind individuals to institutions may account for the growing intrusion of law into relationships that traditionally were immune from legal penetration. For example, interactions between physicians and their clients now reflect growing social distance. As medical practice has shifted from personal interactions between patients and family doctors to large, impersonal health organizations, clinics, and hospitals, medical malpractice suits have proliferated. The growing relational distance between patients and physicians is one reason leading to the willingness both of patients to bring suits against physicians and of legal forums to hear these claims. The breakdown in agreed-upon norms that had marked intimate relationships have led to their growing vulnerability to legal intervention (Lempert & Sanders, 1986).

The increased penetration of legal forums in many arenas in modern life in large part reflects growing social distance. In some cases, this stems from a change in relationships once marked by interpersonal closeness to impersonal interactions within large organizations. In other cases, the former fiduciary relationship between organizations and their members has broken down (Lieberman, 1981). Legal agents step into this gap to assert state responsibility into what previously had been private matters. More law emerges with the growth of impersonal and temporary relationships.

Disputes among Distant Parties

Law is rarely directed at intimates but is increasingly invoked with growing social distance between people. When conflicts emerge between strangers, an impersonal forum for dispute resolution may be desirable (Abel, 1979). Third parties become likely to adjudicate rather than negotiate disputes with growing social distance between disputants.

One cross-cultural study of 30 societies indicates that settlement agents almost always use adjudicative methods with coercive enforcement to resolve conflicts among strangers but strive to reconcile disputants who were intimates (Cooney, 1988, p. 60). When community ties are weak, individuals have little to lose by calling the police or other legal authority against others. Hence, in an urban housing project in an American city, blacks and whites who frequently moved in and out of the project and rarely saw their neighbors were not reluctant to use the courts to settle disputes. Chinese residents, in contrast, were linked to each other through cohesive networks of overlapping associations and did not invoke legal assistance for disputes (Merry, 1979).

Although integrated persons will rarely invoke law against each other, they do commonly direct it against marginal members of communities. In medieval communities, law was disproportionately directed against strangers, especially in cases of robbery, rape, and counterfeiting (Hanawalt, 1979, pp. 26, 170). In early modern Europe, the law was mainly used against the most marginal members of the community such as beggars, vagrants, and prostitutes (Spierenburg, 1984). Historically, the police developed to protect integrated members of the community from marginal ones:

> From the twelfth century onward, the police had a special function with reference to vagabonds, vagrants, and the "sturdy, unworking poor." The Assize of Clarendon of 1166 required sheriffs to enforce restrictions against "entertainers of strangers and the harbourers of vagabonds." A Statute of King Edward III . . . ordered town bailiffs "to make inquiry every week of all persons lodging in the suburbs, in order that neither vagrants, nor people against the peace might find shelter." (Robinson & Scaglion, 1987, p. 147)

Police activities continue to be directed toward those persons least tied to their communities (Black, 1976).

What is the likelihood of law where marginal members of a group confront each other? Two contrasting possibilities exist. On the one hand, the presence of informal controls is weak between marginals so they should frequently use law (Black, 1976). In addition, neither party can benefit from a future relationship with the other so will not risk alienating the other party by invoking law. On the other hand, marginals have little recourse to law so should be more likely to take unilateral means to resolve disputes (Black, 1983).

In general, it appears that marginals are quicker than integrated persons to mobilize legal authority. In both traditional (Auerbach, 1983; Wrightson, 1980) and modern (Engel, 1984; Greenhouse, 1982) societies, marginals are more likely than the integrated to initiate as well as to receive legal action. The use of the legal system often involves the repudiation of community norms. Marginal members of the community may not share the normative restraints that account for the reluctance of the integrated to use the law against other community members. Among the Waigali of Afghanistan, an integrated member would be ostracized for using the courts against a fellow villager. Marginal members, however, have little to lose by doing so. They are most likely to use official courts against their superiors because they are unable to attain justice from informal village mediators who will support the dominant parties (Jones, 1974). Marginal members of a Bavarian village, as well, were more likely than the integrated to bring grievances to court because they did not share the normative restraints against using law found among integrated members of the town (Todd, 1978).

In a Zambian city, the greatest proportion of legal cases stemmed from disputes among members of the non-dominant ethnic group who were immigrants lacking kin, social, and residential networks (Canter, 1978). In contrast, members of the dominant group had strong informal ties who acted to settle disputes within kin and village networks. In all, although the dominant ethnic group accounted for 65% of the population, only 22% of disputes among its members entered the court whereas 20% involved a dominant member suing a non-dominant one, and 9% a non-dominant against a dominant. In 49% of cases, both parties were members of the non-dominant group.

When the availability of law is high, litigation can be common when marginals have grievances against integrated people. In the Plymouth colony of seventeenth-century United States, most litigious individuals were outsiders (Nelson, 1975). In a number of settings in the contemporary United States, as well, marginals do not share the reluctance of integrated members to litigate their disputes. In a study of cattle ranchers in a rural California county, the only two cases of legal invocation uncovered occurred when both victim and offender were outsiders to the community and viewed as "bad apples" (Ellickson, 1986). A similar pattern holds in a rural Illinois county. Although long-time residents are very reluctant to use the law when disputes arise, newcomers and marginals use the courts more frequently to press grievances. They neither face the normative constraints against integrated persons who use law nor have the resources to allow them to press claims informally (Engel, 1984).

In other cases, marginals may make ready use of courts because they have few resources, including time and money, to lose. For example, in cases involving automobile accidents, very low-status persons may be the most likely to continue a case to trial because they have no resources to lose and everything to gain (Ross, 1970). Similarly, prisoners, who have nearly unlimited time, may expend many hours attempting to obtain legal redress. The use of law is thus greater both toward marginals, from marginals toward the integrated, and between marginals themselves.

One factor that may account whether marginals use law is the extent to which they can use unilateral self-help. When self-help is maximally available, little use of law may occur. Young males, for example, who quickly resort to violence against each other are less likely to report victimizations than females or older males (Hindelang & Gottfredson, 1976).

In contrast, elderly people, who lack the means to use self-help, are most likely to report criminal victimizations (Skogan, 1976).

Whatever the social context, the use of law expands as social distance increases. Intimates rarely invoke legal authority against each other, and the decline of intimacy leads to more judicial intrusion into formerly close relational space. Law also is rarely invoked in disputes between integrated members of communities. Marginal individuals are more likely to be both the targets and the utilizers of legal authority. An expansion of legal mobilization in the modern world is the inevitable result of the growth of social distance.

Not only the marginality of disputants but also that of lawyers affects the probability of litigation. Lawyers who are weakly integrated into communities have less reluctance to litigate than more integrated attorneys (Macaulay, 1979). Over the past three decades, tremendous changes have occurred in the composition and structure of the profession. The number of female and minority lawyers who are less integrated than white males into traditional legal structure and culture has greatly increased over this time period (Abel, 1986). If these changes continue, the rate of litigation should also continue to rise.

Hierarchy

Social Class

There are two competing perspectives regarding social class and the use of law. On the one hand, we expect more use of the legal system by upper status people. Legal organization is inherently tied to the sorts of concerns of this group (Mayhew & Reiss, 1969). In modern American society, the legal profession is organized to solve problems that arise in business and property matters. The rules regulating institutions of property are organized in such as way that inevitably bring participants in contact with attorneys. Higher status persons perceive more grievances, have greater access and knowledge of law, and are involved in more affairs defined as legally relevant than lower status people. They are more likely to possess the prerequisites to assert legal rights, including a greater knowledge of legal alternatives, higher consciousness of legal rights, and the ability and means to assert their rights through the legal process (Sarat, 1977). In addition, higher status people may be more likely to press claims because they are used to higher levels of satisfaction and compare themselves to more advantaged reference groups (Coates & Penrod, 1980-1981).

In contrast, lower status persons may be entirely locked out of legal remedies. At the extreme of social status, all forms of redress are denied. Among the Kiowa Indians of North America, the lowest orders of society were "utterly declasse and in effect without the law. They were so far beneath contempt and attention that their thefts went unpunished" (Hoebel, 1954, p. 171). In the Roman Empire, noncitizen aliens had no standing in civil law and so could not seek legal help for any sort of problem (Garnsey, 1968). In many groups, conflicts between parents and children or husbands and wives are classified as private matters of concern only to the individuals involved (Gulliver, 1963; Koch, 1974; Maybury-Lewis, 1967). Children, for example, have virtually no legal opportunity to press complaints about their parents (Baumgartner, 1988, p. 48). In contrast, parents have wide leeway to commit children to coercive control institutions (Lerman, 1982; Warren & Guttridge, 1984).

On the other hand, there are several reasons why higher status persons might mobilize the law less frequently than lower status ones. The use of law in certain situations indicates a loss of respectability that may be particularly important for higher status people. Going to court indicates a breakdown of authority and respect that is an integral value among higher status groups. Therefore, higher status people would be more likely to keep their disputes out of the public eye and avoid using courts. This is especially true if court personnel are perceived to be of lower social status than the grievants themselves (Baumgartner, 1988). Lower-class people have less reputation to lose, although the law is also less accessible to them. In addition, higher status and integrated members of communities often possess internal sanctions for deviance so have less need to rely on legal means when disputes arise among them.

The result of these contrasting factors may lead higher status people to make more use of law for property matters but less use for interpersonal disputes: *The use of law in interpersonal disputes is inversely related to social class,* but *the use of law for property conflicts is directly related to social class.*

Higher status persons are more likely to use legal institutions than lower status ones for property disputes (Mayhew & Reiss, 1969; Silberman, 1985, p. 146). Surveys of consumers indicate that low income and minority status are associated with failure to press complaints against merchants and businesses (Miller & Sarat, 1980-1981). On the other hand, calls for police intervention in the personal disputes of higher status people are extremely rare (Silberman, 1985). Members of higher status households rely less on police services in general than those in lower status households (Bittner, 1980). When disputes do not involve property, higher status persons avoid legal confrontations.

Lower status people, on the other hand, much more readily invoke police assistance for interpersonal conflicts. Cases of violence among intimates in the contemporary United States that come to police attention disproportionately involve unmarried couples who have little education, minority or mixed race backgrounds, and are jobless (Sherman & Berk, 1984). In addition, lower class women are far more likely than higher status women to summon the police in conflicts with their husbands or boyfriends (Black, 1980, Chapter 5). In contrast, middle-class people display a strong aversion to invoking the police for any sort of domestic conflict. In one predominantly middle- and upper-class suburb the result of this tendency was that virtually all court cases involving complaints between family members involved working-class people (Baumgartner, 1988, pp. 50-55, 88). Higher class persons may make more use of law for impersonal matters while lower class ones more readily invoke legal authority in interpersonal affairs.

Gender

The use of trilateral forums need not be the province of the strong against the weak. In some cases, law can be a tool that weaker people can use against more powerful ones. For powerless people, trilateral authority can provide a resource they can use to gain control over an oppressive situation, especially when they have little recourse to self-help.[1]

This is illustrated by the ways that men and women use the law. Women use courts against men more than men do against women (Smith & Klein, 1984). When women do use courts, it is usually against their husbands. In many settings, women are more likely than men to seek judicial remedies against kin, whereas men almost never use courts against female kin or spouses.

For example, in a Zapotec town in Mexico, if a woman took a man to court, it was likely to be her husband, whereas if a man went to court against a woman, it was unlikely to be his wife (Nader, 1964). When women took legal action, in more than two-thirds of cases they lacked a male relative such as a father, father-in-law, or husband who might otherwise have defended them. A mother would never take her son to court if her husband was present because he would have enough authority to control the son. If, however, the mother was a widow, she

[1]For example, a study of disputes among children in a day care center found that "it was more often children who appeared to be losing their struggles who invoked adult authority, rather than those who were faring well on their own" (Baumgartner, 1990, p. 13).

might have no choice but to take legal action. Courts substituted for informal social control and raised the social control resources available to the dependent party. LIkewise, in sixteenth- century Europe, the courts were used by widows, particularly those without male kin groups, to protect their dowries. Law substituted for informal networks to protect the rights of the weak. (Kagan, 1983). In one study of a modern American suburban community, all but 1 of 17 complaints involving family members were initiated by women, including wives against husbands, mothers against sons, and sisters against brothers (Baumgartner, 1988, p. 46).

The use of commitment proceedings to mental hospitals may be another way for women to gain control over their husbands. A study of commitments of male alcoholic patients in Boston around 1900 indicates that many were committed by their wives who had suffered from long histories of beatings (Lunbeck, 1984). Commitment was a means of redress for working-class women for a skewed balance of domestic power and a rare way for them to gain control over husbands in a setting where divorce was time consuming and difficult but commitment easier and more immediate. It is still true that women are more likely to commit men to mental institutions than vice versa (Horwitz, 1982, pp. 75-78).

Victimized women are particularly likely to mobilize the police when they are employed and are not financially dependent on spouses (Black, 1980, Chapter 5). Women are less likely than men to have strong systems of informal control or to have the ability to use violent means of self-help against those who victimize them. Law can be a resource to overcome a situation where women lack alternative means of social control.

CONCLUSION

There is an inherent association between trilateral social control and social distance. Trilateral authority emerges with growing relational distance in groups and is invoked in conflicts between people who share few social ties. In contrast, intimates rarely bring trilateral authority to bear on their disputes but resolve conflicts through less formal means. The intrusion of formal third parties into disputes is a sign that intimacy has disappeared. As societies become increasingly marked by relationships between people at growing social distance and as once inviolable family ties are more easily broken, law expands throughout social life.

The association of trilateral control and social status is more complex. Lower status people use more law for interpersonal matters so law can be a valuable resource for dependents, such as abused wives, who exert social control over more powerful parties. Higher status persons, in contrast, avoid the use of trilateral control for interpersonal disputes but readily use it to resolve conflicts over property. The growing status and organizational ability of previously disenfranchised groups such as women, racial minorities, the handicapped, or children predicts a greater use of legal means to handle conflicts that previously were informally resolved, usually to the disadvantage of the dependent party.

9

The Response of Trilateral Control

INTRODUCTION

The previous three chapters examined the conditions under which private citizens invoke the legal process. This chapter looks at the responses of official third parties to the disputes that enter trilateral forums. I consider what factors predict these responses at several stages of the legal process including police, prosecution, and final disposition.

My major concern is with how the position of a case in social space shapes the discretion of legal officials. At each stage of the legal process, general rules serve as ideals that guide formal control agents. Yet, these agents also function within situations and agencies that have their own imperatives. A range of officials including police, insurance adjustors, housing inspectors, mental health screeners, and the like serve to mediate between the citizenry and the formal system of rules. Situational contingencies and administrative considerations, in addition to legislative or judicial mandates, shape which rules officials will enforce and which they will overlook, as well as which offenders they will sanction.

These officials not only act as conduits for the formal system but also apply their own morality and judgment to situations, which in turn changes legal rights. For example, if formal penalties for some crime are increased to an extent that seems unfair to those who must apply them, gatekeeping agents often find ways of subverting them (Ross, 1986). Drunken drivers may be sent home instead of arrested, housing code violators warned but not fined, or brawlers separated rather than sanctioned. I examine how this discretionary power varies according to the characteristics of the parties involved in a conflict.

I take a sequential view of formal systems of social control. These systems are "loosely coupled" in the sense that each separate segment has a high degree of internal discretion (Reiss, 1971). This leads to a tendency for each subsystem such as the police, prosecution, or courts to create its own practice of justice that may differ from the others.

In addition, each segment deals only with those cases that have been funneled through the previous segments. Because each prior stage screens the cases that enter subsequent stages, a greater uniformity in case characteristics results as cases proceed through the system. For example, if the police only arrest in cases of high seriousness and prosecutors only indict the most serious of these cases, cases that reach a judicial solution reflect only a homogeneous portion of the most serious cases that originally came to police attention. Therefore, the correlates of discretion in any particular stage of the legal system can only properly be specified after the correlates of previous stages are examined (Silberman, 1985).

I develop several themes in this section. First, contrary to the impression of much social control literature, the dominant reaction of legal control agents is to avoid, mediate, or negotiate solutions rather than to pursue penal responses. Second, the preferences of citizen complainants is a predominant determinant of formal responses. Third, several underlying social factors, especially relational distance, the presence of informal control, and the respectability of victims and offenders, affect legal responses. The predictive power of these factors varies at different stages of the legal process so that, in general, autonomous rules become increasingly important as cases proceed through formal systems. However, the grounding of cases in their social fields always, to some extent, influences their processing.

POLICE

Situations

The police are the major gatekeepers processing criminal matters into the legal system. Research regarding citizen-police encounters in modern societies indicates that the police typically settle cases without referring them to further stages of legal processing. Police-citizen encounters rarely involve arrests (Black, 1971). For instance, of 1,688 incidents called to police attention in a midwestern city, 82% did not even receive investigative efforts (Bynum, Cordner, & Greene, 1982). In another study of police-juvenile encounters, only 15% of incidents resulted in arrest (Lundman, Sykes, & Clark, 1978). Studies of decisions in interpersonal conflicts among adults also indicate that only about 15% of cases lead to arrests (Berk & Loseke, 1981; Black, 1971; Smith & Klein, 1984). In most disputes, police are typically reluctant to refer cases to further stages of legal processing.

Instead, the police typically strive to negotiate solutions, serve as mediators, or separate the parties in conflict. When conflicts arise among intimates, police usually reconcile or separate the parties involved. In one study of encounters where both parties to a conflict involving interpersonal violence were present, 28% of cases resulted in arrest, 34% in mediation, and 37% in separation (Smith, 1987). When arrests were made, it was only after less coercive alternatives had failed. When police are mobilized to deal with disputes, they usually do not make vigorous responses.

What explains the tendency of police to avoid making arrests in most potentially legal cases they confront? The essential aspect of police response lies in the *situational* nature of their tasks. Police are mobilized to deal with trouble as, or shortly after, it occurs. When they arrive they are usually faced with distraught individuals, highly charged situations, or overt violence. The primary goal of the police must be to restore order to a troubled situation. The police tend to take those actions that they feel will create an orderly situation. Responses such as mediation, separation, or avoidance often better serve to bring order within situational contexts than arrests so are preferable alternatives to formal processing. The necessity to deal with disputes within their situational context is a major determinant of police response.

Offenders

Many studies focus on how offender characteristics are associated with arrests. They indicate that characteristics of offenders, in themselves, explain little variance in modern arrest patterns. For example, the research that focuses on social class characteristics of suspects shows that these differences have virtually no effect on arrest decisions (e.g. Black & Reiss, 1970; Liska and Tausig, 1979).[1]

The race of offenders has a somewhat greater effect than their social class as a determinant of arrest, although there is no consistency in the

[1]Police response may, however, vary more by the class composition of the community in which encounters occur than by the social status of the offender. As the economic status of the community declines, the probability of arrest in interpersonal disputes rises, regardless of the characteristics of victims and offenders (Smith, 1984). In contrast, police are more likely to search for and implement alternatives to arrest in high- and middle-status neighborhoods (Smith & Klein, 1984).

direction of findings. Most studies show no variation in arrest rates by race when other factors, such as the nature of the crime and victim preference for arrest, are controlled (Black & Reiss, 1970; Worden & Pollitz, 1984). Some research shows that the race of the suspect leads to a greater number of black arrests in urban, but not suburban, counties (Dannefer & Schutt, 1982). In contrast, one major study concludes that whites are somewhat more likely to be arrested than blacks (Petersilia, 1985). Overall, however, offender characteristics are not good predictors of police arrest practices.

Complainants

The wishes of complainants are better predictors of police response than characteristics of offenders. A uniform finding regarding police-citizen encounters in the United States is that complainant request is the most important predictor of police arrest decisions (Berk & Loseke, 1981; Black & Reiss, 1970; Gove *et al.*, 1985; Smith, 1984; Smith & Klein, 1984; Smith & Visher, 1981). This is true to such an extent that in one large study the police complied with complainant wishes in *every* case (Lundman *et al.*, 1978). Even serious cases of physical violence that do not enter the official system are screened out by victims rather than police (Gove *et al.*, 1985). Private, as well as public, control systems also refer few suspects to further stages of legal processing, although their rates of referral vary greatly (Rojek, 1979). Because private concerns, such as merchants and department stores, are very frequent victims of crimes, their tendency not to prosecute reinforces the general tendency of the citizenry not to mobilize the formal control system.

The wishes of complainants in some cases accounts for demographic variation in arrest rates. For example, some studies indicate that blacks are more likely to request arrest than whites. At least in some settings, the higher rate of arrests of blacks results from the wishes of black citizens rather than police practices. Black and Reiss (1970) found that police arrested 21% of black juveniles but only 8% of white juveniles because of the greater tendency of black complainants to request arrests (see also Lundman *et al.*, 1978). Other studies, however, show that police are more likely to comply with the preferences of whites so are more likely to make arrests when victims are white (Smith, Visher, & Davidson, 1984). In both cases, the race of the victim, rather than of the offender, is the crucial predictor of arrest patterns. In addition, police are more likely to comply with the wishes of victims in middle- and high-status neighborhoods than in lower status ones (Smith & Klein, 1984).

Complainant preferences are also related to gender patterns of arrests. Because victims seem reluctant to pursue cases against female offenders, males are somewhat more likely to be arrested than females (Visher, 1983). This pattern was also true in seventeenth century England (Beattie, 1986). The somewhat lower arrest rates of females compared to males results more from victim preferences than police responses.

In the psychiatric system as well, the preferences of complainants, usually family members of disordered persons, determine who enters the formal system. Citizens use lay definitions of when troublesome, annoying, or weird behaviors are appropriate reasons for psychiatric referral (Horwitz, 1982). The willingness of family members to commit disordered relatives is a major predictor of who is committed to mental hospitals. In one study, the disposition of the patient deviated from the wishes of the family in only 13% of cases (Tischler, 1966). In another study, 38 of 43 persons were committed when families were unwilling to care for them, whereas 13 of 21 potential patients were released where relatives were available for care (Warren, 1977). Psychiatric screening agents, like the police, tend to rely on the wishes of complainants in deciding who to admit into the formal system or return to the community. Formal control of all sorts is activated in the absence of appropriate community control and support.

The reliance on citizen preferences means that in most cases the citizenry, not the police, make the basic adjudicatory decision. The police largely act as conduits between citizens and the criminal justice system just as psychiatrists serve as funnels between the families of the mentally ill and the mental health system. Because citizens use informal, rather than formal, norms in pressing their claims, the police and other control agents typically act to reinforce the culture of the community rather than impose the rules of an official system. In addition, this means that the police and other formal control agents are responding more to *victim* requests than to characteristics of offenders (Black, 1971). The initial decision on who enters formal control systems turns on lay rather than official definitions.[2]

[2]An implication of police reliance on citizen preferences is that studies that examine social control processes through correlating aggregate crime rates with social characteristics are virtually impossible to interpret. For example, police arrest rates are positively correlated with high economic inequality, low socioeconomic status of areas, and large concentrations of minority groups (Horwitz, 1984). Yet, if the police mainly respond to citizen preferences, these findings would result less from the imposition of elite control than from the preferences of less powerful victims.

Victim-Offender Relationships

Understanding the relationships between disputants and between disputants and control agents enhances our ability to predict arrest practices. In particular, arrests increase with growing distance between parties and an absence of informal social control.

Relational Distance

Victims are uniformly less likely to request police action when offenders are close to them in relational space. For instance, in three large American cities, the proportion of requests for arrests decreased as victims and offenders moved from family members to acquaintances to strangers (Black, 1971). Victims are reluctant to use public authority in private matters. If official agents are mobilized, it is usually to restore order in a troubled situation, not to impose lasting sanctions.

Victimizations of intimates are less problematic than those of strangers because the police, like others, define interpersonal relationships as private transactions that feature their own sanctions. Thus police operators do not take domestic disputes as seriously as others, and the police are slower to respond to them (Oppenlander, 1982). If the police are summoned, they are rarely likely to make an arrest (Berk & Loseke, 1981). Their typical response is to avoid forceful action and to try calm the parties down or have one party leave the situation (Baumgartner, 1988, pp. 43-44).

The police do not impose a uniquely paternalistic response to domestic problems. Rather, their response mirrors that of the general public: Neither views legal intervention as the most appropriate reaction to the problems of intimates. On the other hand, if the police are unable to restore order into an emotionally charged situation between intimates, they may make more arrests in domestic situations because of the imperative of order maintenance (e.g., Smith, 1984).

The tendencies mentioned refer only to disputes that occur among intimates. When outsiders victimize people in their homes police responses may be more vigorous than when offenses occur in public places (Gottfredson & Hindelang, 1979; Stenross, 1984). Thus police may preserve the status quo of private orders in two disparate ways: first, by not arresting when disputes arise between intimates and, second, by acting more vigorously when outsiders threaten the integrity of the intimate order.

In contrast to disputes among intimates, legal controls are the only available social sanctions to deal with offenses between strangers (Lunsgaarde, 1977). Arrests are correspondingly more likely when strangers confront each other. Yet, it would be a mistake to differentiate sharply the police response to the disputes of more distant parties from those of intimates. The police are reluctant to arrest in *all* types of interpersonal disputes, not only in domestic matters.

Not only the relational distance between victims and offenders but that between them and control agents influence arrest patterns. When the distance between the police and citizens is greater, arrests become more likely. Therefore, large bureaucratic departments that mandate impersonal transactions between police and the public tend to enforce rules more often and make more arrests than smaller, more informal departments (Brown, 1981; Smith, 1984). Fraternal and service departments that are less rule oriented rarely make arrests in interpersonal disputes but tend to conciliate disputes. This tendency is deducible from the greater relational distance that exists between police and offenders in bureaucratic than fraternal police departments.

Informal Control

The reluctance of the police to intervene in matters between intimates reflects not only small relational distance but also the presence of much informal control in a situation. The tendency of police to make arrests increases as the presence of informal control declines. In general, women face more informal control than men, married people more than single ones, and juveniles more than adults. Therefore, arrests are most likely when disputes occur between males, least likely when two women are involved, and equivalent when females dispute with males or males with females (Smith & Klein, 1984). The police may also be somewhat more likely to arrest if the parties involved are unmarried rather than married (Worden & Pollitz, 1984). The greater informal control over female adolescents also makes them a less appropriate target than male juveniles of police control (Hagan, Simpson, & Gillis, 1987).

Police activity is maximal when informal control is minimal, as with vagrants, the homeless, and skid row alcoholics (Black, 1980, p. 30). Intoxicated suspects and those showing little respect similarly have a higher probability of arrest (Berk & Loseke, 1981; Smith & Klein, 1984; Worden & Pollitz, 1984) perhaps indicating a lack of internal control over their behavior. The penetration of legal control in social space depends on the extent that informal control is present to resolve troubled situations.

Future Processing

Although police decisions are largely determined by situational needs to restore order and by the relationship between victims and offenders, they also look ahead to the future fate of cases. Those that will be amenable to easy processing and conventional handling are more likely to lead to arrests. Therefore, those crimes that seem more likely to result in prosecution are also more likely to lead to arrests.

When evidence is present and victims can identify suspects and are willing to testify, police will make more arrests. In some cases, the ease of processing can change the direction of the impact of the demographic factors already discussed. For example, the police may make more arrests in sex offenses between acquaintances than strangers because victims can more easily identify suspects with whom they have had some prior acquaintance (Myers & LaFree, 1981). Or, arrests in cases involving minorities may be less frequent because of the belief that minority victims may be less willing to testify against offenders (Petersilia, 1985). When chances of an ultimate legal resolution are small, police make fewer arrests.

Summary

The sorts of cases that move from the police to the prosecutorial stage are in large part determined by the situational nature of police work. Police tendencies to rely on complainant preferences, arrest in disputes among parties at greater relational distance, and in the absence of informal control, all reflect the crucial imperative to restore order within situations. Intimates have a greater potential to handle disputes themselves, whereas legal control may be the only alternative when disputes arise at greater distances. Similarly, the lack of informal control indicates a lower probability of restoring order without public intervention. Correspondingly, the failure of individual attributes to explain police response stems from the minor role these characteristics play within situational frameworks. For the most part, victim preferences and situational contingencies rather than rule enforcement shape which cases are funneled to the next stage of legal processing.

Prosecution

The decision to prosecute represents the next major stage of legal processing. In contemporary legal systems, this marks a further escalation of formal control.[3] A representative of the state, rather than the victim, becomes responsible for the pursuit of justice (Hagan, 1982). The principal client of the prosecutor is not the immediate victim of the crime but the state. In the contemporary United States, in particular, prosecutors are given tremendous discretion regarding whether or not to pursue a case, who to charge, what charges to make, what bail to set, what penalties to seek, and whether or not to plea bargain (Feeley, 1979).

Because the police response to cases occurs within troubled situations, their reactions tend toward mediation, separation, and order maintenance. Prosecutors, on the other hand, are more likely to be guided by general rules. Cases that enter their domain have been disengaged from troubled situations and are more amenable to purely formal processing. Prosecutors must be particularly concerned with the ability of a case to produce evidence of legal guilt in court, so they must closely attend to questions of victim and witness testimony, material evidence, and eyewitness identification that are potentially relevant if a case eventually leads to a formal trial.

In addition, prosecutorial response will be driven more by organizational than situational imperatives. Although police reactions are primarily present oriented, prosecutorial actions must look more toward the future. The police may have made arrests to calm an outraged wife, end a barroom brawl, or pacify an angry shopowner. Prosecutors do not respond to these immediate circumstances but to their categorization within a system of legal rules (Feeley, 1979). Like all organizations, deviance processing agencies can only handle a large number of cases through the use of general rules that determine which cases will and will not enter and remain within the system.

The central question prosecutors face is whether a case can successfully be resolved within existing organizational resources. Cases that can most readily be handled will be the ones most likely to escalate into further stages of legal processing. If situations and order maintenance are key to police response, organizational imperatives and formal rules are central to prosecutorial reactions.

[3]In the initial development of legal systems, however, there was less differentiation in stages of legal processing. For example, in England before the nineteenth century, prosecution of criminal offenses essentially occurred through private initiatives. Victims themselves had to initiate cases, make the decision to prosecute, chose the court where the case would be tried, determine the charge against the offender, and pay for prosecution and witnesses (Beattie, 1986). In the Colonial period in the United States, as well, victims both initiated and pursued complaints themselves (Steinberg, 1984). By the latter quarter of the nineteenth century, public prosecutors gained much more power and were expected to exercise their discretion in forwarding cases to trial.

In examining the escalation of control at the prosecution stage, it is important to keep in mind the prior narrowing of cases that has already occurred. Prosecutors are reactive to the decisions that citizens and police have already made that have defined what incidents enter the legal system. Prosecutors only receive about 15% of incidents that initially come to police attention (Feeley, 1979). These cases reflect incidents involving greater relational distance, less informal control, and more amenability to prosecution. Prosecutors have a great deal of discretion whether to pursue further processing of these cases.

Victims

The claims of victims remain critical factors at the prosecutorial stage. The ability of prosecutors to pursue a case depends on the presence of a credible victim. Prosecutors need victims who can make potentially convincing cases to juries. The *credibility* of the victim thus becomes an important organizational problem and insures that the funneling of cases will be unevenly distributed in social space (Stanko, 1981-1982).

On the one hand, victims who provoked their offenders or participated in the crime are not likely to see prosecutors vigorously pursue their cases (Feeley, 1979, p. 162; Williams, 1976). In one study, victim-provoked offenses decreased the probability of prosecution by 59% (Albonetti, 1987). When victims are prostitutes, pimps, alcoholics, or homosexuals, credibility is damaged, and the offense may appear to be part of the typical range of interactions such people engage in, rather than criminal offenses (Stanko, 1981-1982). The participation of victims in a crime may also in part explain why crimes of self-help where offenders respond to some perceived deviant action of victims are treated leniently in the legal system (Black, 1983). Prosecutors believe that chances of conviction are minimal when victim provocation or participation is an element in the case so are unlikely to press complaints of victims who may share responsibility for an incident (Feeley, 1979, p. 162).

In addition to the credibility and involvement of the victim, a major determinant of prosecutorial discretion is the *willingness* of the victim to prosecute (LaFree, 1981; Myers & Hagan, 1979). Indeed, this is virtually a necessary condition for a case to proceed. Without victim cooperation, enough evidence for successful prosecution is unlikely to be gathered. Because victims may refuse to cooperate at the prosecutorial stage, a high proportion of those cases that are funneled through the police drop out at this point. (McLeod, 1983).

The willingness of victims to testify varies in social space. Black victims may be less likely than whites to testify against offenders (Petersilia,

1985). This may lead blacks to be prosecuted less often than whites because most crime is intraracial and blacks are more likely than whites to be victims (Radelet & Pierce, 1985). Or, women complainants are more likely than male ones to pursue domestic assault cases. In one study, although 4% of domestic assault cases of men who assaulted women were adjudicated, less than 1% of those involving female defendants and male victims reached the trial stage (McLeod, 1983).

Similarly, the characteristics of the offender may shape victim willingness to testify. For example, men are unwilling to pursue charges when their assailants are women (Visher, 1983). Victims are also more willing to drop charges against younger than older juveniles, so that cases of older offenders have a greater probability of going to court (Stables, 1987).

The necessity of cooperation from victims is particularly important in shaping the response to white-collar crime. The social organization of white-collar offenses is distinctive in that they often have diffuse victims and most potential witnesses are themselves somehow implicated in the offense. Successful prosecution often depends upon providing immunity or filing lenient charges to obtain testimony from witnesses. A study of 9,000 cases in American federal courts between 1974-1977 shows that the court district that was most aggressive in seeking out and prosecuting white-collar offenders was forced to negotiate lower charge seriousness to obtain the cooperation of potential witnesses (Hagan, Nagel, & Albonetti, 1980). In contrast, the districts that waited for victims to come forward had less need to bargain and did not show a corresponding pattern of leniency.

The *status* of the victim is a third factor influencing the probability of prosecution. Victims who are reputable, blameless, and credible are less likely to have prosecution dropped and more likely to have offenses against them considered as serious. One study concludes: "A pleasant appearance, residence in a good neighborhood, a respectable job or occupation, a lack of nervous mannerisms, and an ability to articulate clearly are decided advantages" (Stanko, 1981-1982, p. 230). On the other hand, victims with the opposite characteristics have little chance of pursuing legal cases. For example, among victims who were chronic alcohol abusers: "One-half of cases were dropped at screening and another 60% later dismissed by the prosecutor, leaving only 8 cases which went to trial" (Williams, 1976, p. 191).

Charges are more likely to be serious and cases to go to trial when victims have characteristics that indicate respectability such as being white, married, or employed, and having no prior arrest record. Cases involving employed victims are more likely to be prosecuted than when victims are unemployed (Boris, 1979; Myers & Hagan, 1979; Williams, 1976). Or, homicide cases involving white victims are more likely to result in prosecutors requesting the death penalty (Bowers, 1983; Paternoster, 1984; Radelet & Pierce, 1985). In South Carolina between 1977 and 1981, the probability that prosecutors sought a death sentence was two and a half times greater for white-victim, compared to black-victim, homicides (Paternoster, 1984). Blacks who killed whites in this state were substantially more likely to receive death penalty requests, whereas blacks who killed other blacks were substantially less likely to receive such requests.

Both the organizational need for credible and willing victims and the status of the victim affect the funneling of legal cases. This insures that more respectable and integrated victims are advantaged in the pursuit of justice. Socially marginal and disreputable victims, in contrast, are less likely to see their cases pursued to an adjudicated solution.

Offenders

Several social characteristics of offenders also have some impact on prosecutorial response. As with police responses, studies find varying impacts of offender attributes on prosecution. For example, some studies indicate that blacks and whites are treated equally at the prosecution stage (Albonetti, 1987; Dannefer & Schutt, 1982; Feeley, 1979). Others, however, find more harshness toward blacks so that blacks are less likely than whites to be released but more likely to have charges filed against them (Liska & Tausig, 1979; Petersilia, 1985).

Prosecutors closely attend to the respectability of offenders. For example, defendants who support children, have steady employment, and no prior criminal records typically receive reduced charges (Maynard, 1982). Unemployed offenders, in contrast, are more likely to be prosecuted than employed ones (Boris, 1979). Prior arrest records are especially likely to serve as an indicator of unrespectable status (Black, 1976, Chapter 6; Feeley, 1979).

Respectability is especially important in explaining the response to female offenders. Women who are attached to reputable men or who have young children living with them are typically seen as "respectable" and are more likely than males to obtain pretrial release (Kruttschnitt, 1981, 1984). Those who are not under male control are viewed as "unrespectable" and receive a more vigorous reaction from legal control agents.

Not only respectability but also the lack of informal control predicts escalation at the prosecutorial stage. The probability that cases will proceed into further stages of legal processing varies according to the embeddedness of the offender in informal networks of social control. Offenders who are subject to other forms of control are more likely to have their cases dropped or bargained rather than adjudicated. Those who are subject to no informal control face the greatest intensity of legal control. For example, in medieval Bologna, people could not be held in jail except when they had no relatives to take care of them (Blanshed, 1982). Offenders without family, school, employment, or community ties are still most likely to be held in detention centers or jails before coming to trial (Lizotte, 1978).

The grounding of age and gender in systems of informal control illustrates the impact of informal control on prosecutorial decisions. On the one hand, juveniles may be subject to less law than adults when they are subject to more informal authority in family and school settings. On the other hand, when parents themselves make legal referrals, the juvenile is part of a broken family, or a dropout or truant, juveniles are more likely to be referred to the juvenile court (Dannefer, 1984; Horwitz & Wasserman, 1980; Stables, 1987; Thomas & Cage, 1977). Hence the effect of age is conditioned by its grounding in systems of informal control.

Gender provides another example of how the degree of informal control affects legal responses (Kruttschnitt, 1981). Women are more likely than men to be in dependent statuses that connote a greater amount of informal social control. Girls both face more informal surveillance than boys over behavior and are socialized to have personality traits such as passivity, compliance, and dependence that indicate submission to social control (Kruttschnitt & McCarthy, 1985).

The result is that fewer women than men are indicted and tried for crimes, a finding that held in the Middle Ages as well as now (Hanawalt, 1979, p. 117). Marital status is a better predictor of legal escalation for females than males because it is more likely to indicate the presence of informal control for women than men (Steffensmeier, 1980). A study of several thousand male and female offenders in Minneapolis indicates that offenders who are more economically dependent on others for support and, hence, who are subject to more informal control, are more likely to gain pretrial release (Kruttschnitt & Green, 1984). Conversely, female status offenders are more likely than male ones to be referred for legal adjudication because the lack of informal control is viewed as more serious for females than males (Krohn, Curry, & Nelson-Kilger, 1983). Gender, in itself, however, does not affect the extent of charge reduction (Bishop & Frazier, 1984).

In addition to respectability and presence of informal control, offenders who pose a greater threat to social order are less likely to have cases dropped at this stage of legal processing. In particular, characteristics such as use of a dangerous weapon, greater offense severity, and prior criminal record (Albonetti, 1987; Myers & Hagan, 1979; Stables, 1987) indicate greater threat and, hence, predict further escalation. There is a threshold of seriousness beyond which anyone, regardless of social status, will be prosecuted. For example, when murders are accompanied by multiple felonies, social disparities in rates and types of prosecution disappear (Paternoster, 1984). If the crime involved is considered heinous enough, the influence of offender characteristics is eliminated completely.

Victim-Offender Relationships

A structural, rather than an attribute, perspective enhances our understanding of the escalation of formal control. Prosecutors look less at the individual characteristics of victims and offenders and more to the relationship between them within the context of the crime event (Maynard, 1982).

Offenses between lower status persons or blacks pose less threat to conventional social order and hence are more likely to be dropped or receive more charge reduction (Bernstein *et al.*, 1977; LaFree, 1980). Correspondingly, cases of blacks victimizing whites are viewed as more threatening. Such offenders are more likely to be charged with more serious offenses and be processed through further stages of the criminal justice system (LaFree, 1980; Radelet & Pierce, 1985).

Prosecutors reflect the tendency of all third party intervenors to keep affairs of intimates private and are not likely to pursue prosecution in domestic cases. In contrast to the more rigorous prosecution of assaults between strangers, cases between family members and friends are more likely to be screened out and dismissed. Cases between spouses, usually assaults, are especially unlikely to reach the trial stage. In Washington, DC, only one-sixth of reported marital assaults resulted in a legal plea compared to three-quarters of those involving more distant victims and offenders (Williams, 1976). Similarly, cases that involved past or present romantic involvement, such as ex-spouses, cohabiting couples, and girlfriends or boyfriends resulted in very high rates of dismissal (Williams, 1976). In one large city in Texas, 40% of persons arrested for killing relatives, 37% who killed friends, but only 24% who killed strangers were released without prosecution (Lundsgaarde, 1977, p. 32). In another study in Detroit, only 14% out of a sample of 6,200 cases of domestic assault reached the prosecutor's office, and only 2.6% were adjudicated (McLeod, 1983).

In part, the rare prosecution of domestic violence cases reflects the wishes of victims: The willingness of victims to testify declines as their intimacy with offenders grows. Even if they have initially requested legal intervention, victims are reluctant to continue to press charges against intimates. Married women, for example, are far less likely than separated or divorced women to pursue assault cases against spouses to the trial stage (McLeod, 1983). If victims of domestic assaults are still willing to prosecute, prosecutors usually have a credible case with a willing victim who will testify. In such circumstances, there is more prosecution when victims and offenders know each other than when they are strangers (Myers & Hagan, 1979).

In addition, if intimates have been rejected by their families, they become more vulnerable to strong legal sanctioning. When parents initiate cases against juveniles, indicating the abandonment of informal control, rates of prosecution are very high (Dannefer, 1984; Stables, 1987). Conversely, parents who assault their own children and come to legal attention may be vigorously prosecuted become of the absence of other alternatives that could control their behavior (Williams, 1976).

This factor may be particularly important in explaining gender differences in legal processing. One estimate is that three out of four girls are brought to legal attention by their parents, often when their daughters have failed to live up to demands for obedience and chastity (Chesney-Lind, 1977). This explains why in the past a higher proportion of girls than boys have been prosecuted for status offenses and a lower proportion for criminal offenses, although these differences have been dramatically dropping in recent years (Sarri, 1983). To the extent that the juvenile justice system is paternalistic, it reinforces community standards of morality and the demands of parents for legal discipline of disobedient daughters.

When victims and offenders have a close social relationship, cases are more likely to be settled outside the court setting. If such cases result in an initial complaint, victims are less willing to cooperate in later stages of prosecution, and their cases are more likely to be dropped. When crimes involve strangers, problems of victim testimony are less likely to occur (Williams, 1976). Offenses between strangers will more likely involve a victim who will sustain the charges and be convincing to a jury so are more likely to proceed to further stages of legal processing (Albonetti, 1987).

Summary

Prosecutors are an important stage in the funneling process. Unlike the police, they need not be influenced by situational exigencies. The pressures they face stem from the organizational contexts in which they operate. The credibility, willingness, and respectability of victims are important components of prosecutorial decisions. Prosecutors, like all legal authority, also respond most vigorously in the absence of informal social control and apply the formal authority of law according to standards of community morality. When informal control is high, as in most disputes among intimates, adjudicated outcomes are rare. When, however, legal control is the only available mode of sanctioning, whether in cases between strangers or between intimates who are estranged from each other, adjudicated solutions to cases become more likely.

OUTCOMES

Only a very small proportion of cases that enter the legal system reach adjudicated outcomes. Victims do not pursue most cases. Negotiation between victims and offenders settles many others. Police and prosecutors screen out many cases that still remain. Most cases that reach adjudicative outcomes in modern legal systems are decided through bargaining between prosecutors and defense attorneys. Defendants agree to plead guilty in return for charge reduction. Typically, between 90% and 95% of cases are disposed of in this matter (Feeley, 1979). Similarly, about 95% of contested automobile injury claims are settled without trial (Ross, 1970). Even 30% of cases that do reach the trial stage are not formally contested (Galanter, 1983). The small number of remaining cases reach verdicts through jury trials.

Those few cases that are funneled into the final stages of the legal process should be ones that involve particularly threatening offenses, especially disreputable offenders or reputable victims, and a vacuum of informal control. The few "atypical" cases that have passed through the screening of complainants, police, and prosecutors, such as ones that involve high status or female offenders, should usually have especially dramatic offsetting factors such as the commission of particularly heinous offenses. Because of the homogeneity of cases that remain in the official system by this stage, we would expect there to be little social variation in legal responses at the final stages of processing. The rest of this chapter explores how outcomes vary according to the characteristics of offenders, of victims, and the relationship between offenders and victims, as well as the relationship between adjudicators and the parties to a case.

Distance between Adjudicators and Offenders

One predictor of the severity of outcomes is the social distance between adjudicators and defendants. Growing distance predicts a higher number of guilty verdicts and a greater severity of sentencing. Conversely, when the social distance between those making judgments and defendants is small, the severity of outcomes should be low. This implies that *the severity of legal outcomes is directly related to the social distance between adjudicators and defendants*. This principle indicates that growing social distance leads both to a higher proportion of guilty verdicts and to stiffer severity of sentencing (Black, 1989a).

Before the modern era, the social distance between adjudicators and defendants was often very low. Judges or juries were usually members of the same communities as those they judged and shared common social and cultural characteristics. Early English jurors were chosen by their ability to judge the respectability of offenders and their accusers including their reputations, character, work habits, and social integration. Until the nineteenth century, particularly in rural areas, jurors had to live among the same offenders they were called on to judge. According to Blackstone, "One excellence of the trial by jury is that the jury are triers of the credit of the witnesses, as well as of the truth of the facts" (quoted in Beattie, 1986, p. 126). In this period, releasing defendants because of family and employment considerations was considered highly appropriate rather than extraneous (Langbein, 1983).

As we would expect in a context with small social distance between jurors and defendants, rates of conviction were very low (Hanawalt, 1979, p. 53). Medieval English juries allowed prominent families to help each other out when they became involved with the law because most jurors knew offenders who were often neighbors, kin, or acquaintances. The close social distance between jurors and defendants resulted in very high rates of acquittals—about 80% in the medieval period (Hanawalt, 1979, pp. 56-57). The acquittal rates of English juries between 1660 to 1800 were also very high, ranging from 35% in property offenses to 83% in rape cases, perhaps because relatively small social distance led jurors to dislike the harsh penalties the guilty would be subject to by the formal law (Beattie, 1986).

Not only were acquittal rates low in this period, but the impact of social characteristics on verdicts was high. When defendants were marginal members of communities or outsiders, they could expect both convictions and very harsh sentences. Juries reacted most harshly to offenses of distant, marginal, and disreputable offenders and were most lenient toward intimates and integrated and respectable offenders. In the medieval period, juries were unable to convict members of established village families because they themselves would be liable to revenge. Strangers and more marginal members of medieval communities who lacked ties of friendship and protection were more liable to indictment, conviction, and hanging (Hanawalt, 1979).

Outsiders with no ties to jurors were at particular risk of harsh sentencing. One study of courts in seventeenth-century England indicates:

> A considerable prejudice existed against all strangers, but those who were accused of crimes were at special risk because they had no local family or neighbors to vouch for them. . . . None of the criminals for whom indictments and recognizances survive took property from anyone in their own parishes. While only 13 percent of the known recidivists were ordered executed, 56 percent of the felons identifiable as strangers in East Sussex were ordered hanged. (Herrup, 1985, p. 118)

Those who were sentenced to hang tended to be marginal, disreputable, and lower status offenders:

> Many of those who were executed for crimes against property shared two characteristics: they had been convicted of one of the serious offenses; and they were men who appeared to be "old offenders," or at least vagrants, and wanderers, men who lived anonymously in the larger urban parishes, strangers, Irishmen, men with no fixed place who could not bring an employer or a group of neighbors to speak for them to remove the impression that they were detached and dangerous. (Beattie, 1986, p. 448)

Clemency was likely to be granted when prisoners were of good character, young, elderly, or infirm (Langbein, 1983).

As population size increases and defendants become increasingly anonymous, juries have less information to use in making their decisions. Both legal officials and jurors become more socially distant from offenders. Growing social distance between judges and juries and defendants led rates of acquittal to decline and severity of sentencing to increase during the seventeenth and eighteenth centuries (Green, 1985, 1988). The personal system of justice emphasizing the character and reputation of offenders was transformed into a system that stressed equality and uniformity of treatment.

Enhanced social distance gives rise to greater severity as defendants are more likely to lack close contact with judges or juries. Conviction rates have increased dramatically in the modern world so that between 80% and 90% of those tried by juries are found guilty. Nevertheless, juries still seem to acquit more defendants than judges would in comparable cases (Kalven & Zeisel, 1966). This is deducible from the greater social distance that exists between judges and defendants than between jurors and defendants. However, as the social composition of jurors becomes more heterogenous, more jurors come to share social characteristics with predominantly poor, black, and socially marginal defendants. A decline in the social distance between jurors and defendants should lead to a growing rate of acquittals in jury trials.

The greater social distance between settlement agents and those they judge has dramatically changed the way legal outcomes are produced in the modern world. On the one hand, acquittal rates decline as offenders are judged by persons who have little in common with them. Yet, on the other hand, a greater uniformity in outcomes is produced because the distance between settlement agents and cases does not vary much from case to case (Black, 1989a). This leads to a declining importance of status characteristics of offenders to predict case outcomes (e.g. Feeley, 1979; Hagan, 1974). In most modern, bureaucratic settings, the uniformly high social distance between control agents and defendants dictates that the influence of social characteristics on legal outcomes is now less than ever before.

Offenders

The degree to which characteristics of offenders shape legal outcomes should vary according to their social distance from settlement agents. When this distance is small, adjudicators explicitly use qualities of the person in their decision making, and characteristics of offenders have large impacts on outcomes. This is particularly true in legal systems when the number of offenders is small and much information about the character of offenders is available. When this distance grows, the impact of offender traits should diminish.

Social Status

When there is little distance between settlement agents and defendants, social status has an important impact on case outcomes. In the Roman Empire, qualities such as social prominence, wealth, and good character were seen as proper considerations in deciding the outcome of cases and the quality of witnesses' evidence (Garnsey, 1968). Members of the upper class in Rome who committed crimes were subject to exile or fines whereas the lower classes faced death, hard labor, or slavery for similar conduct. In the courts of medieval Bologna, immigrants were three times more likely than Bolognese to be convicted and punished (Blanshed, 1982). Punishment in early Renaissance Venice reflected the same pattern:

> In rape cases, among 84 nobles successfully prosecuted 37 received fines (44 percent); 14 received jail sentences (17 percent); and 33 received a combination of jail sentences and fines (39 percent). Among 173 workers, 24 received fines (14 percent); 89 received jail sentences (51 percent); and 60 received a combination of jail sentences and fine (35 percent). (Ruggiero, 1980, p. 46)

Likewise, in English society, crimes of the wandering and rootless, gypsies, and unpropertied were disproportionately likely to result in capital punishment (Beattie, 1986; Hay, 1975). In Colonial New Haven, as well, although high-status defendants were commonly accorded dispositions in civil law, crimes of low-status persons were handled through criminal proceedings (Baumgartner, 1978). In this setting, high-status defendants were also more likely to be acquitted than low-status ones, especially if the complainant was of low status.

Status does not always result in legal advantage. In many cases, a greater amount of blameworthiness attaches to persons of higher status if they violate the trust placed in them. This may be particularly true if their victims are also of high status. In feudal Europe, nobles were subject to heavier fines than common people (Rusche & Kircheimer, 1939). In eighteenth-century England, a well-off person was sometimes held to higher standards because he, in the words of one justice of the time, "under the mask of a fair and upright character, was enabled to make depredations on his neighbours and the public, without being suspected, therefore was not to be guarded against, and consequently, in his eye, was much more culpable than the poor man, who commits such acts from real want" (Hay, 1975, p. 119).

In Socialist societies, there is a tendency to punish the affluent more severely in order to set examples for the population (Braithwaite, 1982; Feifer, 1969; Salas, 1979). Some studies of white-collar crime also find a positive relationship between social class and the probability of incarceration (Wheeler *et al.*, 1982). Prison sentences of whites in some states are more severe than of minorities: In Georgia, for example, whites receive prison terms that are more than 2 years longer than blacks, perhaps because they are held to higher standards, whereas the intraracial crimes of blacks are more tolerated (Myers & Talerico, 1986). Likewise, black drug users are sometimes less likely than whites to be sentenced to jail (Peterson & Hagan, 1984). The disadvantaged can be treated more leniently because of lower expectations of proper behavior and more tolerance for their offenses.

In the modern world, when the distance between adjudicators and offenders is uniformly high, characteristics of offenders do not have a strong impact on trial outcomes (e.g., Hagan, 1974; Kleck, 1981). The impersonality of the typical trial and large distance between jurors and defendants leads to relatively similar outcomes for offenders of different social status. Although social status usually results in legal advantage when the distance between judges, jurors, and defendants is small, social distance negates this advantage. The small impact of offender status on legal outcomes is predictable from the uniformly large social distance in the contemporary criminal justice system.

Gender

Settlement agents have a greater tolerance of female than male deviance. In medieval times, only 12.3% of women who were indicted were convicted compared to nearly double that rate for men (Hanawalt, 1979, p. 54). Likewise, in Elizabethan England, women were acquitted in 48% of cases that went to trial compared to an overall acquittal rate of 29% (Samara, 1974). Women accused of homicide in eighteenth-century England were more likely than men to be discharged by grand juries and acquitted by trial juries. Less than a quarter of women were convicted in this period, compared to about half of men (Beattie, 1986, pp. 437-438). In both nineteenth-century Britain and France, the rate of acquittal for females who murdered their husbands was consistently higher than of men who murdered their wives (Hartman, 1977, p. 214). French juries of this time period were also less likely to convict women than men, perhaps because they viewed them as less responsible for their crimes and as less of a threat to social order (Donovan, 1981).

In the contemporary United States, female defendants still usually receive more lenient sentences than males (Farrell & Swigert, 1978; Nagel & Hagen, 1983; Zingraff & Thompson, 1984). Indeed, gender, unlike other social characteristics, seems to have its greatest impact at the sentencing stage. Both juvenile (Stables, 1984) and adult (Curran, 1983; Kruttschnitt, 1984; Nagel & Weitzman, 1971) females are less likely than males to be incarcerated, controlling for other factors. Among a study of white-collar offenders, for example, gender was the best predictor of any variable of who was sentenced to prison (Wheeler *et al.*, 1982). Similarly, wives who kill husbands are less likely to go to prison than husbands who kill wives (Lundsgaarde, 1977). Imprisonment is especially incompatible with the female gender role and is avoided in all but the most extreme circumstances.

The greater tolerance of female offenders is widespread. In a wide variety of times and places, women are viewed as a lesser threat to lives, property, and social order. This tendency seems to result from the nonthreatening nature of the female gender role and from the fact that most female offenders victimize family members who are relationally close to them.

Informal Control

Another predictor of legal sanctioning is the degree to which people are subject to informal social control. Law is less in the presence of other control (Black, 1976). Therefore, all social statuses subject to more informal control should receive less legal control and vice versa.

Defendants who have responsibility for families are often treated more leniently than those without dependents (Daly, 1987a). Persons with family responsibilities are viewed as more socially integrated and are subject to more informal social control. In early modern Seville, women violators appeared less threatening to authorities because they faced more normative and marital constraints (Perry, 1980). Hence, men were disproportionately punished in the courts of this city. In addition, the consequences of jailing such defendants are greater because children and spouses also must suffer from the costs of punishment. The presence of dependents brings the perception of greater social integration, responsibility, and social costs of punishment (Daly, 1987a,b).

Women who are economically independent are subject to less informal social control and, hence, more law. In one contemporary study, women who were independent of male control were more likely to incur severe sentences than those subject to male authority (Kruttschnitt, 1981). Like young boys or older men, women whose daily lives contain much control should be ignored by the law, whereas those who lack daily supervision are seen as in more need of formal social control. The extent to which juveniles are subject to nonlegal control also predicts whether or not they will be incarcerated. Juveniles with strong family and school ties are less likely than others to be placed in reformatories, whereas the absence of these ties consistently predicts patterns of confinement (Cohen & Kluegel, 1978; Horwitz & Wasserman, 1980; Stables, 1987).

Summary

The most common finding of studies that predict sentencing outcomes is the relatively small proportion of variance that any factor explains (Feeley, 1979). In particular, social characteristics of defendants account for very little difference in sentencing pattern. Hence, one literature review concludes that "knowledge of extra-legal offender characteristics contributes only relatively little to our ability to predict judicial dispositions" (Hagan, 1974, p. 379). Similarly, offender characteristics minimally affect rates of conviction and length of sentence. For example, when charge seriousness and prior conviction record are controlled, race differences are small or nonexistent (Feeley, 1979; Spohn, Gruhl, & Welch, 1981-1982).[4]

This small impact of offender characteristics is predictable from several factors. First, the funneling process from initial offense to the outcome stage leads to a homogeneous group of offenders. This social homogeneity predicts a homogeneity of outcomes. Second, the greater distance between settlement agents and defendants also leads to a greater uniformity of outcomes. Third, characteristics of offenders in themselves are relatively unimportant compared to the relationship between offenders and their victims. The influence of social status changes, depending on the relational configuration between victim and offender. It is, therefore, no surprise that offender characteristics are usually not strongly predictive of legal outcomes in the modern world.

Victims

Respectability

A medieval writer noted that "beautiful and noble women, the wealthy who can pay for justice, and the nobles who can use their influence and their private armies" were more likely to attain success when they brought cases to court (Hanawalt, 1979, p. 47). Several centuries later in England, when witnesses were of good character, convictions would likely result whereas disreputable witnesses often led to acquittals (Beattie, 1986, p. 442). In seventeenth-century New England, courts were more likely to convict rapists when a child or a married woman had been raped. At this time, the death penalty for rape applied only for women who were married, engaged, or under the age of 10 (D'Emilio & Freedman, 1988).

Despite the importance of impersonal legal rules in modern legal systems, the respectability of victims still influences legal outcomes. In many places, the law still permits the introduction of victims' person-

[4]It is possible, however, that if discretion in a sequential system is in the same direction at each stage, a small amount of discretion can cumulate to produce a high degree of discretion across the whole system. Hence, if there is a small tendency for citizens to request arrest for black offenders, for police to arrest blacks, and for prosecutors to indict blacks, these small differences may cumulate to produce a large effect at the final stages of the legal process (Liska & Tausig, 1979).

ality, character, and reputation (Lundsgaarde, 1977, p. 154). Defense attorneys emphasize factors such as bad moral character of victims, past criminal records, or culpability in the offense. Persons with prior criminal records, drug or alcohol abusers, prostitutes, and otherwise unrespectable victims are less likely to obtain convictions. On the other hand, the degree of sympathy juries display grows as the respectability of victims increases (Lunsgaarde, 1977).

The importance of victim traits explains why convictions are more probable for victims who are young, married, and have upright reputations (Myers, 1980; Reskin & Visher, 1986). In sexual assault cases, jurors are more likely to acquit offenders when victims had sex outside of marriage, were taking drugs or drinking, were acquainted with the offender, or were black (LaFree, Reskin, & Visher, 1985). The power of these victim characteristics to predict verdicts increases as the strength of legal evidence declines (Reskin & Visher, 1986). Especially when evidence is limited, respectable victims are more likely to see their offenders punished severely.

Organization

Whether victims and offenders are individuals or organizations can affect the sanctioning process. Although little research examines how organizations fare as victims compared to individuals, they appear more likely than individuals to be successful claimants. Offenders who victimize institutions or corporations are more likely to be prosecuted than those who victimize individuals (Albonetti, 1987, p. 310). One study in suburban Toronto found that corporate victims of crimes are about 14% more likely than individual victims to have offenders convicted (Hagan, 1982). Organizational plaintiffs in civil cases tend to win a majority of cases, particularly against individuals. Individual defendants, in contrast, win only a little over 10% of the time (Wanner, 1975). Galanter (1974) estimates that the rate of complete victories of organizations suing individuals is about ten times as high as when individuals sue organizations. This evidence supports Black's (1976, p. 92) claim that organizations are more likely than individuals to be successful in legal systems.

Several reasons may account for the greater success of organizations in the legal process. Galanter (1974, p. 360) states that courts in the United States "are forums which are used by organizations to extract from and discipline individuals." Alternatively, the impersonal, formal, and rational norms of the legal system may be amenable to corporate goals of rationality (Hagan, 1982). Another possibility is that organizational victims are at a greater relational distance from their offenders, so not organization but relational distance explains the greater severity of outcomes in such cases.

It may also be the case that organizations only pursue cases when the strength of evidence is very high. Organizations tend to settle most complaints of individuals informally and only bring to court cases where both settlement is impossible and they are sure of winning. Therefore, organizations will avoid going to trial in all but the most certain cases, so have higher success rates when they do pursue litigation. What reasons explain the higher success of organizational victims are open to question.

Victim-Offender Relationships

Relational Distance

Legal outcomes mirror the reluctance of decision makers at prior stages to judge the affairs of intimates. Cases when the victim has some prior relationship with the defendant are less likely to result in guilty verdicts, whereas cases between more distant parties result in more guilty pleas (Feeley, 1979, p. 132). For example, French juries between 1825 and 1914 accorded more severe outcomes to property crimes than to violent ones because the former offenses were more likely to occur between strangers than the latter (Donovan, 1981). Defendants most likely to be acquitted were accused of crimes at the most intimate distances: abortion and infanticide. Other murders between intimates, which usually involved vengeance, adultery, and domestic quarrels, resulted in fewer convictions than those when victim and offenders were strangers.

In the contemporary United States, cases with prior or present romantic involvements between victim and offender including spouses, ex-spouses, cohabitants, and girlfriends and boyfriends still result in a higher proportion of not guilty verdicts (Williams, 1976). A study of homicide cases in Houston shows that 32% of relatives charged with homicide compared to 49% of friends or associates and 60% of strangers were found guilty (Lundsgaarde, 1977). The death penalty is in nearly all cases reserved only for killings between strangers (Cooney, 1988, pp. 40-41).

More guilty verdicts result with greater relational distance between victims and defendants, although the predictive power of these characteristics is often low (Myers, 1980). This is not surprising because the few cases in close relational space that proceed to adjudicated outcomes are likely to involve particularly heinous offenses that increase the severity they incur.

Social Status

The relative status of offenders and their victims is a crucial consideration in explaining sentencing differences. Social attributes have variable effects, depending on their grounding in structural relationships. Assaults against higher status victims result in more severe penalties (Beattie, 1986, p. 458). This explains why in many cases the delicts of higher status offenders are treated severely: Their victims are other higher status persons. For instance, in early Renaissance Venice:

> In some cases, nobles could be penalized severely for minor crimes. Aluysio Venier, son of Doge Antnoio Venier, along with a friend from an important family, Marco Loredan, left some objects on the bridge that led into campo San Ternita—a set of horns and a sign designed to insult the virtue of Giovanni dalle Boccole, also a noble, and his wife, sister, and mother-in-law. Although it was no more than a youthful joke in bad taste, the commune responded without humor. Both pranksters were given two-month jail sentences, fined 100 ducats, and forbidden to enter the campo of San Ternita for ten years. An incident like this at any other level of society would not have warranted communal attention, but insults among the ruling class could not be overlooked. (Ruggiero, 1980, p. 69)

In the modern world, the highest severity upon conviction in capital cases occurs when persons with low occupational status kill ones with higher standing; the lowest severity in cases of homicide between lower status persons (Farrell & Swigert, 1978).

Because court records in contemporary societies are more likely to indicate the race than the social class of offenders and victims, most studies use race, rather than social class, as an indicator of social status. Black offenders, as a group, are not treated more severely than whites (Feeley, 1979). Yet, the grounding of crimes in relational networks does produce racial differences in legal outcomes. Black intraracial cases are least likely to result in strong sanctions, whereas blacks who victimize whites are most likely to receive severe sentences (Kleck, 1981; LaFree, 1980; Radelet, 1981).

The most severe punishment occurs when black offenders kill or rape white victims. In the seventeenth century in the United States, the harshest penalties for sexual assault applied to blacks who attacked white women (D'Emilio & Freedman, 1988). In one contemporary study of rape, black intraracial crimes were treated most leniently in seven of nine stages of criminal processing but black on white crimes received the harshest sanctions in eight of nine stages (LaFree, 1980). When rapes occur between blacks, offenders are increasingly likely to be funneled out of the criminal justice system in each stage from case reporting to sentencing, whereas the proportion of cases with black suspects and white victims steadily increases with each succeeding stage. The effect of dyad characteristics were particularly important in the latter stages of sentencing, incarceration, and sentence length. Black-on-black rapes accounted for 45% of all reported cases but 26% of offenders sentenced to prison and 17% of sentences of more than 6 years. In contrast, black-on-white offenses accounted for 23% of reported cases but 45% of prison sentences and 50% of sentences of more than 6 years (LaFree, 1980).

In homicide cases, as well, black offenders who kill white victims are in greatest jeopardy of receiving death sentences or long terms of imprisonment (Radelet & Pierce, 1985). A large study of death sentences in four states indicates that blacks who kill whites are in substantially more danger than others for receiving death sentences, followed by whites who kill whites, blacks who kill blacks, and whites who kill blacks (Bowers & Pierce, 1980). The relationship between offenders and their victims also accounts for why blacks are treated more leniently than whites for typically intraracial crimes such as theft and assault but less leniently for the typically interracial crime of robbery (Myers & Talerico, 1986).

The gender composition of victim-offender dyads also influences legal outcomes. Men are held to different standards than women when violence crosses gender lines. In homicide cases, women are handled more leniently than men when they commit homicides, whereas killers of women receive more severe sanctions than killers of men (Cooney, 1988, p. 116). In the contemporary United States, males who murder females receive the harshest sanctions whereas females who kill males are underpenalized (Farrell & Swigert, 1978). Female gender is a mitigating factor for defendants but an aggravating one when men victimize women (Farrell & Swigert, 1978, p. 574).

CONCLUSION

As cases progressively move through legal systems, different sorts of factors predict how they will be resolved. The main concern of the police is to preserve order within situational contexts; of prosecutors to resolve cases within organizational contexts; and of judges and juries to apply legal rules. These goals lead different factors to be important at each stage—the police are highly responsive to victim preferences, whereas prosecutors focus on aspects of cases that can produce strong evidence and plea-bargained agreements. Judges and juries that are close in social distance to victims and offenders closely attend to social characteristics, whereas the importance of social characteristics declines as the distance between adjudicators and offenders grows.

Some aspects of the social structure of cases are consistently related to third-party response. At each stage, the willingness of victims to press the case to legal resolution, greater social distance between victim and offender, and the lack of informal social control is associated with an escalation of official response. In these ways, formal legal institutions are not autonomous bodies that impose formalistic rules on offenders who are divested of social personalities. Instead, in important ways, they reflect and reinforce the moral order of the surrounding communities. The bureaucratic structure of modern legal systems reduces, but does not eliminate, the impact of social characteristics on case outcomes.

Legal authority in the modern world is often viewed as a monopolistic, all-encompassing power that intrudes into the informal realm. Yet, the importance of community norms persists in many respects. Inaction and self-help respond to most grievances. This is especially true when trilateral institutions are weak, inaccessible, or unavailable. Others, especially among status equals in tightly knit communities, are resolved through bilateral resolution. Trilateral institutions emerge with growing social distance and tend to be used in disputes among strangers where alternative means are not available to resolve conflicts.

Few grievances enter trilateral systems. Those that do are typically filtered out of the system before reaching adjudicated solutions. The small number of cases that are ultimately resolved through adjudication usually involve marginal and disreputable people who are not subject to informal control and people who have offended social superiors, as well as those who have committed the most heinous crimes.

To be sure, there is a strong legal presence in modern life. Law intrudes when strangers confront each other and no informal control is possible. Similarly, it is strong when disreputable, marginal, and low-status persons offend the upright, integrated, and well-off. In addition, in recent years the domain of law has greatly expanded to encompass schools, businesses, government, medicine, and many other organized settings (Lieberman, 1981). As these institutions are increasingly marked by a greater relational distance, impersonality, and breakdown in authority and trust, law is more likely to order their affairs.

The atomization of individuals and simultaneous growth of corporate entities has led to two very different trends. On the one hand, exit and avoidance flourish among disputants as it becomes ever easier to walk away from or ignore grievances (Baumgartner, 1988). On the other hand, as more and more relationships, involvements, crimes, accidents, and grievances occur within or against organizational entities, the resort to law becomes more frequent (Black, 1989a). As claims are increasingly made against organizations, the routine processing of grievances should become more institutionalized (Abel, 1979). Malpractice claims, consumer disputes, personal injuries, and the like may come to be handled like automobile accidents are today. Then, individuals might use avoidance in disputes with other individuals but routinely receive compensation from organizations that have harmed them. By that time, however, the structure of social organization may have changed into some new and as yet unknown shape, which will engender a new configuration of the forms of social control.

III

The Effectiveness of Social Control

The previous chapters explored how the style and form of social control vary in social space. The next two chapters examine how the nature of social life shapes the effectiveness of social control. Effective social control indicates that social control agents have accomplished their goals. It has two major components: first, the goals of the sanctioning agent or agency; and, second, the extent to which people's behavior conforms to these goals. Social control is effective to the extent that the efforts of controllers change the behavior of potential deviants.

This chapter examines how networks of social ties shape the effectiveness of social control. Its premise is that the nature of social relationships determine whether or not controllers can succeed in changing aberrant behavior. The influence of family, friends, and valued community members is more important than that of the state in maintaining conformity and preventing deviance. The success of official control attempts depends upon whether family, friends, and community members reinforce or reject the efforts of police, courts, mediators, psychotherapists, and the like.

This emphasis on the importance of informal networks contrasts with most schools of thought that examine the effectiveness of social control. These focus on how various aspects of *formal* systems of social control influence rates of deviant behavior. Deterrence theorists, for example, assume that actors are responsive to changes in the certainty and severity of legal controls and study variation in the types of formal sanctions that are applied (e.g., Blumstein *et al.*, 1978; Ehrlich, 1973). They usually neglect how informal relational networks shape responsiveness to sanctions. Labeling theorists, as well, focus on how formal agents of control such as police, courts, or mental hospitals shape deviant identities (e.g., Goffman, 1961; Schur, 1971). They rarely examine how the responses of intimate others alter rates of deviant behaviors. The voluminous research on the effectiveness of psychotherapy also almost exclusively examines formal therapeutic techniques (e.g., Eysenck; 1952; Smith *et al.*, 1980). We know little about how the reactions of intimates to personality problems shape change efforts.

An adequate theory of effectiveness must encompass informal as well as formal responses. Effectiveness encompasses not only state-imposed suffering but also all social efforts that respond to deviant behavior. If the responses of formal and informal controllers are incongruent, the impact of the formal effort is likely to be neutralized or even reversed. Praise from peers for a daring theft may negate legal punishment; continued patronage of consumers neutralize fines for illegal business practices; shame from relatives and friends counteract insight gained from psychotherapy. The greater the congruence in the aims of formal agents of social control with those of informal social networks, the greater the effectiveness of social control.

This process accounts for much of the variation in the effectiveness of control efforts. It explains, for example, both why small, homogeneous groups are able to exert effective social control and why modern, heterogeneous societies have such great difficulty in this endeavor. It also predicts why the effectiveness of control efforts in modern societies vary by factors such as relational and cultural distance, gender, age, and social class. In addition, it indicates what sorts of programs are more or less likely to produce desired change in deviant populations. Not only the properties of formal control systems but also the reactions of informal networks as well as the interaction between official and lay response predict the effectiveness of social control.

A social theory of effectiveness predicts and explains the varying effectiveness of control efforts in social space. To what extent does the way people are embedded in different types of social groups and relationships affect whether social control efforts are successful, counterproductive, or without effect? There is no inherent reason why the same social forces that are related to other dimensions of social control cannot predict how successful control efforts will be (compare Black, 1972). Effectiveness is an empirical phenomenon defined by the ends of control agents rather than by some ideal standard.

In practice, it is very difficult to specify any particular aim of a control effort. The goals of the control process are often vague. Diverse groups involved in control efforts often hold different aims that may differ from the principles set forth in legislation or judicial opinions. For instance, a statute may emphasize the punishment of offenders in order to reduce family violence. A police officer, however, may be more interested in restoring order to a troubled situation, a prosecutor in gaining assurances that the offense will not be repeated, or a judge in the impact of sentencing on family stability. Although none of these control agents may actively subvert the intention of the legislation, their positions in the social control system alter their implementation of the policy.

Faced with the problem of defining the goals of control efforts, many researchers substitute their own values of what goals control efforts ought to achieve as the measure of effective control efforts (Black, 1972). Vague and abstract notions such as justice, due process, or equality are viewed as standards by which to judge a law's success, although these values are difficult to specify or ground in the empirical world. The values of the investigator become the standard used to judge the effectiveness of the social control system under study. When, however, the goal of social control is not set by any abstract set of values but by the actual intentions of control agents, effectiveness can be defined and studied as an empirical phenomenon.

In addition to the problem of defining the goals of control efforts, the measurement of effectiveness is inherently difficult. The most effective sanctions ought to be the ones that are rarely invoked and hence impossible to measure directly. For example, suppose shaming and ridicule are effective sanctions against deviance in adolescent peer groups. Yet, their very effectiveness would lead youths to refrain from behaviors that would invoke them. The problem for investigators is to measure the effectiveness of sanctions that might be so powerful that they need not be used.

The obstacles in measuring deterrence are especially large (Blumstein *et al.*, 1978; Gibbs, 1975; Zimring & Hawkins, 1973). By definition, people who are deterred would have committed some forbidden act but did not because of the threat of punishment. Therefore, deterrence inherently is not directly measurable (Gibbs, 1975). The measurement of specific deterrence—the impact of penal sanctions on particular offenders—is also difficult because we usually cannot determine how much deviance would have been committed had sanctions not been applied.

Another measurement problem arises because seemingly effective control efforts can displace, rather than prevent, deviance. Additional police might be assigned to patrol subway stations with a resulting drop in the crime rate on subways accompanied by an increase in crime on streets surrounding subway stations (Chaiken, Lawless, & Stevenson, 1974). A proper evaluation of effectiveness must focus not just on particular social control measures but also on any resulting displacement effects. The appropriate measurement of effectiveness must be broad in time as well as space. For instance, many studies show that new laws have substantial initial deterrent effects that diminish to initial levels over time (Ross, 1986). The demonstration of effectiveness cannot be shown adequately at one point in time.

A complete explanation of effectiveness would involve introducing numerous independent variables such as the type of deviant behavior in question, characteristics of norms, the difference between actual and perceived sanctions, and personality characteristics of offenders and sanctioners, as well as the nature of social groups and relationships (Tittle, 1980). In contrast, I limit my study to how the nature of social relationships shapes the effectiveness of control efforts. In particular, I emphasize how group ties influence the ability of control systems to detect deviance, treat cases, and prevent deviant behavior. Groups that feature strong bonds between members are better able to exercise effective social control. In contrast, growing individualism and heterogeneity lead to greater difficulties in controlling deviant members. This view of effectiveness as a social process neither contradicts nor competes with psychological perspectives of this process but provides a complementary picture of factors that shape the effectiveness of social control.

I deal with three aspects of effectiveness. The *detection* of deviant cases is the first. No social control system can be effective if it lacks access to relevant cases. Control agencies acquire cases in two ways. In proactive methods, social control agents themselves observe cases; in reactive methods, deviants or lay observers bring the case to the attention of the control system (Black, 1971). The greater the ability of a control system to gather cases either proactively or reactively, the greater the potential effectiveness of the system.

Once the system has acquired cases, the effectiveness of control systems depends on their ability to treat and reintegrate people into the community. Social control systems must be able to apply effectively the sanctions of coercive social control or the rewards of consensual social control. Maximally effective control systems will not only punish or reward deviants but also reintegrate them into the group once the control process is over.

Finally, social control systems may engage in *prevention*. The goal of preventive systems is to keep deviance from arising in the first place. In effective preventive systems, no deviance emerges, and no subsequent social control is necessary. To prevent deviance, control agencies must either negate the root causes of deviant behavior or raise the costs of sanctions or rewards from conformity high enough to outweigh the rewards from deviance. These two chapters consider what factors are related to successful detection, treatment, and prevention.

10

Detecting and Treating Deviance

Social control agencies can only be effective to the extent that they gain access to cases and apply sanctions and rewards. This chapter considers the factors that shape how successfully social control systems can detect and treat deviants.

Detecting Cases

Introduction

Social control systems cannot be effective if they do not acquire cases. Perfectly efficient systems would have immediate and direct access to all appropriate cases of deviance. Yet, the nature of deviant behavior insures that detection is not easy. Deviance, by definition, usually involves the sorts of activities that people try to hide from agents of social control. These agents must find ways either to observe instances of deviance or to generate case reporting from bystanders, victims, or deviants. There are two general ways through which social control agencies acquire cases (Black, 1971). In *proactive* systems, social control agents directly observe the offending action. These agents are the initial reactors to offenses. Familiar types of proactive control include traffic control, undercover police work, or arrests in public places. Proactive systems are potentially efficient detectors of deviance because the norms of the citizenry do not filter the sorts of acts brought to official attention.

The social organization of much deviant activity, however, is often hidden so does not lend itself to direct observation. For example, most criminals conceal their actions to avoid detection and sanctions; symptoms of mental illness are often invisible or hidden from nonintimates; accidents occur in random and unpredictable ways. Because deviants hide their actions, because coercive styles of control cannot rely on the cooperation of offenders themselves to report violations, and because deviant acts emerge too often and too randomly to be directly observed, proactive social control usually is not a practical strategy of gaining access to cases.

In addition, proactive control is almost never a viable strategy in obtaining cases for consensual systems of social control. Effective therapeutic and conciliatory systems require voluntary clients who see clear benefits from involvement in the control effort. Yet, individuals who are forced to enter therapy or conciliation by official agents can rarely be convinced of the benefits of these processes. Patients who enter psychotherapy through court referrals are unlikely to remain in therapy; addicts who are forced to seek drug treatments return to the streets as soon as they are able; or battering husbands that police send to marital counseling quickly drop out (Berk *et al.*, 1982). Because proactive efforts typically impose unwanted control, they are ineffective ways of obtaining clients for persuasive systems of social control. Instead, consensual systems must be able to persuade potential clients that it is in their own interest to enter and remain in therapeutic or conciliatory efforts.

Because control agents often are unable to observe deviance directly, most social control activities are *reactive* rather than proactive. In reactive systems, social control agents respond to help-seeking efforts by bystanders, victims, or deviants themselves. Although the norms of social control agents guide case gathering in proactive control systems, the norms of citizens who mobilize official social control systems filter cases into reactive systems (Black, 1971). When sanctioning agents cannot observe wayward acts, victims, observers, or deviants themselves must report them. Typical examples of reactive case gathering are when observers call the police after muggings, troubled people visit psychiatrists, or drivers notify insurance agents after automobile accidents.

Effective reactive systems require either that people have suffered some moral outrage or believe that the rewards from reporting will outweigh the costs of doing do. People who believe they have suffered some serious harm that authorities can remedy are likely to take some action to bring the case to official attention (Miller & Sarat, 1980-1981). When observers' senses of right and wrong have been violated they will be likely to report offenses. Therefore, offenses such as serious crimes that generate moral outrage are most likely to generate reactive reporting of offenses (Gove *et al.*, 1985).

When the demands of morality are not high enough, the promise of instrumental rewards can motivate reactive mobilization. This is especially important for seekers of compensation. They should report harm to the extent that they expect monetary rewards. When official systems make reporting easy and maximize the chances of reward, as with damages suffered from automobile accidents, reporting of cases is nearly universal (Ross, 1970).

For many victimizations, however, the costs of reporting exceed the rewards from doing so. The time and expense involved in going to the police, mental health facilities, or counseling agencies may prevent official notification. If systems providing care are thought to be inefficient and ineffective, reactive utilization should correspondingly decline. In other cases, victims may not even be aware that their problems could be helped through legal recourse or therapeutic assistance.

Observers should be less likely than victims of crimes to mobilize official control agents. They have less interest than victims in seeing that justice is served and rarely gain any instrumental benefits from reporting. The intangible rewards from being a good citizen for reporting incidents often seem less than the costs of time, involvement, or accruing the enmity of the offender. Especially in large, heterogeneous societies where observers are unlikely to know victims, reporting may be unlikely.[1] When neither proactive nor reactive case gathering methods provide access to cases, social control systems cannot be effective. The critical question for securing successful social control is: What social conditions are conducive to gathering cases?

Visibility

Several aspects of social organization shape the effectiveness of case gathering. Whenever the conditions of social life increase the visibility of deviant behavior, social control systems have easier access to cases. These conditions include small group size, intense scrutiny over behavior, and a highly predictable structure of deviant occurrences.

Group size is related to how visible offenses will be: *The visibility of deviance is inversely related to group size.* The small size and intense interaction found in certain forms of social organizations lead themselves to effective case gathering because deviance becomes more visible to control agents. The encapsulation and visibility of social life promotes the

[1]The notorious Kitty Genovese incident in Queens, New York, where many neighbors watched and listened without taking any action even to call the police while a woman was murdered is the most dramatic illustration of this tendency (Black, 1989a, pp. 79-80).

direct observation of deviance. When groups are small and tightly interconnected, everyone is aware of what others are doing. Most social behavior is visible and easily detected. Crimes, accidents, marital disputes, or symptoms of mental disorder are all difficult to conceal.

Members of tribal societies, for example, are almost completely lacking in privacy. Tribal living conditions make anonymity impossible, and everybody knows virtually everything about all members. Such settings need not rely on specific social control agents to detect deviance because the entire population act as potential police and informers.

Another reason control systems in small, tightly knit groups can effectively detect cases is that offenders have few opportunities for leaving the group. If people can readily escape immediate detection from the sanctioning body they should be less fearful of sanctions and therefore violate rules more freely. In many small, interdependent groups, wrongdoers are not able to detach themselves from the group and join alternative groups (Furer-Haimendorf, 1967; Roberts, 1979). Not only is their behavior more likely to be observed, but their inability to leave the group makes detection more certain.

Effective case gathering occurs not only in tribal groups but whenever interaction occurs in small, tightly integrated, and closed communities such as communes, monasteries, or small towns. Small and stable groups can exert more effective social control because deviance is more visible and easier to detect (Bayley, 1976). In stable neighborhoods where adults are present, residents can supervise the area, watch each other's property, and challenge outsiders (Skogan, 1986). Or, married couple families have a greater ability to watch over their own and other children than divorced or single households (Sampson, 1986). Youths who grow up where familial and neighborhood controls are strong have both less opportunity to generate deviant activities and a greater chance of detection because of the greater supervision and surveillance of their activities (Sampson, 1986).

Totalitarian societies provide another setting that can generate effective proactive means of deviance detection. Such groups reproduce the qualities of intense, localized group interaction that enhance the ability to observe cases of wayward behavior. In totalitarian societies, the state penetrates all relationships between individuals through creating widespread networks of informants who assist police and report potential subversive actions and speech (Hollander, 1982). Street committees are often established on every block of a city to closely scrutinize the daily life of all residents (Feifer, 1969; Frolic, 1980; Salas, 1979). When such strong interconnections exist between formal and informal agents of social control, few cases of deviance can go undetected. Hence, effective proactive detection of deviance is maximal under conditions of intense group interaction that allow for the close scrutiny of behavior.

In contrast, the size, diversity, and heterogeneity of modern life insures that most deviance arises in unpredictable times and places. Most ordinary crimes such as muggings, rapes, burglaries, and robberies are unexpected, and offenders can flee before capture. Loose social boundaries, mechanized transportation, and easy mobility allow offenders to leave the scene of their offense, enhancing problems of detection. In modern societies, case gathering is difficult not only because of the inability to observe offenses directly but also because of the ease with which offenders can escape detection after they engage in deviant behavior.

Only a few nontotalitarian settings in the modern world lend themselves to effective systems of case gathering. The enforcement of traffic rules provides one example in modern life where the visibility of deviant behavior lends itself to proactive control. Authorities can predict where and when violations are likely to occur and take proactive steps to catch offenders. Radars can detect speeders; hidden police cars at busy intersections can observe many violations of traffic signals; and blockades on major highways at midnight can predictably capture many drunken drivers. Highways, however, are one of the few areas of modern life that generate a high volume of deviance in visible and predictable ways.

Another setting conducive to proactive control is when much social life occurs in public settings. For instance, hot, crowded, and deteriorated housing conditions often lead lower-class people to interact in public arenas rather than in the private settings middle-class life offers (Stinchcombe, 1963). This renders their deviant behaviors more visible and, hence, more detectable than those of the middle class. Correspondingly, juveniles whose deviance would be observed by parents in their homes are often forced to interact in public or semipublic settings, so their behaviors are more visible to police and other adult agents of social control. Hence, the behavioral patterns of youth render their deviance more visible and detectable than those of adults. Likewise, when symptoms of mental illness become visible to others in public settings, social control efforts are more likely to be forthcoming (Clausen & Yarrow, 1955).

The public visibility of deviance does not necessarily lead to effective case gathering. For example, certain ecological areas in most cities become centers of drug dealing, prostitution, gambling, and other deviant activities. Social control agents know when and where offenses are likely to take place so have the capacity to observe deviance. Because offenders share this knowledge, symbiotic relationships of bargaining and exchange often develop between deviants and control agents. Deviants are ignored as long as they keep actions within defined places or compensate control agents. In such cases, the predictability of deviance leads not to detection but to the corruption of social control agents.

The social organization of deviant behavior is also related to its visibility. Some types of offenses are especially difficult to detect not only because they are not visible to control agents but also because they have no direct victims. The social organization of many white collar offenses, for example, limits their visibility and prevents the establishment of effective case gathering mechanisms. Many white-collar offenses such as embezzlement, price overcharging, collusion, fraud, or insider trading may be unknown to victims as well as to control agents. Unless informants who are participants in the criminal activity come forward, agents of social control have no means of uncovering cases.

Infiltration

When control agents are unable to observe deviant activities, infiltrating deviant groups is an alternative means of case gathering. Because the difficulties of observing deviance in most settings are so great in modern societies, control agents often attempt to infiltrate deviant groups (Marx, 1988). This is especially likely when deviance is both hidden from direct observation and victims are unlikely to report offenses. For example, victims involved in potentially shameful activities such as patrons of prostitutes or drug dealers who are robbed; dupes of get-rich-quick schemes who are swindled; or buyers of drugs who obtain oregano rather than marijuana are not likely to bring offenders to police attention. Conversely, if offenders are able to involve victims in shameful activities, they should become more immune to official control. Undercover agents, however, might be able to witness or provoke these activities.

Politicians taking bribes, securities dealers trading inside information, businessmen defrauding consumers, or members of groups with politically unpopular opinions may not be detectable without the use of undercover agents. Social control systems can often only gain access to such cases by infiltrating deviant groups.

In contrast to other forms of proactive control, social conditions in large, heterogenous societies may enhance the possibility of infiltration: *The ease of infiltration of deviant groups is related to the anonymity of social life.* Because many transactions in modern societies involve relative strangers, anonymous social control agents can more readily penetrate deviant networks.

Exchanges of contraband materials in networks that rely on contacts with many relative strangers should be relatively easy for control agents to infiltrate. Lucrative drug trading, for instance, depends on dealing with a high volume of people who are not well-known to dealers. Control agents who adopt appropriate dress, speech patterns, and demeanor become indistinguishable from genuine clients. However, such strategies are typically only effective in detecting relatively low-level dealers because leaders of networks shield themselves from direct interactions with all but a few closely trusted accomplices (Ekland-Olson *et al.*, 1984).

In contrast, when criminal activities occur within tightly knit groups whose members know one another, penetration is extremely difficult. For many years, organized crime groups based on strong ethnic and kin ties were strongly resistant to official penetration because of the intimate ties between members. In such cases, social control agencies must somehow obtain the cooperation of individuals who are known and trusted by the deviant subculture. Often, they must turn to vulnerable insiders, such as members of the subculture who have already been caught. In such cases, authorities can trade lenient punishment in exchange for the undercover reporting of deviant activities through mechanisms such as wiretaps, hidden cameras, or pocket tape recorders. However, such members have inherent problems of credibility before juries so their efforts often ultimately fail. Nevertheless, when criminal activities are hidden, infiltration is often the only possible method of gathering deviant cases.

Settings that rely on transactions between strangers lend themselves not only to infiltrating deviant networks but also to provoking illegal actions. For example, rules that forbid discrimination in housing are easily enforced through proactive methods (Mayhew, 1968). Housing sales or rentals are publicly advertised, and undercover social control agents are indistinguishable from other strangers who might be interested in obtaining housing. Further, control agencies can readily vary the racial, gender, or marital composition of potential buyers. When such circumstances exist, motivated social control agents can readily elicit deviant behavior through proactive means.

Victim-Offender Relationships

The relationship between the victim and offender predicts the effectiveness of case-gathering systems: *The effectiveness of case gathering is inverse to relational distance.* People victimized by intimates are unlikely to mobilize official social control agents (see Chapter 8). Emotional bonds, dependence on the victimizer, and norms of privacy render reporting unlikely.

Control agents have more limited access to institutions that are considered private (Laslett, 1973). Because victimizations between intimates are also the most likely sorts of deviance to occur in private settings, social control agents are unlikely to observe them. Official social control systems will always face great difficulties in gathering cases of deviance between intimates.

When harm arises within intimate social space, victims themselves are unlikely to mobilize official agents. Husbands who abuse wives, parents who beat their children, or children who harm elderly parents have traditionally been invulnerable to official social control. Victims of such abuse are often restrained by norms of privacy or fearful of retaliation if they mobilize official control agents. Especially when households do not include nonfamily members and interactions of family members take place in the home, official social control over families is minimal (Laslett, 1973).

Not only conflicts within families but also conflicts between friends and neighbors are unlikely to generate reactive mobilization. In intimate social space, informal norms of cooperation are supposed to prevail over legal ones in decision making. The long-term costs of lasting bitterness, alienation, and retaliation from mobilizing legal control are usually higher than the short-term benefits from prevailing in the particular conflict (Ellickson, 1986). When people balance the potential gains from mobilizing social control with tolerating or avoiding problems, they are likely to choose the latter.

Much deviance among intimates occurs in private space and is not observed by any outsiders. However, even if deviance among intimates is witnessed, bystanders are often unwilling to mobilize official control. In some cases, norms of privacy dictate that strangers "mind their own business" when they observe deviance among intimates. In other cases, neighbors, friends, or acquaintances have ties to both parties in conflict and do not wish to take sides. Authorities such as teachers, social workers, or physicians also may fail to recognize or report possible violence among intimates. Official control agents have always been reluctant to intervene in the affairs of intimates. In addition, physical abuse is usually only one of various interpretations of the causes of the symptoms they observe. Formal control is not only ineffective in intimate social space because victims will not come forward but also because observers are less likely to report violators.

Finally, case gathering is most difficult for violence between intimates because official agents who are mobilized are reluctant to apply severe sanctions to offenders. Officials share community norms that dictate offenses between intimates are inappropriate for official intervention. In addition, police, prosecutors, or judges face great practical problems in dealing with such cases. Victims are unlikely to pursue cases, provide evidence, or testify in court (McLeod, 1983). The low probability of ultimate sanctioning, combined with cultural norms against official penetration of private spaces, renders case gathering difficult when offenders and victims are intimates.

The legal control of intimate social space is inherently problematic. Because proactive penetration of intimate space is not viable and victims will not readily mobilize official control, deviance in private relationships is relatively immune to official social control. Unless the harm created generates an unusual degree of moral outrage, people victimized by others in close social space will rarely mobilize official control. Although much recent legislation mandates case reporting for cases of violence among family members (Crystal, 1987; Ferraro, 1989; Kalmuss & Strauss, 1983), programs that try to prevent the abuse of spouses, children, or elders will find it difficult to gather cases of deviance among intimates.

Several developments in modern life, however, increase the possibility of detecting cases of intimate violence. When intimates do not have dependent relationships, victims are more likely to mobilize official control agents (Black, 1980, Chapter 5). As spouses, parents, and children become less dependent on each other and norms of privacy weaken, the reluctance of intimates to report victimizations decreases. Violence in intimate space should increasingly come to engender the same mobilization behavior that once marked only distant relationships.

In addition to the weakening of interdependence among intimates, victims and potential victims have banded together in organizations that promote victims' rights. The presence of such organizations of victims and their advocates promotes awareness of harm, efficient reporting, and rewards for reporting. When feminists, civil rights advocates, or victims of family violence organize, consciousness of harm and resulting reporting of perceived victimizations increases. Organizations of victims not only promote rights consciousness but also diminish potential shame from reporting. For example, women who find support in groups or shelters for battered women lose their reluctance to report victimizations (Browne & Williams, 1989).

The emergence of organizations devoted to victims' rights has increased the willingness of victims, observers, and control agents to report harm. For example, people who experience discrimination in their jobs or finding housing may be uncertain whether they have a sustainable legal claim (Miller & Sarat, 1980-1981). Those who are isolated are unlikely to pursue a grievance. Successful claimants are ones who band together with other victims and enlist the aid of government and private organizations (Burstein & Monaghan, 1986).

The growing organization of victims and declining privatization of intimate space has also led to a change in the behavior of social control agents. Police, physicians, teachers, and social workers are losing their reluctance to intervene in formerly private spaces, rendering abusers of intimates more vulnerable to official action. The exertions of women's groups, for example, have led control agents to be increasingly likely to view women as victims rather than participants in rape and family violence (Ferraro, 1989). In the same vein, the efforts of civil rights organizations have led crimes by whites against blacks to be viewed as equally severe as those of blacks against whites. Correspondingly, victims, observers, and control agents now seem more likely to pursue cases against victimizing males, whites, and higher class offenders.

The decline of interdependence among intimates coupled with the growth of organizations has promoted awareness of harms and help seeking that increase mobilization among formerly powerless segments of the population. The changing nature of social relationships is leading violence among intimates to become indistinguishable from violence at greater social distances (Sherman & Cohn, 1989). The reporting of such incidents has increased dramatically over the past decade and, if current trends continue, should continue to grow.

Control Agents

The costs of reporting not only to victims and observers but also to control agents shape the effectiveness of case gathering. These agents are unlikely to report deviance when the costs of processing are too high or the future rewards for doing so are too low.

When the time and effort involved outweighs the gain in enforcing the law, control agents may fail to process cases. Police may release petty offenders or the mentally ill who are not amenable to routine processing (Bittner, 1967); insurance adjustors may settle even claims they know are false to avoid the excessive paperwork involved in proving their suspicions correct (Ross, 1970); therapists may turn away severely ill patients who take too much time and effort (Peyrot, 1982). At the aggregate level, social control systems that have more capacity to acquire and process cases are more effective. With crime rates held constant, the greater the number of police and expenditures on police forces are among the best predictors of the proportion of crimes cleared by arrests, prosecutions, and convictions (Liska, 1987).

Although instrumental aspects such as the size, funding, and convenience of control agencies are important predictors of case acquisition, the values of controllers toward the control effort are also crucial predictors of effectiveness. Social control agents have the capacity to subvert rules if they do not share the values promoted by legislation, judicial decisions, or higher bureaucratic authorities. Police, prosecutors, and judges may not consider the control of violence within families a high priority (Berk *et al.*, 1982). Police may release obviously drunken offenders if they believe that the punishment mandated by drunken driving legislation is too harsh (Ross, 1986). Screeners for mental health agencies may turn away clients such as drug abusers, persons referred from the criminal justice system, or involuntary patients if they believe they are not "appropriate" subjects for treatment (Peyrot, 1982). Social control system are likely to be ineffective when official agents are unwilling to process cases, whether through instrumental or normative factors.

Distance of Victims from Control Agents

Not only factors influencing victims and offenders but also the distance between victims and control agents shape the probability of reactive mobilization: *The mobilization of social control is inversely related to the social distance between victims and control agents.* Victims who are socially and culturally akin to control agents are more likely than distant ones to mobilize official control. In contrast, victims at a great social distance from control agents underreport crimes and other harm. When problems arise, people utilize generalists such as physicians and clergy at a close distance before calling upon specialists at a greater social distance (Eklund-Olson, 1984; Horwitz, 1977b).

Victims who share a common culture with control agents will be more likely to report crimes, seek compensation, pursue negotiation, or enter therapy. Cultural congruence is especially important for systems of persuasive control. People who voluntarily mobilize therapeutic and conciliatory control are those who share the social, cultural, and psychological characteristics of control agents (Horwitz, 1987). The result is that the problems that enter these systems are predominantly those of higher status, well-educated, and professional people (e.g., Marmor, 1975).

In contrast, people with similar problems at a greater social and cultural distance from therapists resist entry into treatment. Hence, persuasive control systems are especially ineffective in bringing their services to the poor, minority, and isolated people who may need them the most. On the other hand, when reporting outlets such as shelters for battered women or rape hot lines that diminish the social space between crime victims and reporting outlets emerge, the likelihood of reactive official mobilization should increase (Browne & Williams, 1989).

Summary

The nature of modern social life insures that social control agencies do not have ready access to deviant cases. The number of cases that arise, the low visibility of behavior, and the ease of exit for offenders makes direct detection of deviance difficult. Although, in theory, proactive control provides the most direct and efficient case gathering for social control systems, in practice the nature of deviant activity and of social organization usually prevents the establishment of such systems. Proactive control can occur when deviance arises in tightly knit groups or in public places and when offenders cannot exit the settings of their deviant activity. In addition, criminal networks that depend on dealings with strangers are vulnerable to penetration by undercover control agents. In most settings, however, proactive case gathering is not feasible.

The inability to gain proactive access to deviance forces most social control systems to rely on reactive methods of gaining cases. The size, fluidity, and heterogeneity of modern populations make most social control efforts dependent on reactive notification by victims, observers, or offenders. Several factors affect the ability of social control agencies to acquire cases. Victims or observers must believe that they have more to gain from reporting some offending behavior than from tolerating the victimization. The likelihood of reporting grows when victims and bystanders are socially close to control agents and socially distant from offenders. The promise of instrumental rewards enhances reporting whereas factors such as the time and cost involved in reporting diminishes the chances of official mobilization. Finally, the costs and values of control agents, as well as of victims and observers, encourage or impede the efficient acquisition of cases. When social factors are not conducive to the reporting of harm, social control processes cannot be effective.

The willingness of victims, observers, and control agents to report crimes is not constant over time but constantly changes. The most effective control systems will be ones that can promote value congruence between themselves and the citizenry. This congruence can occur not only when the values of citizens come to coincide with those of controllers but also when the behavior of controllers changes. However, the heterogeneous nature of modern societies insures that many cases of deviance will not be reported, so many offenders will inevitably escape sanctioning.

EFFECTIVE TREATMENT

Introduction

Once they acquire cases, effective social control systems must apply sanctions or rewards that produce desired change in deviants. Coercive control systems must administer sanctions that punish, deter, or rehabilitate. Consensual systems must apply techniques that achieve changes in relationships and personalities. In both cases, effective change only results if efforts within the control system carry over into the natural social setting of clients.

In consensual control systems, social control personnel work cooperatively with clients to achieve desired change in relationships and individuals. The key aspect of effective therapeutic control is the establishment of a strong relationship between therapist and client that generates change. Considerable research in psychotherapy indicates that, with some exceptions, particular therapeutic techniques have no impact on shaping outcomes (Bergin, 1977; Casey & Berman, 1975; Frank, 1973; Smith *et al*, 1980). Regardless of their particular intellectual allegiances and techniques, therapists of all schools who display "interests, understanding, respect, dedication, and trust" that characterize all strong interpersonal relationships produce more positive outcomes than others (Bergin, 1977, p. 10). Therapeutic relationships that feature powerful bonds between therapist and patient that are marked by warmth, empathy, and genuineness promote positive change (Lofland, 1969).

The essential qualities of effective conciliation are those that generate consensus between the parties in conflict. Settlements reached by consensus are more likely to generate obligation than orders imposed by authorities. The consent of both parties to a solution generates a sense of duty and leaves both sides with a just feeling that produces compliance with decisions (McEwan & Maiman, 1984).

The treatment of deviants through coercive control is inherently more difficult than through consensual control. Coercive systems can easily incapacitate deviants for defined periods of time but cannot create the conditions that promote conformity after the period of punishment is over. As with therapeutic control, strong and positive bonding must develop between control agents and offenders if the motivation to change will occur. Yet such bonds are extremely unlikely to develop within coercive situations. Because individuals are involved in a punishment process against their wills, they will be more likely to resist than to cooperate with imposed efforts at change. Rehabilitation is always problematic in any punishment-oriented setting (Lipton, Martinson, & Wilks, 1975).

In addition, coercive systems face a basic contradiction in reintegrating offenders into the community after they have been sanctioned. On the one hand, one of the purposes of sanctions is to stigmatize offenders and uphold the social norms they have broken. On the other hand, this stigma must be eliminated if offenders can be reintegrated effectively into the community after the punishment process is over. It is difficult to accomplish both ends simultaneously. Because of these inherent difficulties in administering coercive sanctions, coercive systems should not have much ability to apply effective and lasting sanctions once the immediate period of punishment is over.

Social Ties

The social context of the treatment effort predicts the types of societies within which treatment is likely to be effective, the types of programs that are likely to produce effective change, and the types of individuals who are likely to benefit from treatment.

Different types of societies are more or less conducive to effective treatment: *Effective treatment is related to the degree of social integration.* Small, close-knit, and tightly integrated societies are better suited than large, individualistic, and heterogeneous societies to treat deviants. Treatment in socially integrated groups is effective for several reasons: limited differentiation of healers from other members of the group; shared beliefs in the ideology of the healing system; mutually reinforcing informal and formal treatment efforts; and the ease of reintegration of the treated individual into the group. Each of these factors serves to strengthen the bonds among controllers, deviants, and the social network.

Small, homogeneous groups should be the most likely settings for bonds productive of positive change to develop. In such groups, healers are not highly differentiated from patients but share most life circumstances and identity categories with them (Lofland, 1969). The close social distance between therapists and patients in such groups is conducive to the development of strong bonds.

Faith that a therapeutic technique will work also predicts how effective that technique will be (Frank, 1973). Change efforts are enhanced when both healers and patients share a common culture and belief system that produces mutual confidence in the change effort. This self-fulfilling nature of change efforts should be most common among patients and therapists in small, homogeneous groups (Horwitz, 1982).

A third reason for the greater success of healing in tightly integrated groups lies in the involvement of the change effort in many aspects of a patient's life. The therapeutic effort is not radically differentiated from the rest of the patient's life but is integrally involved with it. Family members, kin, neighbors, and other members of the group all participate in healing efforts (Horwitz, 1982). Hence, the efforts of informal group members reinforce those of the healers.

Finally, in tightly knit settings, once treatment has occurred, the deviant is considered cured and is accepted back into the group. Deviance does not become a master status that defines the basic identity of the individual (Becker, 1963). Rather, because people know so much about each other, it is only one aspect of a more complex social identity. Therefore, stigma does not linger, and the treated individual is not placed in a special social role (Waxler, 1974). After people have complied with any penalties that have been imposed on them, they resume their normal status and roles and are not considered persons of any special kind (Furer-Haimendorf, 1967, p. 211). In addition, the nature of roles in societies that are not technologically advanced is such that the available opportunities for work may conform to realistic possibilities for performance (Lefley, 1987). Work roles are neither too complicated nor too demeaning to perform.

Large, heterogeneous societies, in contrast, lack the social conditions that underlie effective treatment. Indeed, typical modern therapeutic relationships display precisely the opposite characteristics from those that should facilitate positive change.

In modern societies, treatment agents engage in highly differentiated activities that are an aspect of a formal occupational position. The job of a therapist is to relate to strangers in specialized ways (Lofland, 1969). Exposure is limited to the confines of an office for a limited amount of time each week. Therapists offer no practical aid other than the therapy itself.

Therapists in modern societies are typically trained in esoteric knowledge systems not shared by their clients. The absence of a common culture is exacerbated when much relational distance exists between highly educated, older, white therapists and their often poor, young, and minority clients. Such conditions are unlikely to lead to highly charged yet warm and positive relationships between therapists and clients.

Modern life lacks not only relationships between patients and therapists conducive to effective treatment but also mutually reinforcing efforts between informal relational networks and formal treatment efforts.

Change attempts typically occur solely between identified deviants and therapists. Members of the informal network are rarely involved in treatment. Instead, families are often rejected, blamed, or confused by what professionals do (Lefley, 1989).

The responses of informal groups in modern societies rarely reinforce those of professionals. In some cases, the informal network may display hostile and rejecting attitudes toward the identified patient (Vaughn & Leff, 1976). In other cases, group pressures can convert intended stigmata into status symbols (Zimring & Hawkins, 1973). For example, juvenile gang members who are released from jail may find their status enhanced in the eyes of their peers because they have been incarcerated (Werthman, 1967). In heterogeneous modern societies, informal reactions often do not reinforce official efforts.

Finally, once sanctions have been applied, modern societies have difficulties reintegrating the sanctioned or treated individual. Because people in individualistic societies know much less about each other, a deviant status such as "criminal," "mental patient," or "alcoholic" becomes an easy way to categorize individuals (Wilkins, 1964). Deviant labels can provide a master status that overrides other possible identity categories (Becker, 1963). In addition, the provision of skills that would make the rewards from conformity greater than those from deviance are a necessary aspect of any successful change effort. Control processes that have produced criminals who have learned job skills, patients who are aware of oedipal conflicts, or delinquents who are motivated to obtain high-school diplomas must be reinforced by opportunities within the community. Yet, socially desirable and lucrative jobs may be beyond the capacity of ex-deviants to attain. Legitimate opportunities may be confined to unrewarding, low-level, or demeaning jobs. Clients who have no skills that would allow them to earn a decent living are unlikely to find that the rewards of normality outweigh the benefits of deviance. The nature of opportunity in modern societies insures that many people will find deviance more rewarding than conformity.

Despite the presumably more powerful knowledge base and technological capabilities of modern societies, the treatment of deviants is more effective in simpler settings. For example, even serious mental illness in tribal groups is of relatively brief duration and has minimal lasting consequences for the disordered member. In Mauritius, 62% of schizophrenics had favorable outcomes compared to 49% in Great Britain (Murphy & Raman, 1971). Another study of over 1,300 cases of schizophrenia in 10 countries indicates that the outcomes for core cases of this disorder are more favorable in developing countries than in modern Western ones (Sartorius, Jablensky, & Shapiro, 1978). The researchers who conducted this study were so surprised at these results that they conducted a further follow-up a decade later. In this latter study, 56% of schizophrenics in developing countries compared to 39% in developed societies had favorable outcomes. In contrast, 40% of patients in the developed countries but only 24% of those in developing countries had very negative courses of illness (Sartorious, Jablensky, Korten, Ernberg, Anker, Cooper, & Day, 1986). The presumably more advanced knowledge and techniques underlying therapy in modern societies produce worse outcomes than supposedly more primitive techniques based upon mistaken beliefs.

Within modern societies, as well, the greatest positive changes among the mentally ill occur among persons who are tightly integrated into highly accepting social networks (Jenkins *et al.*, 1986). Regardless of the therapeutic technique or belief system involved, tightly bonded groups that respond to deviance through solidifying family and community ties are best able to quickly and easily reintegrate errant members into the group with little stigma, blame, or sense of difference (Braithwaite, 1989; Waxler, 1974). In contrast, efforts at therapy that ignore the family, peer, and community networks that influence individual behavior are usually unsuccessful (Coates, 1981).

The effectiveness of conciliatory styles of social control is also higher in egalitarian groups where disputing parties share a common culture (Todd, 1978). In such settings, both parties share common ties to others who can push them to accept compromise settlements. In modern societies, conciliation is most effective when the parties involved want to or must continue their relationship in the future (Braithwaite, 1989, p. 135-136; Felstiner, 1984; Witty, 1980) Where social bonds are fragmented, successful conciliation is less common. When disputes arise at greater social and culture distance, they are more likely to engender efforts to maximize individual gain rather than to reach mutually acceptable outcomes (Felstiner, 1984; Witty, 1980; Ynvesson, 1978).

Treatment Programs

The nature of social bonds predicts not only the sorts of groups that should apply the most effective treatment but also the types of programs that generate the most effective change: *Effective treatment is related to the degree of bondedness between clients, their social networks, and the treatment program.* Treatment programs that involve more aspects of individuals' lives, that provide all-encompassing belief systems, and that mobilize members of the informal network should be effective in all social settings. In contrast, individualistic relationships between patients and therapists applied in cultural and social vacuums should have little ability to change behavior.

Successful treatment programs in modern societies reproduce some of the control techniques that are effective in premodern settings. Programs that create enveloping environments, provide powerful ideologies, have minimal differentiation between therapists and clients, and involve network members as well as patients appear to achieve better results.

The Alcoholics Anonymous (AA) program is a prototypical program that provides clients with a powerful ideology, wide-ranging and time-consuming therapeutic activities, and therapists with similar identities to clients. In addition, family members are recruited into the therapeutic process. The AA program involves an enveloping round of group activities that provide members much moral and emotional support as well as practical aid and advice (Fingarette, 1988; Trice & Roman, 1980). Group meetings take place every night of the week, special activities are held on weekends and holidays, and members are encouraged to have only other AA members as friends. Spouses and children of AA members also often become involved in the therapy process through adjunct programs such as Al-Anon and Al-Ateen. Membership in AA becomes as encompassing as possible for a middle-class person in American society (Lofland, 1969). In addition, AA provides members with an ideology regarding the causes and control of drinking that is grounded in a more embracing world view. It thus enlists members' beliefs as well as allegiances. Although it has proven difficult to conduct conclusive evaluations of AA programs, they do appear to have higher success rates than traditional professional therapies (Emrick, Lassen, & Edwards, 1977).

Programs that mobilize the beliefs and involvement of social network members, as well as clients, provide the most effective treatment. Likewise, particular therapists who engender powerful emotional bonds with clients provide the most effective therapy regardless of their intellectual allegiances or technological skills. This means that formal psychotherapy in modern societies should be no more effective than nonprofessional alternatives. Sympathetic and empathic individuals may provide as good or better therapeutic intervention than professionals in times of need.

Many studies indicate that the clients of therapists who lack formal credentials do as well or better than the clients of credentialed professionals (Anthony & Carkhuff, 1977; Berman & Norton, 1985; Durlak, 1979; Hattie *et al.*, 1984). Likewise, professional treatment for alcoholism does not seem to result in better success rates than what would occur naturally without professional intervention (Fingarette, 1988, p. 77). At best, professionals achieve comparable levels of improvement with clients across different types of problems, treatments, and outcome measures (Berman & Norton, 1985). Helping persons in the natural environment also may provide therapy as good as that from trained mental health experts (Bergin, 1971, p. 244). Much of what is called "spontaneous remission," when people become symptom-free without professional help, may actually result from the healing efforts of friends and family.

It should be much more difficult to produce effective change through coercive rather than consensual means, so overall success rates should be lower in coercive settings. Nevertheless, the same factors predict success in both settings. Relatively unbureaucratic, nonprofessional programs that use counselors who share many characteristics with clients produce the most positive change among inmates in the criminal justice system (Woodson, 1981). Inside correctional institutions, nonprofessionals trained in empathic skills produce positive effects on inmate change (Anthony & Carkhuff, 1977, pp. 109-111). Programs that link therapeutic efforts with intensive efforts to strengthen community and family ties also produce the most successful results (Coates, 1981; Currie, 1985, pp. 240-241). The treatment of criminals is most effective when community members actively participate in both shaming and reintegrating offenders (Braithwaite, 1989, p. 8).

Programs that enlist the beliefs and allegiances of clients are most successful in creating effective change. The nature of social life leads treatments in premodern settings to mobilize more aspects of individuals' lives, social networks, and belief systems. Nevertheless, those programs in modern societies that can develop these features seem more successful than those that apply particular techniques in isolation from other aspects of clients' lives. Likewise, therapists who engender strong emotional ties produce the most positive change. Neither professional credentials nor particular therapeutic systems, but the creation of strong, positive bonds between therapists and clients provides the most effective treatment.

Social Distance

The principle that indicates the sorts of groups and programs where therapy is successful also predicts the kinds of individuals who benefit most from therapeutic relationships: *Effectiveness is inversely related to the social and cultural distance between therapists and clients.* Therapists who share many social and cultural characteristics with clients should produce more positive change.

Similarity in social and ethnic backgrounds between therapists and patients leads to more accurate diagnoses (Loring & Powell, 1988) as well as higher success rates in therapy (Lambert, 1979). In modern societies, therapists tend to be of relatively high social status, education, and cultural sophistication. Clients who share these characteristics have more success in treatment. The best results are seen with those young, attractive, intelligent, and verbal clients who are close in cultural distance to therapists (Rosenberg, Prola, Meyer, Zuckerman, & Bellak, 1968). As therapists become more socially and culturally heterogeneous, social differences in effectiveness decline (Stern, 1977).

Psychotherapy is least effective with lower social class patients. They are less likely than higher status clients to seek therapy, be accepted for treatment, be regarded as suitable clients for therapy, and remain in treatment (Brody, 1968; Lambert, 1979; Lesse, 1968). Similar findings hold within coercive systems. Delinquents who are matched with therapists who share personality and social characteristics have somewhat lower recidivism rates than those who are used as unmatched controls (Palmer, 1973). Although social and cultural similarities do not inevitably produce strong and positive bonds between patients and therapists, they are conducive to the development of these relationships.

Conclusion

The location of change efforts in social space influences the effectiveness of social control attempts. Control efforts are most successful when they occur within tightly knit societies or encompassing treatment programs and when control agents and deviants share a common culture. Modern societies, however, have serious problems in implementing effective sanctioning systems. In many groups, the rewards from deviance are high enough and benefits from conformity low enough to offset potential sanctions. Informal reactions to deviance often do not reinforce official efforts. Further, access to cases becomes more difficult as societies grow and become more differentiated. Finally, treatment and reintegration rarely succeed in modern societies. Therapists provide isolated efforts at change that cannot mobilize faith or participation of network members in the change effort. Traditional styles of social control, in general, may have little effectiveness within the bounds of modern social structure. The next chapter examines the factors that shape whether social control systems can prevent deviance from arising at all, so that there would be no need for either detection or treatment.

11

Preventing Deviance

INTRODUCTION

The most effective possible social control system would be one that prevents deviance from arising at all. It could prevent deviant acts from occurring in the first place (primary prevention) or, if they have occurred in the past, prevent their reoccurrence (secondary prevention).[1] Successful prevention either attacks the root causes of deviance or raises the costs of deviance or rewards of conformity so high in the minds of potential deviants that they will not commit the action.

Social control systems cannot easily accomplish these goals. In some cases, genetic or biological sources that preventive efforts cannot influence lead to deviance. For example, rates of core cases of schizophrenia are relatively stable across widely varying cultural contexts, so little can be done to prevent these cases from emerging in the first place (Goldhamer & Marshall, 1953; Sartorius *et al.*, 1978). Many other matters that enter modern legal systems such as accidents, malpractice cases, or personal injuries are inevitable consequences of modern technology that might be limited in number but never entirely prevented.

Even actions that individual actors can control are very difficult or impossible for control systems to influence at an aggregate level. Demographic changes in the numbers of people at risk for behaviors such as delinquency, homicide, drug use, suicide, and depression are strongly correlated with rates of these behaviors (Hirschi & Gottfredson, 1983; Klerman, 1988). For example, an increase in the number of males between the ages of 15 and 24 will also result in higher rates of deviance, apart from any measures social control authorities might take. Other trends

[1]I do not distinguish primary from secondary prevention in this chapter because both try to stop the emergence of the deviant action rather than react to it.

linked to broad social changes such as growing divorce rates, single-parent households, or geographic mobility also influence rates of deviance but are impervious to the actions of control agents (Kramer, 1983). Still other factors that contribute to the production of deviant behavior such as domestic troubles, relational conflicts, or intergenerational tensions may resist intervention from social control authorities. Therefore, much deviance in modern societies will inevitably occur regardless of the efforts of social control agents.

In addition to factors that are impervious to preventive efforts, social control agencies themselves are not likely to have major preventive impacts. These agencies are established to respond to deviance once it has occurred, not stop it from happening in the first place. The entire social control apparatus from police and therapists to courts, prisons, and mental hospitals is designed to apprehend, process, and punish or treat deviants rather than to prevent their behavior from arising.

Despite the limited ability of social control agencies to prevent deviance, here, I examine the *variance* in the success of preventive efforts. Prevention ought to be more or less successful depending on the nature of social relationships. I examine two essential elements of prevention. First, controllers must communicate their ability to impose severe sanctions or to provide rewards to potential deviants. Effective social control efforts require that people believe the costs imposed by sanctions outweigh the benefits of engaging in deviant activities. Consensual systems should be able to communicate the rewards that will follow from help-seeking efforts. Second, official efforts must coincide with or be able to alter informal definitions of rewards and punishments. I consider these aspects of prevention in turn.

AWARENESS

Sanctions cannot have their intended impact if potential deviants do not know what they are. Yet the literature on prevention assumes rational choice based on complete awareness of formal sanctions (Williams & Hawkins, 1986). Most theories of effectiveness assume individuals weigh the costs and benefits of various alternatives and then, out of self-interest, fear, or respect for norms choose their course of action. In fact, however, the degree to which the objects of control efforts are aware of sanctions is highly variable.

Successful prevention depends not on the level of actual costs or benefits from control efforts but on the *perception* of these punishments or rewards (Tittle, 1980). Peoples' actions are based on their beliefs about what punishments or rewards will be forthcoming if they engage in certain behaviors. The sorts of communications they receive about the characteristics of sanctions and the sorts of direct experiences they have with social control systems shape these beliefs.

In coercive systems, effective sanctioning occurs when people believe that severe sanctions will be forthcoming after deviant acts. People must think that the penalties associated with sanctions are more powerful than the rewards they receive from deviating. The expected harm from sanctions does not inhere in penalties themselves but diverges across social locations. Some people may find the experience of arrest to be catastrophic, whereas others would regard it as a minor inconvenience. Definitions of harm diverge to such an extent that people at the bottom edge of the social scale may view the prospect of spending time in mental hospitals or prisons as a relief from wretched conditions in the outside world (Braginski, Braginsky, & Ring, 1969; Brown, 1987).

Not only the perceived costs of sanctions but also the expected rewards for conformity vary considerably in social space. Ghetto youth who do not view college as a realistic career alternative will not value school achievement highly. Nor will a job that pays the minimum wage have much appeal, especially compared to exciting and lucrative opportunities from drug selling (Sviridoff & Thompson, 1983). People who do not expect long-term opportunities in the conventional labor market will not be inclined to look for legitimate employment but will be receptive to criminal opportunities (Currie, 1985).

Consensual systems require awareness of the benefits that control systems can offer suffering individuals. These benefits must be defined as greater than the costs of seeking help. The sorts of messages that are communicated to the population about the operation of social control systems are a key aspect of preventive systems.

The nature of social ties shapes both the accuracy of communication of rewards and punishment and the interpretations of the communications that are received: *Group size and bondedness predict the accuracy of communications about sanctions.* Small, homogeneous groups are marked by the accurate communication of rewards and sanctions. Information flows more easily through highly connected, morally homogeneous networks (Merry, 1984). In contrast, the communication of the costs and benefits of deviance in modern, heterogeneous societies is highly problematic. People in large, heterogeneous settings have few ways of obtaining accurate information regarding sanctions and must largely rely on transmissions from the mass media. Informal sanctions such as gossip, shaming, ridicule, or dishonor also atrophy as they pass through loosely connected, morally heterogeneous networks.

The communication of sanctions in small, homogeneous societies is not problematic. Indeed, the knowledge of sanctions is impossible to escape. Communication is direct and immediate so all members should have accurate knowledge of what consequences an erring member can expect. Gossip is an especially potent way to communicate information about deviance in closely knit groups where people are concerned about their reputations (e.g., Gluckman, 1963; Merry, 1984; Radcliffe-Brown, 1933b). Everyone knows who has been punished, stigmatized, or undergone therapy. For the members of small, tribal groups, the disapproval of fellow group members is a far more serious sanction than for members of modern societies where people are unaware of their past offenses (Furer-Haimendorf, 1967, p. 209).

Social control agencies in large, heterogeneous societies cannot take the awareness of sanctions for granted. Most persons will be unaware of how effective control systems actually are. The size, distance, and heterogeneity of the population prevents effective communication of rewards and sanctions. The citizens in most modern societies typically are ignorant, have mistaken knowledge, or misinterpret what information they have about laws (Ellickson, 1986). They know neither the probabilities of being caught if they engage in deviance nor the degree of punishment they will receive if they are caught. Analogously, knowledge of the potential benefits consensual agencies might provide is limited. Modern life is marked by a pervasive ignorance of how social control systems actually operate.

Further, informal channels in the modern world such as gossip and ridicule are also less likely to communicate sanctions or rewards. Growing size and heterogeneity means that persons who have in fact been sanctioned are more anonymous and less visible to others. Gossip as a force for social control atrophies and has little power to influence people who are unconcerned with their own or others' reputations (Merry, 1984). In addition, once sanctions have been applied they are easier to conceal. No one, other than those most intimate with deviants, need know of possible stigmatizations. Friends and neighbors may be unaware of mental hospitalizations, stays in reformatories, or treatment in alcoholism programs. In many modern communities, the loosely structured nature of social ties means many members have little information about each other and no social reputations to protect (Baumgartner, 1988; Christie, 1977).

Alternatively, people may exit from potentially stigmatizing situations by changing jobs, friends, or neighborhoods. Stigma is avoidable in direct proportion to the size and heterogeneity of the population. Hence, sanctions have little value as deterrents when people can easily move from situations where others are aware of their deviant status.

Because members of small, homogeneous groups ought to have a more accurate awareness of the certainty and severity of sanctions need not mean these systems are more effective in preventing deviance. This would be the case only if the actual sanctions for deviance are certain and severe. If, in fact, people can engage in deviance without being punished, this awareness would also be widely known. Hence, although information transmission in small close-knit groups should be more accurate, it is not necessarily more effective in preventing deviance.

Likewise, the widely mistaken beliefs about punishments or rewards in modern society does not necessarily lead to less effective social control systems. When the actual sanctions in coercive systems or rewards in consensual systems are low, communications that inflate estimates of costs and benefits are more effective than accurate ones. For example, it would not aid preventive efforts if people knew that they have about a 10% chance of being caught for a mugging in New York City and about a 10% chance of imprisonment if arrested (Shinnar and Shinnar, 1975). Similarly, messages that emphasize that therapy from professional psychotherapists has not proven to be more effective than help that nonprofessionals provide would not attract many clients.

It is not surprising that communications in societies that rely on the mass media to transmit information about the consequences of deviance emphasize the maximum penalties from sanctions or rewards from help seeking, not the actual chances of punishment or benefit. Both entertainment and news presented in the mass media focus on crimes such as murder that are most likely to lead to arrest and imprisonment and devote much attention to the legal processing of those persons who do get caught (Geerken & Gove, 1975). Likewise, the focus on therapeutic efforts emphasizes the rewards they bring to suffering people. Regardless of the actual state of affairs, effective control systems are ones that promote an awareness of swift and severe sanctions or immediate and beneficial treatments.

Another paradox of the communication of sanctions in modern societies is that those people who are most likely to engage in deviance will also have the most accurate information about sanctions. Under conditions of low certainty and severity of punishment, people who engage in crime or live in criminal environments will have the most accurate perception of punishment (Geerken & Gove, 1975). Based on personal experience, they can disregard communications that emphasize the swiftness and harshness of penalties. Hence, such messages may deter only those who would not have committed crimes in the first place. Modern societies face the problem of being able to deter those who are unlikely to commit crimes while having little impact on criminally prone individuals.

Large and heterogeneous societies thus face the double dilemma of communicating sanctions and rewards to distant and interspersed individuals about a system with minimal actual sanctions and rewards. The emphasis on the harshness of punishment may influence only those who are not prone to deviate in the first place. The people most prone to criminal activity, in contrast, obtain their knowledge of penalties directly, and what they learn might only encourage them in the direction of deviant behavior.

Interactional Costs

Effective preventive efforts require that people believe that sanctions will be forthcoming if they deviate and that these sanctions will outweigh rewards from deviance. However, official sanctions and rewards are never interpreted in a vacuum but are always defined relative to lay norms. What officials may define as punishing or rewarding may be defined in entirely different ways by the intended objects of sanctioning agents. Sanctions gain their power through individual desires to win the approval or avoid the disapproval of their fellows (Radcliffe-Brown, 1933b). How sanctions are interpreted and their resulting effectiveness are embedded in networks of interpersonal relationships.

Both relational costs and reputational damage are affected more by the responses of informal networks than by the characteristics of the formal sanctions themselves: *Interactional costs predict the effectiveness of preventive social control.* The most powerful aspects of sanctions lie in the interactional costs that result from a loss of reputation or social attachments (Williams & Hawkins, 1986). Formal sanctions, in themselves, have little power to alter behavior. Official social control is effective to the extent to which it has negative consequences on networks of interpersonal relationships.

Deviants or potential deviants look more toward the significant others in their intimate environment than toward formal rules and sanctioning agencies in weighing the consequences of potential actions (Ellickson, 1986; Macaulay, 1963; Tittle, 1980). Informal sanctions are more powerful than formal ones because coercive social control is effective to the extent that it harms reputational status and social attachments. Persons whose social position is such that sanctions will lower their esteem and standing in the group will be more responsive to control efforts. In contrast, when threatened or imposed punishments do not disgrace, their power is considerably lessened (Braithwaite, 1989; Zimring & Hawkins, 1973). Without shame that lowers social standing, punishment is inconvenient or physically unpleasant but has no lasting impact. In addition to reputational damage, the most costly sanctions are those that most intensely harm and disrupt valued attachments to informal networks (Ekland-Olson *et al.*, 1984).

The extent of reputational and attachment costs is highly variable. A prison term or stay in a mental hospital may leave social esteem and relational networks unchanged for some people but destroy them for others. If sanctions do not lead to a severing, loss, or weakening of social relationships, their costs will be low. Conversely, consensual rewards that lead to greater integration and enhancement of interpersonal relationships will be most effective in changing behavior.

Threatened or actual sanctions from friends and family are the best predictors of the effectiveness of sanctions (Andenaes, 1974; Anderson, Chiricos & Waldo, 1977; Braithwaite, 1989, p. 69; Paternoster & Iovanni, 1986). These sanctions have immediate and direct impact. When the values of subgroups contradict official values, they neutralize the impact of formal penalties. For example, marijuana use is up to six times more prevalent among college students when its use is approved by family and friends than when informal others disapprove this behavior (Anderson *et al.*, 1977; Meier & Johnson, 1977). When anticipated punishment from intimates increases to outweigh the rewards of deviance, rates of errant behavior are low. Hence, adolescents who have strong ties to parents and teachers refrain from delinquent activities (Hirschi, 1969; Shannon, 1982). As the importance of conventional family and work roles grows, previously delinquent youth become conformist.

Among adults, as well, informal sanctions have a stronger effect on deviant behavior than the perceived certainty of formal sanctions. The potential loss of respect from people one knows personally is the best predictor of self-reported deviance among adults (Tittle, 1980). In the workplace, the belief that co-workers will apply sanctions explains property and production deviance far better than expectations of the more formal responses of management (Hollinger & Clark, 1982). Or, among drug users, the most powerful predictor of behavioral change as a response to the threat of AIDS is whether one's friends are also changing their behaviors (Friedman *et al.*, 1987).

Informal sanctions are more powerful than formal ones because they have a greater impact on reputation, interpersonal attachments, and identity. People are more concerned with their standing in the eyes of family, friends, and colleagues than on impersonal legal authority (Braithwaite, 1989). The impacts that formal sanctions do have depend on the fear of possible informal sanctions that would follow from the formal ones (Tittle, 1980).

Individuals

The importance of interactional costs predicts the sorts of persons who are most likely to be influenced by preventive efforts at social control. Those who fear more loss of respect from intimate others if they are sanctioned should be more likely to refrain from deviance. Therefore, individuals who are tightly integrated into strong informal groups will be most affected by the impact of lay rewards and punishments: *Social integration predicts the effectiveness of preventive social control.* Hence, married people are more easily deterred than unmarried ones; the employed more than the unemployed; females more than males; older people more than younger ones; and middle more than lower status individuals. In contrast, efforts at prevention will be most difficult for socially isolated, marginal, and unconventional people who have least to gain from conformity and least to lose from deviance.

Age

In many times and places, adolescent males are most likely to participate in sanctionable activities (Hirschi & Gottfredson, 1983). Adolescents who have outgrown ties with families and rejected ties with school but have not yet acquired marital or work bonds are especially difficult to deter. Because many younger people have not yet acquired a strong stake in conforming to conventional roles, the costs of sanctions will not harm either reputational or social position. In many cultures, only unmarried sons can afford to commit acts of violence because such acts by married men or any woman would result in too dire consequences for their reputations (Schneider, 1971). In the United States, in both contemporary and Colonial times, groups with surpluses of young unmarried males feature high rates of violent crime (Greenberg, 1982). Many youths do not feel that contacts with the criminal justice system will lead to negative effects on interpersonal relationships with either family or peers (Mahoney, 1974).

Although young people in general should perceive fewer negative sanctions for nonconforming behavior than adults, there is much variation in the effectiveness of sanctions to prevent deviance among youths. Young people who have strong attachments to parents and teachers and who anticipate rewards from conventional activities in the future have low rates of deviance. In contrast, youths with few ties to family and school but strong attachments to nonconforming peers display the highest rates of deviance (e.g., Braithwaite, 1989, p. 28; Hirschi, 1969; Meier & Johnson, 1977; Silberman, 1976). The proposition also predicts the widely noted "maturing" effect on crime. Youths naturally mature into work, marital, and parental roles that are jeopardized by nonconforming behavior, so rates of deviance decline dramatically following adolescence and young adulthood (Greenberg, 1985). Thus, crime rates in England, France, and the United States indicate a sharp increase through the teen years to age 20 and a decline through the adult years (Cohen & Land, 1987; Hirschi & Gottfredson, 1983). When young people marry, have children, and get steady jobs, they become far more responsive to potential social sanctions.

Social Status

The success of prevention also varies by social status. Control efforts are least effective with persons who have the least reputational and interpersonal resources to lose if sanctioned. In all groups, people with the least status are most immune to reputational and attachment costs, so may engage in deviance with less fear of the consequences of sanctions than those higher on the status ladder (Homans, 1950). Poor members of the community, especially those who do not depend on wealthier members for their livelihoods, have little to lose from sanctions because their reputation will not suffer if sanctioned. Lower status people also reap the greatest rewards from deviance relative to their small gains from conformity. A universal problem social control systems face is that the nature of sanctions insures that they work least well for those people who are most prone to deviate. The combination of the ineffectiveness of punishment for deviance and inadequate rewards for conformity insures that social control will be least effective in responding to the deviance of lower status people.

The life chances of middle-ranking persons are more likely to be spoiled by criminal labels. They can lose jobs, homes, families, money, social position, respectability, and reputation, so typically should be highly responsive to potential control efforts (Braithwaite, 1982). For example, among the Sarakatsan shepherds in northwestern Greece, the middle-ranking four-fifths of families are roughly equal in wealth but are dependent on the wealthy few (Merry, 1984). Middle-ranking persons are most vulnerable to the economic pressure of kin, most in need of respect, most concerned to marry well, and least able to leave the community. Therefore, they are greatly concerned about the reputations of themselves and their families and refrain from committing deviant acts.

The position of many middle-class people in the modern world is similar: "A trusted cashier committing embezzlement, a minister who evades payment of his taxes, a teacher making sexual advances towards minors and a civil servant who accepts bribes have a fear of detection which is more closely linked with the dread of public scandal and subsequent social ruin than with apprehensions of legal punishment" (Andenaes, 1966, p. 964). This means that objectively similar sanctions in the criminal justice system have a more powerful impact on middle than lower status people because the same degree of sanctioning leads to more interactional costs. Lower- or working-class individuals may not lose their positions in the labor force or standing in the community, whereas middle-class people may have their entire future jeopardized as a result of criminal convictions. Therefore, prosecutors often provide more lenient sanctions to middle or higher status people while justifying them in the name of equality (Feeley, 1979, pp. 164-165).

For the same reasons, white youths are more strongly affected by criminal labeling than black adolescents, who are more likely to ignore or reject such labels (Jenson, 1972; Harris, 1976). Criminal labels have less impact on the psychological well-being of blacks than of whites because whites are more likely to be excluded from their reference groups after such labeling (Harris, 1976).

If sanctions are least powerful for lower status persons and most powerful for middle-ranking ones, they should produce the most variable impact among higher status persons. In some circumstances, the effectiveness of control efforts should vary curvilinearly with social class so that neither lower- nor upper-class people are strongly influenced by penalties. In other circumstances, however, sanctions have powerful impacts on higher as well as middle status people.

Social control may be ineffective in controlling the most powerful members of the group when they have resources that insulate them from the consequences of interactional costs. If their deviance is discovered, their influence and ability to countersanction control agents might prevent the application of sanctions so they have less risk of engaging in deviance. In some settings, the wealthy are insulated from sanctions by their economic power, which can amend for a lost reputation. For example, in Mediterranean societies, the reputation of a girl that has been damaged by involvement in premarital sex can be recovered through the payment of a large dowry (Loizos, 1978). Among the Greek Sarakatsans, already mentioned, the wealthy few were able to ignore gossip and other potential informal sanctions. Therefore, both the wealthiest and the poorest members of this group were relatively immune from sanctions:

> In general, people who ignore gossip are those who have significantly more or less power and resources, those who are not subject to economic and political control of those gossiping about them, those who are not entirely dependent on their local community for political support, economic assistance, or irreplaceable social relationships, and those who can leave the community easily. (Merry, 1984, p. 286)

In the contemporary United States, when physicians are sanctioned for malpractice, they typically suffer no negative effects on their practices but in some cases actually see an improvement because their colleagues sympathize and refer more patients to them (Cressey, 1978, cited in Braithwaite, 1989, p. 128). Likewise, politicians who resign from public office because of their misdeeds often find lucrative positions in the private sector. In these cases, there is no stigma attached to the deviance of higher status persons so sanctions will not have negative consequences. Both the people with the least status and those with the most wealth can ignore sanctions because their reputational status is not lowered.

In other circumstances, however, high-status persons should be highly sensitive to reputation and, like middle-ranking ones, be strongly influenced by control efforts. This may explain why some research finds strong deterrent impacts of punishment on higher status people, whereas other studies indicate no impact of punishment on this group (Grasmick, Jacobs, & Mccollum, 1983; Tittle, 1980). When punishment will disgrace them in the eyes of their colleagues, powerful people are easily deterred by sanctions (e.g. Braithwaite, 1989, Chapter 9; Clinard & Yaeger, 1980; Zimring & Hawkins, 1973). High-level executives, politicians, judges, or academics may suffer total disgrace if sanctioned. When sanctions have the power to alter the reputation and interpersonal networks of high-status people, they should have a powerful impact in shaping behavior.

Gender

In general, women are more sensitive than men to interpersonal relationships and personal reputations (Gilligan, 1982). The maintenance of respectability and interpersonal attachments has traditionally been of special importance for women, especially when they are not centrally engaged in economic and political institutions. Women are typically more integrated than men into families, friendships, and other informal relationships so should be more sensitive to the impact of informal sanctions (Hagan, Simpson, & Gillis, 1979). In addition, stigmatizing criminal labels should be more incongruent with female than male self-concepts (Toby, 1981). Because sanctions have more interactional costs for women than men, prevention should be more effective with women.

Most research indicates that women are more responsive than men to threats of social control. For example, after drugs were criminalized in the early twentieth century, females were far more likely than males to desist in the newly illegal behavior (Waldorf, 1973). Females seem especially concerned about the loss of respect from personal acquaintances if they commit deviant acts (Tittle, 1980). The greater female sensitivity to the feared reaction to deviance from important people leads them to have a far lower rate of delinquency than males (Braithwaite, 1989, pp. 92-94; Hagan *et al.*, 1979; Jensen & Erickson, 1978). Where gender role differences are slight, as among college students, gender differences in deterrability are small (Tittle, 1980, p. 15). This is predictable because the social location of male and female college students is very similar.

Women may also be more responsive than men to the benefits conferred by the patient or client roles in therapeutic or conciliatory control. Men resist adopting these roles, hampering preventive efforts at consensual control (Horwitz, 1977a, 1982, pp. 75-78). Women should be both more deterred by the costs of coercive sanctions and more influenced by the benefits of consensual control, rendering preventive efforts in both cases more effective with females than males.

Whenever the interactional costs of sanctions are high, preventive social control can be more effective. It is least effective among the young, lower status people, and men, who face less damage to reputation and social attachments from sanctions. Because these groups are also the most prone to develop deviant motivation, preventive social control is least effective with the kinds of people who need it the most.

Groups

Bondedness

The nature of attachment and reputational costs predict not only the sorts of individuals but also the kinds of groups that can exert the most effective social control. Groups that are small, intimate, and tightly knit have the power to influence reputation and attachment so can exert the most effective preventive social control: *The strength of group bondedness predicts the effectiveness of social control.* Groups with strong bonds, interdependent members, and shared norms are more likely than individualistic groups to have members who wish to do what is right in the eyes of their fellows. Sanctions in such groups create more attachment costs and reputational damage than those in individualistic groups. Just as individuals who are more socially integrated are more responsive to preventive social control, groups that are more homogeneous and tightly knit are better able to exert preventive social control over their members.

In tightly bonded groups, each individual is linked to the group through many interrelated elements. Sanctions produce harm in a greater number of important relationships, extend to a greater area of activity, and create more loss to the individual. Social roles are not segregated from one another so sanctions affect the whole person, not a limited area of life. In close knit communities, the threat of exposure to ridicule and shaming is a powerful deterrent because it bears on the entire self and cannot be escaped (Roberts, 1979). Individuals are enmeshed in networks of relationships that entail strong senses of obligation to the group. Therefore, the group can exert greater control over each individual.

Societies that feature strong interdependence between members and strong senses of communal obligation can provide the most effective preventive social control (Braithwaite, 1989). Modern Japan, for example, has extremely low crime rates because the close bonds between members lead to great shame when a deviant act occurs (Bayley, 1976). People refrain from crime because they do not want to disgrace their families, colleagues, or companies. Likewise families, schools, or companies that feature strong bonds can exert more effective prevention because their members are more concerned with the disapproval that will result from their deviance (Braithwaite, 1989).

As societies evolve from traditional to modern structures, they face great difficulties in exerting effective social control (Reiss, 1984). When individuals are not highly dependent on groups, they receive fewer rewards from conformity and face less attachment and reputational costs from sanctions. Individualistic groups are less able to impose informal sanctions that buttress the impact of legal sanctions. Interpersonal relationships become more isolated from collective obligations. In such settings, the ability of groups to impose effective preventive control declines.

The lack of dependency on the group that marks modern life allows individuals simply to disregard to opinions others have of them. For example, one factor associated with the growth of deviance among youth is weakened bonds between parents and children. The decline of close supervision by adults coupled with the rise of the automobile and an independent youth culture has resulted in a decline of informal control over adolescent activities. Compared to their parents and grandparents, adolescents now spend more time in unsupervised activities with other teenagers, and their parents are less likely to know where they are (Felson & Gottfredson, 1984). One result is a rapidly rising rate of youthful deviance in the modern world (Cohen & Land, 1987).

Similarly, attempted sanctions between people who share few or no group affiliations will have little impact. For example, in one urban housing project, gossip was only effective within separate ethnic groups (Merry, 1979). Members of the Chinese ethnic group that featured tight internal connections, much interdependence, and high costs of expulsion closely attended to what others said about them. Like members of tribes, they had no alternative but to continue their group attachments. For the black and white groups, in contrast, the ease of mobility and shifting attachments to different groups neutralized informal sanctioning systems. Sanctions were powerless to influence behavior across groups because people had no concern about what members of other groups felt about them (Merry, 1979).

The atomized nature of ties and easy movement across different groups that allows people to discount informal sanctions is typical in large, heterogeneous societies. As the degree of group bondedness decreases, the effectiveness of social control should correspondingly decline.

Congruence of Lay and Official Norms

Different sanctions and rewards may take on different meanings to community members and official control agents. The greater ability of tightly integrated groups to apply preventive sanctions need not indicate that *official* social control will be more effective when directed toward these groups. The impact of group bondedness on social control depends on whether group norms coincide with or diverge from official norms. The combination of group bondedness and the congruence of lay and official norms produces four ideal typical situations: Group ties may be strong or weak, and lay and official definitions may or may not coincide.

If informal norms contradict official norms, social control efforts will be less effective when directed at tightly knit groups. Only when lay and official norms coincide will preventive efforts likely to be successful: *Congruence between official and community sanctions predicts effectiveness.* Strong, informal groups produce more preventive control when their norms coincide with official norms but less effectiveness when the two sets of definitions diverge.

Official social control efforts are most effective when people are integrated into strong groups with conventional social norms. In such settings, official and lay definitions of deviance correspond. Social consensus validates the moral judgment of authorities. People refrain from deviance not only because they fear punishment but also because they do not want to do what is wrong. Official and informal controls tend to be complementary and mutually reinforcing. Public criticism, shame, and ridicule work to express and augment the stigmatizing aspects of punishment.

People in heterogeneous societies are members of numerous subcultures that do not share official definitions of deviance and conformity. The incongruity between informal norms and official punishments neutralizes or subverts the aims of control efforts. Indignation over crime diminishes as moral diversity grows. Within particular subcultures, offenders may not be seen as deserving of punishment but as entrepreneurs, heroes, or victims of their environments (Zimring & Hawkins, 1973).

When strong informal group influences contradict official sanctions, the degree of integration into social groups has the opposite effect on prevention. Prevention will be most difficult when people are both isolated from conventional groups and integrated into tightly knit groups that reject traditional values. This situation is often the case in modern heterogeneous societies that feature many groups with values that conflict with official ones. The presence of a strong subculture may neutralize or contradict official efforts at control. For example, juvenile gangs may view arrests or prison terms as signs of toughness highly valued by the group, neutralizing the stigmatizing functions of sanctions (Zimring & Hawkins, 1973, pp. 213-217). Rewards from deviance are immediate and direct, whereas rewards for conformity lie far in the future and may be difficult to visualize at all. In such settings, reputation depends on conforming to standards that contravene formal sanctions. For individuals with strong bonds to networks whose values clash with those of formal sanctioners, the rewards of conformity to the subculture outweigh the costs of sanctions. Social integration only prevents deviance when the values of the group coincide with those of controllers.

A corresponding phenomenon exists in consensual systems of social control. Socially and culturally distant populations will be less likely to share the definitions of the rewards from conciliatory or therapeutic control systems. They will be more likely to define psychotherapy as "headshrinking" than "therapeutic" and mental symptoms as "craziness" rather than "illness" (Friedson, 1970; Hollingshead & Redlich, 1958). Troubled individuals in close-knit communities that are suspicious of psychiatry resist entry into therapy (Horwitz, 1987). Just as the shameful qualities of punishment decline as social distance increases, so the perceived helpful qualities of therapy diminish with growing distance between control agents and their intended clients.

Example: The Social Control of AIDS

Efforts to prevent the spread of AIDS illustrate the importance for successful social control of both the nature of group ties and the congruence of lay and official norms. The response to AIDS illustrates that strong group bonds can work either to contravene or to reinforce official control efforts. In contrast, efforts to prevent AIDS among marginal and disorganized individuals have less impact.

Once the deadly effects of the AIDS virus became known in 1981, official reaction first attempted to alter the behavior of gay men. The gay communities in major metropolitan areas, especially San Francisco and New York City, featured tightly interconnected networks whose members had many ties to each other and strong group consciousness. Within these communities, the gay subculture was politically well-organized and activist. Subcultural norms promoted strong hostility and mistrust toward government authorities. Community norms also encouraged active sexuality featuring sexual encounters with many different partners. These often occurred in bathhouses, which were central institutions in the gay community (Bayer, 1989, Chapter 2).

The initial reaction of the gay community to the threat of AIDS was to oppose and resist the efforts of social control authorities (Bayer, 1989; Shilts, 1987). The defense of gay identity seemed to require resistance to any government intrusion on any form or location of gay sexuality. Limits on sexual activity such as efforts to close bathhouses were resisted as attacks on free choice and the gay life-style. Gay leaders also reacted with hostility and fervent opposition to government efforts at testing people who might possibly carry the virus or of notifying those who had contact with infected persons, fearing the violation of civil liberties and confidentiality (Shilts, 1987, pp. 541-542). Many public health officials as well as members of the gay community came to oppose measures such as bathhouse closures, screening of blood donors, or testing of high-risk groups, fearing intrusions on individual privacy, freedom, and choice (Bayer, 1989). Because of the opposition of the gay community, virtually no mandatory public health measures were adopted to combat the spread of AIDS.

As the death toll among gay men rose rapidly, the devastating impact of AIDS could not be ignored, and the attitudes of the gay community changed. The gay subculture began to educate itself on the disease and adopt control measures (Bayer, 1989; Shilts, 1987). Most gay men radically altered their sexual habits to eliminate high-risk sexual activity (Becker & Joseph, 1988; Doll *et al.*, 1987). The degree of change in communities with well-organized gay communities such as San Francisco were higher than in with weaker subcultures (Stall, Coates, & Huff, 1988). In San Francisco, for example, by 1985 one survey indicated that only 1 in 11 gay men was engaging in unprotected oral sex and only 1 in 14 in unprotected anal sex. More than half were involved in stable monogamous relationships (Shilts, 1987, p. 569). Eventually the gay community was fully mobilized to fight the AIDS epidemic through educational and therapy groups, telephone hotlines, fund raisers, and the provision of informal social support to stricken members.

The well-organized and tightly knit nature of the gay community had a different impact on prevention in different time periods. Initially, the strong oppositional nature of the subculture precluded efforts at preventive control. As the crisis worsened, however, the ability of the gay community to take organized action resulted in dramatic changes in high-risk behaviors and effective measures to stop initial infection. At both time periods, the effectiveness of preventive efforts depended less on government activities and more on the response of the subculture. When this subculture resisted change efforts, no preventive control developed, but when it embraced them, preventive efforts succeeded.

Efforts to control AIDS outside of the gay community have produced different results. Heterosexuals who contract AIDS are now nearly always intravenous drug users, their sex partners, or their children.[2] Most of these people are likely to be poorly educated members of minority communities who live in impoverished urban areas. Far from living in an organized and articulate community, they are marginal, disorganized, and isolated. Unlike the homosexual community, there are no organizations of drug users who can urge and implement informal behavioral change efforts. The fragmentation, absence of leadership, and lack of community among drug users render preventive efforts difficult to direct. The political and social integration that marks the gay community has no counterpart among intravenous drug users.

Predictably, efforts to prevent AIDS among intravenous drug users have had less success than among homosexuals. Unlike the gay community, which first actively resisted and then actively embraced preventive measures, drug users show far less substantial behavioral changes

[2]Initially, large proportions of heterosexuals who contacted AIDS were hemophiliacs and other persons who received blood transfusions. After protective measures for insuring an untainted blood supply were developed, almost all heterosexual cases now emerge among intravenous drug users and their sexual contacts.

than members of the gay community (Friedman *et al.*, 1987). Those changes that have occurred are more associated with changes in the behavior of small groups of fellow drug users than with efforts in the mass media, community institutions, or organized subcultures (Friedman *et al.*, 1987). Although AIDS has been contained among the gay subculture, it continues to expand among intravenous drug users.

The failure to prevent AIDS among intravenous drug users illustrates the problems that any effort at prevention will have among people who both lack cohesive organization and are at a great social and cultural distance from conventional social control agents. If, however, formal organizations of drugs users can be developed, effective behavioral changes should result (Friedman, de Jong, & Des Jarlais, 1988).

Successful Prevention

The fragmentation of modern life insures that preventive social control will often be difficult. Yet, in many cases, judicial and legislative rulings have resulted in fundamental and far-reaching changes. Laws regarding school desegregation, reapportionment, police practices, and abortion have created profound changes in the moral climate and social practices. Other laws have changed the behaviors of particular groups to conform with official intentions (e.g. Chelius, 1976; Danzon & Lillard, 1983). How has this occurred?

Many of the most significant judicial and legislative rulings that have produced effective change are not directed at individuals or informal groups but at organized and visible bodies. For example, many of the Warren Court decisions in the 1960s that profoundly altered the criminal law were directed at police departments. Because the actions of police are both centralized and visible, they often have little choice but to comply with new legal rules. Other important laws were also directed at public authorities. The *Brown v. Topeka Board of Education* decision, for example, is addressed to school boards rather than to parents, students, or teachers. Enforcement thus need be directed at only a relatively small number of visible official bodies rather than an immense number of individuals. Most other important court rulings that deal with subjects such as reapportionment or school prayer are also addressed to public officials rather than private individuals.

Other successful legislative and judicial activity is directed at organized private groups. For example, laws that attempt to alter rates of industrial accidents (Chelius, 1976) or medical malpractice claims (Danzon & Lillard, 1983) are directed at visible, regulated, and organized firms or professionals. In such cases, the objects of social control are likely to alter their behavior to conform with the law. Law in modern societies may have lost much of its power to regulate effectively the conduct of individuals, but it can regulate successfully the behavior of public bodies and private organizations. As large public and private organizations become more and more central in modern life, the effectiveness of law as a tool for social change correspondingly grows.

Conclusion

Preventive social control systems are most effective within small, closely knit, and homogeneous groups. Sanctions in these groups are known to all, create high reputational and interactional costs, and are reinforced by informal efforts. Large, individualistic, and heterogeneous societies have great difficulties in preventing deviance. For many people, the costs of formal sanctions are low, and informal reactions may neutralize official efforts. Although preventing socially integrated people from engaging in deviance is relatively easy, it is difficult to develop effective preventive control systems for the socially marginal, lower class people, and young males. The great social distance in modern societies between controllers and those they must regulate creates a demanding and obstinate task for preventive systems of social control.

Social structure shapes the effectiveness of social control. Groups that tightly grip their members are better able than individualistic ones to prevent people from deviating, discover them if they do deviate, and effectively treat them. The strength of social bonds that mark relationships in tightly knit groups at the same time magnifies the consequences of sanctions and prevents people from engaging in deviance. The ability of highly integrated groups to apply effective sanctions leads them to have less need to actually use these sanctions.

Earlier chapters showed how this aspect of tightly knit groups leads them to feature conciliatory and therapeutic styles of social control with a rehabilitative and group-centered focus. Holistic groups typically make little use of stigma or ostracism and easily reintegrate offenders. The paradox of social control in strongly bonded groups is that those sanctions that are maximally effective in preventing deviance are also least likely to be used.

In contrast, the size and heterogeneity of modern societies undermine both the conditions for effective case gathering and the attachment and reputational costs that give sanctions their binding power. Although the decline in the effectiveness of informal sanctioning systems leads to the need for more effective formal controls, the ability of official sanctions to prevent deviance among individuals is low. Modern trends such as urbanization, mobility, divorce, living alone, and the freedom of adolescents from parental control that lead to increasing rates of deviant behavior also produce social control systems that cannot effectively combat deviance.

Modernity is marked by both the need for effective formal social control and the absence of the tools that could provide effective prevention. The problems of social control in individualistic and heterogeneous societies are severe and intractable to simple solutions. We should not see a quick end to the convergence of growing rates of deviance with ineffective social control systems. Modern societies have generated many efforts to overcome their inherent difficulties in developing effective social control systems. The concluding chapter examines several of the trends that respond to the diminished effectiveness of social control.

12
Conclusion

Introduction

The central theme of this work has been that the structure of social relationships shapes the style, form, and effectiveness of social control. Fundamental changes in relational structures should, therefore, produce basic shifts in social control systems. In recent decades, particularly in the United States and some Western European societies, the most central social bonds have radically altered. Weakening ties between individuals and families and between families and communities lead to a deteriorating capacity of families and communities to exert informal social control. On the one hand, the decline of informal control is accompanied by an expansion of trilateral forms of control. The number of police, attorneys, psychotherapists, and other official control agents grows and the range of their functions expands. On the other hand, fragile social bonds often make tolerance, avoidance, or exit efficient strategies of control. People become reluctant to mobilize any sort of social control, and morality atrophies. The future of moral life may feature pendular swings between heavy reliance on formal control or on inaction in the face of deviant behavior. This chapter outlines some of the most important recent changes in social ties and sketches the sorts of transformations in social control systems that may follow.

Relational Change

Growing individualism has been one of the master trends in social evolution (e.g., Maine, 1861; Parsons, 1966; Popenoe, 1988). For most of human history, people were indivisible from their ties with extended kin groups. Identity, social interaction, and social roles were inseparable from one's place in kin and communal groups. Beginning about the seventeenth century in Western Europe and increasing most rapidly during the nineteenth century, ties with extended families declined, and nuclear families came to form the basic unit of social structure. Over the past few decades in the United States and some Western European societies, nuclear families have themselves weakened. Their members have become more autonomous, divorce rates have grown, the family fulfills fewer social functions, and the primacy placed on the value of family ties has declined (Popenoe, 1988). The result of this weakening has been an expansion of individualism as individuals become more isolated from strong family bonds.

Statistics on household composition in the United States illustrate the breakdown of nuclear families and the growth of individualism. Between 1950 and 1984, the number of people living in nonfamily households in the United States increased by 396% from 4.7 to 23.4 million while family households grew only by 60% from 38.8 to 62.0 million (US Bureau of the Census, 1985a). The greatest expansion of households, 405%, occurred among people who live alone. The proportion of people living in married couple households has consistently declined from 78% to 58% between 1950 through 1984. In contrast, over the same period, the percentage of nonfamily households has grown from 11% to 27% and the percentage of people living alone from 9% to 23%.

These figures indicate that people are now more likely to live alone or with others who are not relatives. Children are more likely to grow up in one-parent homes or in homes with a step-parent. Among family households, female householder families without a spouse grew by 175% and male householder families without a spouse by 74%. In contrast, married couple families grew by only 47%. The proportion of female-headed households has grown to encompass 13% of white and 44% of black families (Mintz & Kellogg, 1988).

Several factors account for these changes. Increasing numbers of young adults leave parental homes without establishing family households of their own. Young adults are marrying at later ages, delaying having children if they bear children at all, and having fewer children. Rates of separation and divorce have soared, although they leveled off in the first half of the 1980s. Even married couple households are less likely to have children in them both because of a declining birth rate and because older children have moved out of the home. Continuing geographic mobility splits children from grandparents, grown children from parents, and older siblings from one another. Greater longevity has increased the number of widows because women still live longer than men.

Even for people who remain in families, modern life has become much more individualistic. Families are now extremely loose knit relative to those in other times and places. They are very small, their members follow individuated daily routines, participate in few collective activities, often not even meals, have much spacial separation, few common possessions, and little long-term hold on their members. Middle-class people, in particular, participate in an atomized social structure marked by much mobility from place to place, participation in fleeting relationships, little contact with extended family members, and loose chains of association (Baumgartner, 1988).

The structure of modern communities, as well as of families, has drastically changed. The development of an automotorized society has led to the dispersion of homes, jobs, and shopping over a broad area (Felson, 1987). More and more people live in sprawling suburbs in large metropolitan areas. People can avoid spending time in the household and neighborhood and are freed to interact and spend their leisure hours with widely scattered others. Many married women are in the labor force, so residential areas are largely abandoned by adults during the daytime. High rates of geographic mobility and divorce mean that people frequently move in and out of areas. As interaction within families and neighborhoods declines, communities no longer have the capacity to exercise strong informal social control.

Not only the growth of suburbanization but also changes in inner-city neighborhoods result in the decline of effective systems of informal control. Over the past 30 years growing unemployment, nonparticipation in the labor force, welfare dependency, and the movement of the middle class and stable working class to suburbs has weakened the social organization of inner-city neighborhoods and communities (Wilson, 1987). The resulting high rates of property crime, drug abuse, alcoholism, and violence in turn reinforce the breakdown of community norms and create a self-perpetuating cycle of weak social control and high rates of deviance.

These structural changes lead to a diminished ability of informal groups to care for or control close relatives. Divorced parents have weaker ties to children who do not live with them, individuals who have moved to other parts of the country may be unable to participate in the care of infirm parents or disordered siblings, women who work have less time than housewives to control their children or care for their parents, and neighborhoods that are nearly abandoned by adults during the daytime have little capacity to control the activities of teenagers or strangers. Compared to prior generations, teenagers, especially girls, now face far less supervision of activities, are more likely to be away from home at night, and spend more time with peers and less with parents (Felson & Gottfredson, 1984). American families cannot exert strong informal social control over their children, who can easily evade adult surveillance.

In addition to the dramatic expansion of structural individualization, the interdependence of people that once characterized social life has greatly declined. For the most part, this has resulted from the increased independence of women. Fewer families now depend on men for their livelihoods as more women and children live in families without husbands or fathers. A majority of women, including women with small children, are now in the labor force. Although in 1950 in the United States, only a quarter of married women who lived with their husbands worked outside the home, by the late 1980s about 60% did so (Mintz & Kellogg, 1988, p. 204).

In addition to growing individualism and declining interdependence, a third master trend in social structure has been the growth of organizations. The number of incorporated organizations has expanded fivefold over the first seven decades of the twentieth century (Coleman, 1982). Increasingly, important social transactions are conducted between individuals and organizations (Black, 1989a, Chapter 3). Individuals are now likely to work in hugh organizations, shop in chain stores, send their children to day-care centers, live in condominiums, and play in recreational leagues. Fewer activities are conducted outside of the context of organizations. More and more transactions occur between individuals and organizations rather than between individuals.

Growing individualism, declining interdependence, and the expansion of organization foreshadow basic changes in social control systems. On the one hand, these changes produce a more atomized social structure that cannot exert effective informal control. The lack of strong informal control should produce a growth in formal, state-centered control (Black, 1976). On the other hand, a society composed of isolated individuals may not possess the moral consensus necessary to mobilize formal control, demand punishment, and reinforce formal sanctions with community pressures. The diminution of the informal control system can produce a general weakening of social control rather than a growth of powerful systems of formal control. Although the particular impact of changing structures of relationships is impossible to predict accurately, the new social structure will surely have an important impact on the style, form, and effectiveness of social control systems.

STYLES OF SOCIAL CONTROL

Penal Control

Major changes in relational structures should produce shifts in the styles of social control. Growth in structural individualism predicts a greater use of penal styles of social control. More and more victimizations occur between people who are not only relational distant but who also differ in cultural, ethnic, and social traits. Offenders and victims not only share few or no social ties but also lack ties to third parties who might arrange nonrepressive settlements. In addition, bureaucratization, large case loads, and impersonality within formal control systems increase the distance between control agents and offenders. The growing social distance between offenders, victims, and control agents all predict the expansion of penal styles of social control.

A second trend predicting a growth in penal styles lies in the greater independence of previously dependent populations. Equality between men and women leads women to be more willing to seek punishment instead of tolerating their victimizations. Equality also means that women will become more liable for their delicts and therefore subject to more punishment. As juveniles become more autonomous, their liability to punishment increases as well. Previously dependent populations are now more likely to both seek and be subject to punishment.

These structural changes have led to an expansion of penal styles in the contemporary United States. Overall, the number of persons subject to the legal sanctions of arrest, trial, and sentencing has greatly increased. For example, the rate of persons incarcerated in state or federal prisons more than doubled between 1970 and 1984 from 96 per 100,000 to 195 per 100,000 Americans (Currie, 1985, p. 32). The rate of persons under some sort of correctional supervision increased from 661 per 100,000 in 1965 to 921 in 1976 to 1,043 in 1983 (Cohen, 1985, p. 49). In the United States, capital punishment has been reinstituted and used almost exclusively for those who commit heinous offenses against others at great relational distance (Radelet & Pierce, 1985).

Some behaviors that were previously ignored, tolerated, or mildly sanctioned such as violence among intimates, drunken driving, illegal drug use, and even cigarette smoking (Austin & Garner, 1980) are now potentially subject to punishment. The growth of punishment is particularly apparent in the response to intrafamily violence. Police and courts increasingly intervene in domestic affairs when husbands victimize wives or parents beat children (Ferraro, 1989; Kalmuss & Straus, 1983;

Sherman & Cohn, 1989; Ferraro, 1989). A convergence of social and economic roles between men and women should also lead to greater equality in formal sanctioning (Kruttschnitt & Green, 1984). Likewise, juveniles are now more likely to be tried as adults and sentenced to prison terms. Although growing social distance and decreasing dependence are not the only causes for these changes, they are associated with the growth of punishment-oriented responses in modern life.

Yet, the same forces that lead to an expansion of punishment in some cases also insure that punishment cannot effectively respond to the problems that generate them. The conditions of modern life make it more difficult to create sustained and organized penal reactions to deviance. Victims and offenders are usually anonymous so are unlikely to confront each other again. People who lack powerful incentives to seek punishment, especially when social conditions make tolerance, avoidance, or exit highly feasible, often are inactive in the face of deviance (Baumgartner, 1988). Observers, too, are less likely to be acquainted with victims so rarely form organized support groups that demand vengeance.

The criminalization of some behaviors contrasts with the growing tolerance for divergent life-styles, sexual orientations, and living arrangements. Behaviors that were once stigmatized such as homosexuality, single parenthood, sex outside of marriage, or living with members of the opposite sex without marrying them are now more likely to be tolerated, ignored, or approved. Changes in social structure also predict this decline in penal response. When substantial proportions of people themselves live outside of traditional family arrangements or know others who do, it is difficult to sustain moral outrage at less conventional others (Greenberg, 1988). The growing individualism in social structure at the same time leads to a decline in punishment directed at people with nontraditional life-styles and a growth of penal responses for victimizations between intimates.

In addition, greater social heterogeneity, population size, and distance of control agents from community members predict not only more punishment but also less informal reinforcement of official sanctions. Offenders who have been subject to formal sanctions may not face informal shaming in communities, neutralizing the impact of official control (Braithwaite, 1989). When informal control does not reinforce the impact of formal sanctioning, effective punishment cannot occur.

Although legislators and social control agents strive to increase the scope and severity of penal styles, the social realities of modern life may continuously undermine their efforts. Women whose former spouses or boyfriends leave them alone may not care if legal sanctions are imposed;

communities of strangers may generate initial outrage at crime that quickly diminishes; individual victims can change apartments, jobs, or communities. Penal styles should continue to expand in the modern world, but are unlikely to provide effective responses to the problems that give rise to them.

Compensatory Control

Disputes result in compensation when conflicts arise between individuals backed by collective liability systems or between organizations. The growing presence of organizations and collective liability in modern life has led to a reemergence of compensation as a style of social control (Black, 1987). Compensatory systems can efficiently deal with problems created by accidents, injuries, pollution, and the like. Organizations are increasingly likely to create these harms. In recent decades, the amount of social control over organizations has greatly increased, usually through the imposition of compensation rather than punishment (Reiss, 1984). When harms result from organizational action, as should increasingly be the case in the modern world, compensation should be the resulting style of social control.

Compensation efficiently redresses much of the harm that organizations inflict on individuals and other organizations. Yet, compensatory systems can exacerbate the problems of upholding strong and enduring moral systems in modern societies. Insured people and organizations have little incentive to engage in conforming behavior because both conforming and deviant members will have relatively equal premiums. Strict liability systems, in particular, undermine deterrence by making people who err intentionally or accidentally equally liable (Lempert & Sanders, 1986).

Although compensatory systems provide more efficient methods of redress to victims than penal systems, they do not form the basis for moral order. Nor can compensation effectively redress harm that individuals cause each other (Stables, 1986). Despite the fact that compensation should expand and routinize in an organizationally based society, the growing monetarization of social response cannot provide a moral underpinning for systems of social control.

Conciliatory Control

The sorts of structural changes promoting individuation should undermine the relational ties that give rise to conciliation. The most common settings for conciliation are small, homogeneous, and tightly knit communities that have largely disappeared in the modern world. People in conflict who have little in common save their dispute have no basis for reaching conciliatory resolutions. Therefore, we expect a continuing decline in conciliatory outcomes in disputes between individuals. However, other social changes may enhance the chances of conciliating disputes beyond what would arise from the social relationships of the disputants themselves.

Recent decades have seen hugh growth in the number of lawyers in American society (Curran, 1986). Although the mobilization of these lawyers usually indicates a penal response to some injury, conciliation may be the ultimate outcome of solutions involving attorneys. Instead of directly dealing with each other, disputants purchase the services of lawyers to do their negotiating (Black, 1989a). Between people at an otherwise great relational distance from each other, attorneys can create a social space that is conducive to bargaining and compromise. Between intimates, attorneys can dampen intense hostilities and negotiate agreed-upon solutions (Sarat & Felstiner, 1986). The greater number and importance of attorneys in the modern world need not indicate a growth in litigiousness but rather an expansion of individuals whose professional roles involve the construction of negotiated solutions.

Another common setting for negotiation in modern life is when organizations have conflicts with each other or with individuals. Conciliatory solutions are common when organizations dispute with individuals (Ross & Littlefield, 1978) or other organizations (Galanter, 1974). Although growing individualization and social distance predict a decline in conciliation, the proliferation of lawyers and organizations may create the social space necessary for the persistence of conciliatory styles of social control in modern societies.

Therapeutic Control

The expansion of therapy as a technique of social control accompanies increasing individualism (Conrad & Scheidner, 1980). The number of persons providing therapy has exploded in recent decades (Mechanic, 1989). There has been a hugh expansion of professional therapeutic personnel including psychiatrists, clinical psychologists, social workers, school counselors, and psychiatric nurses as well as of quasi-professional therapists such as drug and alcohol counselors, community mental personnel, or street workers.

The growing number of people entering therapy corresponds to the greater number of therapists. Between 1955 and 1983, treatment episodes in organized mental health facilities increased from 1.7 to 7 million (Mechanic, 1989, p. 10). People also are more willing to utilize psychiatric services. In one large national survey conducted in 1957 and again in 1976, the number of people who would use professional help for personal problems rose from one-third to one-half, and the number who actually used help nearly doubled (Veroff, Kulka, & Douvan, 1981). Indeed, in the 1976 interviews, 26% of adults had actually sought professional therapeutic help.

Not only the numbers of patients and therapists but also the types of problems viewed as appropriate for therapeutic intervention has expanded. Although labels of mental illness were once reserved for only the most bizarre sorts of behaviors, over the course of the twentieth century therapy came to be viewed as the appropriate response to a much wider net of behaviors. Children who are disruptive in school, their parents who compulsively drink alcohol, or their siblings who are addicted to drugs are now likely candidates for therapy and are treated within medically oriented frameworks (Conrad & Schneider, 1980).

What accounts for the growth of therapeutic frameworks and interventions in modern societies? Individualistic styles of therapy are a logical outgrowth of social transformations. Geographic, social, and occupational mobility diminish extended family ties, and soaring divorce rates and declining social cohesion weaken nuclear family bonds. As individuals come to be more and more isolated from each other, the self becomes the central basis of existence. Belief in broader social institutions of religion and nation also weaken, whereas self-reliance and self-fulfillment become cardinal virtues (Bellah *et al.*, 1985). When motives, goals, and problems are grounded within the self, a logical response to deviant behavior is to change the individual personality. The rise of the therapeutic style is an outgrowth of changing social structures (Horwitz, 1982, Chapters 6-8).

Therapeutic social control, however, has only a narrow range of effectiveness. It can promote positive change when clients voluntarily cooperate and share common value systems with controllers. This is usually only the case when people share the educational, class, and cultural orientations of their therapists (see Chapter 10). The benefits of therapy for people who do not share this psychological culture have not been demonstrated.

Even for people who find therapeutic styles attractive ways to resolve problems, the benefits of therapy are limited. The enhancement of psychic gratification produced by successful therapy may only exacerbate the isolation that initially led people to seek the help of therapists in the first place. Modern therapeutic styles can detach people from social relationships, rather than strengthen the interdependence of patients with intimate others (Horwitz, 1982, Chapter 8).

In addition, the conditions of modern life usually prevent establishing effective change relationships within the typical professional interchange. Modern therapists are not able to interact with clients in an encompassing, multistranded way (Lofland, 1969). The therapeutic process is isolated from other aspects of patients' lives. Because of these limitations, the expansion of therapeutic styles of social control cannot solve the most troubling problems of social control that face modern societies.

Summary

Structural changes should produce growth in various styles of social control in different social locations. Each style intensifies in some locations and diminishes in others. Increasingly, the problems of intimates may be punished, middle-class and atomized individuals treated, and those of organizations redressed through compensation or conciliation. At the same time, we expect failure in penal efforts when individualism undermines shared senses of morality; in therapeutic attempts for people who do not share the social and cultural characteristics of therapists; and in arranging compensation or conciliation for disputes between individuals. Each style of control should persist, although with varying intensity, in different places in modern life.

FORMS OF SOCIAL CONTROL

Transformations in social relationships also change the forms of social control. Growing individualism has two divergent consequences. On the one hand, the decline of strong informal ties leads to a growing use of third parties to resolve problems of all sorts. When families, neighborhoods, and community institutions such as schools and churches are unable to control behavior, a growing reliance on state-centered forms of social control often results. As social distance between disputants increases and as more interactions involve strangers, more law should emerge to deal with conflicts (Black, 1976). Problems that once were tolerated become increasingly legalized. Spouse beaters, child abusers, malpracticing physicians, or discriminatory organizations become more liable to legal processing (Lieberman, 1981). Correspondingly, with growing numbers of broken families and more individuals living alone, the number of people seeking help from psychotherapists for personal problems should continue to expand.

On the other hand, modern social conditions often make it easier to walk away from conflicts than to adjudicate them (Baumgartner, 1988). The great social distance between disputants lowers the costs to honor that conflicts produce. Individualism both undermines forceful responses to conflict and makes tolerance, avoidance, or exit more feasible strategies of conflict management. Instead of mobilizing third parties, people may withdraw from conflict situations. Neighbors may avoid rather than litigate conflicts; spouses divorce instead of seeking therapy; apartment dwellers relocate instead of confronting a troubled situation. The decline of the nuclear family and growing diversity of living situations produces a growing tolerance for many divergent life-styles. Such strategies should become more prevalent as individuals can withdraw from relationships at will, freely move from place to place, and live apart from families and other supportive groups.

The decline in interpersonal dependence also has implications for the forms of social control. Growing equality decreases the reluctance of intimates to use law against each other. If growing avoidance is increasingly likely in all but the most serious conflicts between strangers, growing legalization marks the response to conflicts in intimate social space. Wives are more likely to invoke legal authority against husbands; parents to be legally responsible for abusing children; patients to bring lawsuits against their physicians; employees to sue their employers (Lieberman, 1981). At the same time, previously powerless groups including racial minorities, women, children, the handicapped, mental patients, or prisoners and their advocates have become more organized, and their problems consequently more legalized. Children, for example, traditionally had no access to law. Courts allowed parents almost total license to punish their children and schools to discipline pupils according to their own systems of rules. Now, however, third parties are more willing to intervene in cases of possible child abuse and to review matters of school discipline.

The growing status and organization of previously disenfranchised groups does not inevitably lead to a growth of litigation. Although these factors predict that courts and other trilateral forums will be more likely to hear grievances, the greater equality between organized groups also predicts negotiation and mediation rather than law (Black, 1989a). Greater organization and power can lead to more law, although also to more negotiated solutions with other organized entities. It is, therefore, difficult to predict whether the growing organization of previously powerless groups will result in greater bilateral or trilateral control.

As adversaries become more distant, more equal, and more organized, third parties should increasingly provide social control. At the same time, atomized and individuated social structures make inaction a common response to grievances. Official control systems should continue to grow, although forms of inaction will be a common alternative to the use of third party systems. In contrast, bilateral forms of control may flourish among organized groups of adversaries.

EFFECTIVENESS

The social configuration of modern societies is not conducive to the effective application of traditional means of social control. The atomized, fluid, and individualized nature of modern social structures make case gathering difficult. Victims or observers often find few rewards from reporting crimes to officials, whereas offenders can easily exit from situations. Sanctions are more difficult to apply because people are less concerned with reputational and interactional costs. Groups no longer participate in processes of punishment or healing so do not reinforce official control efforts. New strategies of social control are emerging that try to overcome the inability of traditional means to counter rising rates of deviance.

One emergent trend is the growth of *compliance* systems of social control (Reiss, 1984). Compliance strategies establish standards for conformity and enforce these standards regardless of whether or not a deviant action has taken place. Organizations are held to environmental standards, buildings periodically checked for violations of safety codes, drivers stopped on the highway and checked for blood alcohol levels, or employees tested for drug use. In each case, the deviant actor or organization need not have acted in a deviant way to invoke social control. Instead, anyone who has failed to meet certain standards may be subject to sanctioning.

Such proactive methods of compliance can overcome the problems large and heterogeneous societies face in gaining access to cases. Because compliance strategies are easier to implement than alternatives, are efficient to administer, and do not require strong moral underpinnings, social control systems will probably place a growing reliance on them. Organizations are particularly suited for control through compliance strategies because it is far easier to hold organizations than individuals to standards of conformity. Recreational leagues, day care centers, or chain stores can be held to standards that would be more difficult to enforce over pickup sandlot games, neighbors who watch children, or independent merchants. As more and more social life occurs within organizations that can be subject to compliance standards, legal regulation can become more effective.

The expansion of individualism is also congruent with a growing *infiltration* of deviant groups (Marx, 1988). Because so much interaction occurs between strangers, it is easier for disguised social control agents to penetrate or provoke deviant activities. Another stimulus to the use of undercover policing has been growing social control over white-collar crimes involving corporate executives, political officials, or labor leaders. White-collar offenses have been relatively impervious to reactive methods of control because they are typically consensual activities that have no victims in the traditional sense of the term. When affected individuals are not even aware of their victimizations, they cannot report offenses to officials. Yet, the anonymity of social life lends itself to proactive undercover means of policing activities such as fraudulent stock trading, organized criminal activities, or political bribery.

Technological improvements in devices such as hidden video cameras, miniaturized tape recorders, tiny, radio-transmitted body bugs, and the like have vastly increased the ability of social control agents to engage in undercover surveillance (Marx, 1988). Likewise, hugh computer data banks store vast quantities of information that potentially broaden and deepen surveillance over large populations. Both the anonymity of illegal transactions and new mechanisms for observing them enhance the potential effectiveness of covert means of social control.

The danger of these new, proactive strategies is their threat to the civil liberties of both nondeviant and deviant populations who must submit to their intrusions. They violate traditional democratic values of privacy, liberty, and repugnance against covert policing methods. Yet, the inability of modern democratic societies to develop effective reactive strategies of social control may lead them to use more broadly proactive strategies traditionally associated with totalitarian societies. Whether or not these strategies can be congruent with democratic values is an open question. The failure of traditional, reactive forms of social control to respond effectively to deviance may inevitably lead to new, more aggressive strategies of social control.

Shifts in the nature of social relationships produce changes in styles and forms of social control as well as differences in how effective control systems can be. It is impossible to specify the shape of future social control systems. They should, however, reflect a new order of social life where relatively equal individuals freely move in and out of relationships with anonymous other individuals and organizations. The great relational distance in such a society fails to generate strong moral bonds yet in many cases requires repressive official means of control to insure order.

The result of these transformations may be that social control in modern world will vary between heavy reliance on trilateral control institutions, on the one hand, and inaction, on the other hand. For example, the decline in the number of institutionalized mental patients over the past 35 years contrasts dramatically with rapidly growing numbers of prisoners over this period (Mechanic & Rochefort, 1990). Or, the sharp increase in punitive responses toward drug use diverges from the relaxation of responses to nontraditional sexual behaviors. At the same time that inaction becomes an efficient response to deviance, a wide array of professional agents of social control, as well as attorneys, counselors, and psychotherapists are readily available. Proactive strategies of control also become easier to implement, yet undermine the core values of democratic societies. A central issue for students of social control in the twenty-first century will be how systems of social control in individualistic societies can deal with the inherent contradictions between the need for law, order, and efficiency and the desire for freedom, liberty, and privacy.

References

Abel, R. L. (1979). Western courts in non-Western settings: Patterns of court use in colonial and neo-colonial Africa. In S. B. Burman & B. E. Harrell-Bond (Eds.), *The imposition of law* (pp. 167-200). New York: Academic Press.

Abel, R. L. (1986). The transformation of the American legal profession. *Law and Society Review, 20,* 7-17.

Albonetti, C. A. (1987). Prosecutorial discretion: The effects of uncertainty. *Law and Society Review, 21,* 291-314.

Andenaes, J. (1966). The general preventive effects of punishment. *University of Pennsylvania Law Review, 114,* 949-983.

Andenaes, J. (1974). *Punishment and deterrence.* Ann Arbor: University of Michigan Press.

Anderson, L. S., Chiricos, T. G., & Waldo, G. P. (1977). Formal and informal sanctions: A comparison of deterrent effects. *Social Problems, 25,* 103-114.

Anthony, W. A., & Carkhuff, R. R. (1977). The functional professional therapeutic agent. In A. S. Gurman & A. M. Razin (Eds.), *Effective psychotherapy: A handbook of research* (pp. 103-119). Oxford: Pergamon Press.

Aubert, V., & Messinger, S. L. (1958). The criminal and the sick. *Inquiry 1,* 137-160.

Auerbach, J. S. (1983). *Justice without law?* New York: Oxford University Press.

Austin, W., & Garner, S. W. (1980). Light up or butt out: An assessment of antismoking laws in the United States. *Deviant Behavior, 1,* 395-405.

Ayres, E. L. (1984). *Vengeance and justice: Crime and justice in the 19th century American South.* New York: Oxford University Press.

Balbus, I. (1973). *The dialectics of legal repression: Black rebels before the American criminal courts.* New York: Russell Sage.

Barkun, M. (1968). *Law without sanctions: Order in primitive societies and the world community.* New Haven: Yale University Press.

Barton, R. F. (1919). *Ifugao law.* Berkeley: University of California Press.

Baumgartner, M. P. (1978). Law and social status in colonial New Haven. In R. J. Simon (Ed.), *Research in law and sociology, Volume 1* (pp. 153-174). Greenwich: JAI Press.

Baumgartner, M. P. (1984). Social control from below. In D. Black (Ed.), *Toward a general theory of social control: Volume 1: Fundamentals* (pp. 303-345). New York: Academic Press.

Baumgartner, M. P. (1988). *The moral order of a suburb.* New York: Oxford University Press.

Baumgartner, M. P. (1990). War and peace in early childhood. *Virginia Review of Sociology,* forthcoming. Greenwich: JAI Press.

Bayer, R. (1989). *Private acts, social consequences: AIDS and the politics of public health.* New York: Free Press.

Bayley, D. H. (1976). *Forces of order: Police behavior in Japan and the United States.* Berkeley: University of California Press.
Beattie, J. (1966). *Other cultures.* London: Routledge.
Beattie, J. (1973). *The Bunyuro state.* New York: Oxford University Press.
Beattie, J. M. (1986). *Crime and the courts in England: 1660-1800.* Princeton: Princeton University Press.
Becker, H. S. (1963). *Outsiders: Studies in the sociology of deviance.* New York: Free Press.
Becker, M. H., & Joseph, J. G. (1988). AIDS and behavioral change to reduce risk: A review. *American Journal of Public Health, 78,* 394-410.
Beirne, P., & Quinney, R. (Eds.), (1982). *Marxism and law.* New York: John Wiley.
Bellah, R. N., Madsen, R., Sullivan, W. M., Swidler, A., & Tipton, S. M. (1985). *Habits of the heart: Individualism and commitment in American Life.* Berkeley: University of California Press.
Ben-Yehuda, N. (1980). The European witch craze of the 14th to 17th centuries: A sociologist's perspective. *American Journal of Sociology, 86,* 1-31.
Bergeson, A. (1984). Social control and corporate organization: A Durkheimian perspective. In D. Black (Ed.), *Toward a general theory of social control: Volume 2—Selected problems.* (pp. 141-170) New York: Academic Press.
Bergin, A. E. (1971). The evaluation of therapeutic outcomes. In A. E. Bergin & S. L. Garfield (Eds.), *Handbook of psychotherapy and behavior change: An empirical analysis* (pp. 217-270). New York: John Wiley.
Bergin, A. E. (1977). Introduction. In A. S. Gurman & A. M. Razin (Eds.), *Effective psychotherapy: A handbook of research* (pp. xv-xvi). Oxford: Pergamon Press.
Berk, S. F., & Loseke, D. (1981). Handling family violence: Situational determinants of police arrest in domestic disturbances. *Law and Society Review, 15,* 314-344.
Berk, R. A., Rauma, D., Loseke, D. R., & Berk, S. F. (1982). Throwing the cops back out: The decline of a local program to make the criminal justice system more responsive to incidents of domestic violence. *Social Science Research, 11,* 245-279.
Berk, R. A., Berk, S. F., Newton, P. J., & Loseke, D. R. (1984). Cops on call: Summoning the police to the scene of spousal violence. *Law and Society Review, 18,* 479-498.
Berman, H. J. (1983). *Law and revolution: The formation of the Western legal tradition.* Cambridge: Harvard University Press.
Berman, J. S., & Norton, N. C. (1985). Does professional training make a therapist more effective? *Psychological Bulletin, 98,* 401-407.
Bernard, T. J. (1984). The historical development of corporate criminal liability. *Criminology, 22,* 3-17.
Bernstein, B. (1964). Social class, speech systems, and psycho-therapy. *British Journal of Sociology, 15,* 54-64.
Bernstein, I., Kelly, W., & Doyle, P. (1977). Societal reactions to deviants: The case of criminal defendants. *American Sociological Review,* 42, 743- 755.
Best, A., & Andreasen, A. (1977). Consumer response to unsatisfactory purchases: A survey of perceiving defects, voicing complaints, and obtaining redress. *Law and Society Review, 11,* 701-742.
Bishop, D. M., & Frazier, C. E. (1984). The effects of gender on charge reduction. *Sociological Quarterly, 25,* 385-396.
Bittner, E. (1967). Police discretion in apprehending the mentally ill. *Social Problems, 14,* 278-292.
Bittner, E. (1980). *The functions of police in modern society.* Cambridge: Oelgeschlager, Gunn & Hain.
Black, D. (1971). The social organization of arrest. *Stanford Law Review, 23,* 1087-1111.
Black, D. (1972). The boundaries of legal sociology. *Yale Law Journal, 81,* 1086-1100.
Black, D. (1976). *The behavior of law.* New York: Academic Press.

Black, D. (1979). A strategy of pure sociology. In S. McNall (Ed.), *Theoretical perspectives in sociology* (pp. 149-168). New York: St. Martin's Press.
Black, D. (1980). *The manners and customs of the police.* New York: Academic Press.
Black, D. (1983). Crime as social control. *American Sociological Review, 48,* 34-45.
Black, D. (1984a). Social control as a dependent variable. In D. Black (Ed.), *Toward a general theory of social control* (pp. 1-36). New York: Academic Press.
Black, D. (1984b). Jurocracy in America. *The Tocqueville review - La revue Tocqueville, 6,* 273-281.
Black, D. (1987). Compensation and the social structure of misfortune. *Law and Society Review,* 21: 563-584.
Black, D. (1989a). *Sociological justice.* New York: Oxford University Press.
Black, D. (1989b). The elementary forms of conflict management. In *New directions in the study of justice, law, and social control.* New York: Plenum Press.
Black, D., & Baumgartner, M. P. (1983). Toward a theory of the third party. In K. O. Boyum & L. Mather (Eds.), *Empirical theories about courts* (pp. 84-114). New York: Longman.
Black, D., & Reiss, A. J. (1970). Police control of juveniles. *American Sociological Review, 35,* 63-77.
Blackstone, W. (1811). *Commentaries on the laws of England.* Oxford: Clarendon.
Blake, J., & Davis, K. (1964). Norms, values, and sanctions. In R. E. L. Faris (Ed.), *Handbook of modern sociology* (pp. 456-484). Chicago: Rand McNally.
Blanshed, S. R. (1982). Crime and law enforcement in medieval Bologna. *Journal of Social History, 16,* 121-138.
Bloch, M. (1961). *Feudal society. Volume 2: Social Classes and Political Organization.* Chicago: University of Chicago Press.
Block, R. (1974). Why notify the police: The victim's decision to notify the police of an assault. *Criminology, 11,* 555-569.
Blum-West, S., & Carter, T. J. (1983). Bringing white-collar crime back in: An examination of crimes and tort. *Social Problems, 30,* 545-554.
Blumstein, A., Cohen, J., & Nagin, D. (Eds.). (1978). *Deterrence and incapacitation: Estimating the effects of criminal sanctions on crime rates.* Washington, DC: National Academy of Sciences.
Boggs, S. (1971). Formal and informal crime control: An exploratory study of urban, suburban, and rural orientations. *The Sociological Quarterly, 12,* 319-327.
Bohannan, P. (1957). *Justice and judgment among the Tiv.* London: Oxford University Press.
Bohannan, P. (1965). The differing realms of the law. In L. Nader (Ed.), *The ethnography of law.* Supplement to *American Anthropologist, 67,* 33-42.
Boris, S. B. (1979). Stereotypes and dispositions for criminal homicide. *Criminology, 17,* 139-158.
Bowers, W. J. (1983). The pervasiveness of arbitrariness and discrimination under post-Furman capital statutes. *Journal of Criminal Law and Criminology, 74,* 1067-1100.
Bowers, W. J., & Pierce, G. L. (1980). Arbitrariness and discrimination under post-Furman capital statutes. *Crime and Delinquency, 26,* 563-635.
Braithwaite, J. (1982). Challenging just deserts: Punishing white-collar criminals. *The Journal of Criminal Law & Criminology, 73,* 723-768.
Braithwaite, J. (1985). White collar crime. *Annual Review of Sociology, 11,* 1-25.
Braithwaite, J. (1989). *Crime, shame, and reintegration.* Cambridge: Cambridge University Press.
Braithwaite, J., & Biles, D. (1980). Empirical verification and Black's *The Behavior of Law. American Sociological Review, 45,* 334-338.
Braginski, B. M., Braginsky, D. D., & Ring, K. (1969). *Methods of madness: The mental hospital as a last resort.* New York: St. Martin's Press.
Brenzel, B. (1980). Domestication as reform: A study of the socialization of wayward girls, 1856-1905. *Harvard Educational Review, 50,* 196-213.

Brody, E. B. (1968). Status and role influence on initial interview behavior in psychiatric patients. In S. Lesse (Ed.), *An evaluation of the results of the psychotherapies* (pp. 269-279). Springfield, IL: Charles Thomas.

Brogger, J. (1968). Conflict resolution and the role of the bandit in peasant society. *Anthropological Quarterly, 41,* 228-240.

Brown, J. V. (1987). Peasant survival strategies in late imperial Russia: The social uses of the mental hospital. *Social Problems, 34,* 311-329.

Brown, M. K. (1981). *Working the street.* New York: Russell Sage Foundation.

Brown, P. (1964). Enemies and affines. *Ethnology, 3,* 335-356.

Browne, A., & Williams, K. R. (1989). Exploring the effect of resource availability and the likelihood of female-perpetrated homicides. *Law and Society Review, 23,* 75-94.

Brumberg, J. J. (1984). 'Ruined' girls: Changing community responses to illegitimacy in upstate New York, 1890-1920. *Journal of Social History 18,* 247-272.

Bullough, V. L. (1973). Transvestites in the Middle Ages. *American Journal of Sociology, 79,* 1381-1394.

Burstein, P., & Monaghan, K. (1986). Equal employment opportunity and the mobilization of law. *Law and Society Review, 20,* 355-388.

Bynum, T. S., Cordner, G. W., & Greene, J. R. (1982). Victim and offense characteristics. *Criminology, 20,* 301-318.

Canter, R. S. (1978). Dispute settlement and dispute processing in Zambia: Individual choice versus societal constraints. In L. Nader & H. F. Todd (Eds). *The disputing process: Law in ten societies* (pp. 247-281). New York: Columbia University Press.

Casey, J. (1983). Household disputes and the law in early modern Andalusia. In J. Bossy (Ed.), *Disputes and settlements: Law and human relations in the West* (pp. 189-218). Cambridge: Cambridge University Press.

Casey, R. J. & Berman, J. S. (1985). The outcome of psychotherapy with children. *Psychological Bulletin, 98,* 388-400.

Castan, N. (1983). The arbitration of disputes under the Ancien Regime. In J. Bossy (Ed.), *Disputes and settlements: Law and human relations in the West* (pp. 219-260). Cambridge: Cambridge University Press.

Chagnon, N. A. (1977). *Yanomamo: The fierce people.* New York: Holt, Rinehart & Winston.

Chaiken, J. M., Lawless, M. W., & Stevenson, K. A. (1974). *The impact of police activity on crime: Robberies on the New York subway system.* Santa Monica: Rand Corporation.

Chambliss, W. J., & Seidman, R. (1971). *Law, order, and power.* Reading: Addison-Wesley.

Chelius, J. R. (1976). Liability for industrial accidents: A comparison of negligence and strict liability systems. *Journal of Legal Studies, 5,* 293-309.

Chesney-Lind, M. (1977). Judicial paternalism and the female status offender. *Crime and Delinquency, 23,* 121-135.

Chiricos, T. G., & Waldo, G. P. (1975). Socioeconomic status and criminal sentencing: An empirical assessment of a conflict proposition. *American Sociological Review, 40,* 753-772.

Christie, N. (1977). Conflicts as property. *British Journal of Criminology, 17,* 1-15.

Clare, G. (1980). *Last waltz in Vienna.* New York: Holt, Rinehart, & Winston.

Clark, A., & Gibbs, J. (1965). Social control: A reformulation. *Social Problems, 12*: 398-415.

Clausen, J. A. (1983). Sex roles, marital roles, and response to mental disorder. *Research in Community and Mental Health, 3,* 165-208.

Clausen, J. A., Pfeffer, N. G., & Huffine, C. L. (1982). Help seeking in severe mental illness. In D. Mechanic (Ed.), *Symptoms, illness behavior, and help seeking* (pp. 135-155). New York: Neale Watson.

Clausen, J. A. & Yarrow, M. R. (1955). The impact of mental illness on the family. *The Journal of Social Issues, 11,* entire issue.

Clinard, M.,B., & Yeager, P. C. (1980). *Corporate crime.* New York: Free Press.

Coates, D., & Penrod, S. (1980-1981). Social psychology and the emergence of disputes. *Law and Society Review, 15,* 655-680.

Coates, R. (1981). Community-based services for juvenile delinquents: Concept and implications for practice. *Journal of Social Issues, 37,* 87-101.

Cockburn, J. S., & Green, T. A. (Eds). (1988). *Twelve good men and true: The criminal trial jury in England, 1200-1800.* Princeton: Princeton University Press.

Cohen, S. (1985). *Visions of social control.* New York: Basil Blackwell.

Cohen, L. E., & Kluegel, J. R. (1978). Determinants of juvenile court dispositions: Ascriptive and achieved factors in two metropolitan courts. *American Sociological Review, 43,* 162-176.

Cohen, L. E. & Land, K. C. (1987). Age structure and crime: Symmetry versus asymmetry and the projection of crime rates through the 1990s. *American Sociological Review, 52,* 170-183.

Coleman, J. S. (1982). *The asymmetric society.* Syracuse: Syracuse University Press.

Collier, J. F. (1973). *Law and social change in Zinacantan.* Stanford: Stanford University Press.

Colson, E. (1953). Social control and vengeance in Plateau Tonga society. *Africa, 23,* 199-212.

Colson, E. (1974). *Tradition and contract: The problem of order.* Chicago: Aldine.

Columbia Journal of Law and Social Problems (Eds.). 1970. Rabbinical courts: Modern day Solomons. *Columbia Journal of Law and Social Problems, 6,* 49-75.

Conard, A., Morgan, J., Pratt, R., Voltz, C., & Bombaugh, R. (1964). *Automobile accident costs and payments: Studies in the economics of injury reparation.* Ann Arbor: University of Michigan Press.

Conrad, P., & Schneider, J. W. (1980). *Deviance and medicalization: From badness to sickness.* St. Louis: Mosby.

Cooley, C. H. (1909). *Social Organization.* New York: Scribner.

Cooney, M. (1986). Behavioral sociology of law: A defence. *Modern Law Review, 49*: 262-271.

Cooney, M. (1988). *The social control of homicide: A cross-cultural study* (Unpublished doctoral dissertation, Harvard Law School).

Counts, D. A. (1980). Fighting back is not the way: Suicide and the women of Kaliai. *American Ethnologist, 7,* 332-351.

Cressey, D. R. (1978). Testimony to subcommittee on crime of the committee on the Judiciary, House of Representatives, 95th Congress, Serial No. 69, *White-collar crime.* Washington, DC: U.S. Government Printing Office.

Crystal, S. (1987). Elder abuse: The latest "crisis." *The Public Interest, 88,* 56-66.

Cullen, F. T. (1983). *Rethinking crime and deviance theory: The emergence of a structuring tradition.* Totowa: Rowman & Allanheld.

Curran, B. A. (1986). American lawyers in the 1980s: A profession in transition. *Law and Society Review, 20,* 7-18.

Curran, D. (1983). Judicial discretion and defendant's sex. *Criminology, 21,* 41-58.

Currie, E. (1985). *Confronting crime: An American challenge.* New York: Pantheon Books.

Dain, N. (1964). *Concepts of insanity in the United States, 1789-1865.* New Brunswick, NJ: Rutgers University Press.

Daly, K. (1987a). Structure and practice of familial-based justice in a criminal court. *Law and Society Review, 21,* 267-290.

Daly, K. (1987b). Discrimination in the criminal court: Family, gender, and the problem of equal treatment. *Social Forces, 66,* 152-175.

Daniels, A. K. (1972). Military psychiatry: The emergence of a subspecialty. In E. Freidson & J. Lorber (Eds.), *Medical men and their work* (pp. 145-162). Chicago: Aldine-Atherton.

Danzon, P. M., & Lillard, L. A. (1983). Settlement out of court: The disposition of medical malpractice claims. *Journal of Legal Studies, 12,* 345-377.

Dannefer, D. (1984). "Who signs the complaint?": Relational distance and the juvenile justice process. *Law and Society Review, 18,* 249-271.

Dannefer, D., & Schutt, R. K. (1982). Race and juvenile justice processing in court and police agencies. *American Journal of Sociology, 87*, 1113-1132.

Davis, N. Z. (1975). *Society and culture in early modern France*. Stanford: Stanford University Press.

Diamond, S. (1971). The rule of law versus the order of custom, *Social Research, 38*, 42-72.

D'Emilio, J., & Freedman, E. B. (1988). *Intimate matters: A history of sexuality in America*. New York: Harper & Row.

Dobash, R. E., & Dobash, R. P. (1979). *Violence against wives: A case against the patriarchy*. New York: Free Press.

Doll, L., Darrow, W. W., Jaffe, H., Curran, L., O'Malley, P., Bodecker, T., Campbell, J., & Franks, D. (1987). *Self-reported changes in sexual behaviors in gay and bisexual men from the San Francisco City Clinic Cohort*. Paper presented at the Third International Conference on AIDS, Washington, DC.

Donovan, J. M. (1981). Justice unblind: The juries and the criminal classes in France, 1825-1914. *Journal of Social History, 15*, 89-107.

Donzelet, J. (1979). *The policing of families*. New York: Pantheon.

Doo, L. (1973). Dispute settlement in Chinese-American communities. *American Journal of Comparative Law, 21*, 627-663.

Durkheim, E. (1893). *The division of labor in society*. New York: Free Press.

Durkheim, E. (1899). Two laws of penal evolution. *Economy and Society, 2*, 285-313.

Durlak, J. A. (1979). Comparative effectiveness of para-professional and professional helpers. *Psychological Bulletin, 86*, 80-92.

Eckhoff, T. (1966) The mediator, the judge and the administrator in conflict-resolution. *Acta Sociologica, 10*, 158-166.

Ehrlich, I. (1973). Participation in illegal activities: A theoretical and empirical investigation. *Journal of Political Economy, 81*, 521-565.

Ekland-Olson, S. (1984). Social control and relational disturbance: A microstructural paradigm. In D. Black (Ed.), *Toward a general theory of social control, Volume 2: Selected problems* (pp. 209-234). New York: Academic Press.

Ekland-Olson, S. (1986). Crowding, social control, and prison violence: Evidence from the post-Ruiz years in Texas. *Law and Society Review, 20*, 389-422.

Ekland-Olson, S., Lieb, J., & Zurcher, L. (1984). The paradoxical impact of criminal sanctions: Some micro-structural findings. *Law and Society Review, 18*, 159-178.

Ellenberger, H. F. (1970). *The discovery of the unconscious: The history and evolution of dynamic psychiatry*. New York: Basic Books.

Ellickson, R. C. (1986). Coarse and cattle: Dispute resolution among neighbors in Shasta County. *Stanford Law Review, 38*, 623-687.

Emerson, R. M., & Messinger, S. L. (1977). The micro-politics of trouble. *Social Problems, 25*, 121-134.

Emrick, C. D., Lassen, C. L., & Edwards, M. T. (1977). Nonprofessional peers as therapeutic agents. In A. S. Gurman & A. M. Razin (Eds.), *Effective psychotherapy: A Handbook of research* (pp. 120-161). Oxford: Pergamon Press.

Engel, D. M. (1984). The oven-bird's song: Insiders, outsiders, and personal injuries in an American community. *Law and Society Review, 18*, 551-582.

Ennis, P. H. (1967). *Criminal victimization in the United States: A report of a national survey*. Washington DC: U.S. Government Printing Office.

Ericson, R. V. (1977). Social distance and reaction to criminality. *British Journal of Criminology, 17*, 16-29.

Evans-Pritchard, E. E. (1940). *The Nuer*. London: Oxford University Press.

Eysenck, H.J. (1952). The effects of psychotherapy: An evaluation. *Journal of Consulting Psychology, 16*, 319-324.

Falk-Moore, S. F. (1972). Legal liability and evolutionary interpretation: Some aspects of strict liability, self-help and collective responsibility. In M. Gluckman (Ed.), *The allocation of responsibility* (pp. 51-107). Manchester: Manchester University Press.

Fallers, L. A. (1969). *Law without precedent: Legal ideas in action in the courts of colonial Busoga.* Chicago: University of Chicago Press.

Farrell, R. A. & Swigert, V. L. (1978). Legal disposition of inter-group and intra-group homicides. *Sociological Quarterly, 19*: 565-576.

Feeley, M. M. (1979). *The process is the punishment: Handling cases in a lower criminal court.* New York: Russell Sage Foundation.

Feifer, G. (1967). Justice in Moscow: Ten days' normal fare. In P. Bohannon (Ed.), *Law and warfare: Studies in the anthropology of conflict* (pp. 93-116). Garden City: The Natural History Press.

Feifer, G. (1969). *Message from Moscow.* New York: Random House.

Feinberg, J. (1970). What is so special about mental illness? In *Doing and deserving* (pp. 272-292). Princeton: Princeton University Press.

Feinblatt, S., & Gold, A. (1976). Sex roles and the psychiatric referral process. *Sex Roles, 2,* 109-122.

Feinman, S. (1974). Approval of cross-sex-role behavior. *Psychological Reports, 35,* 643-648.

Felson, M. (1986). *The synchronized society.* Unpublished manuscript.

Felson, M., & Gottfredson, M. (1984). Some indicators of adolescent activities near peers and parents. *Journal of Marriage and the Family, 46,* 709-714.

Felstiner, W. L. F. (1974). Influences of social organization on dispute processing. *Law and Society Review, 9,* 63-94.

Felstiner, W. L. F. (1984). The logic of mediation. In D. Black (Ed.), *Toward a general theory of social control, Volume l: Fundamentals* (pp. 251-270). New York: Academic Press.

Ferraro, K. J. (1989). Policing woman battering. *Social Problems, 36,* 61-74.

Field, M. H., & Field, H. F. (1973). Marital violence and the criminal process: Neither justice nor peace. *Social Service Review, 47,* 221-240.

Fingarette, H. (1988). *Heavy drinking: The myth of alcoholism as a disease.* Berkeley: University of California Press.

Finkelhor, D. (1983). Common features of family abuse. In D. Finkelhor, R. J. Gelles, G. T. Hotaling, & M. A. Straus (Eds.). *The dark side of families: Current family violence research* (pp. 17-28). Beverly Hills: Sage.

Firth, R. (1963). *Elements of social organization.* Boston: Beacon Press.

Fisher, L. E. (1985). *Colonial madness: Mental health in the Barbadian social order.* New Brunswick, NJ: Rutgers University Press.

Foucault, M. (1965). *Madness and civilization: A history of insanity in the age of reason.* New York: Pantheon.

Foucault, M. (1977). *Discipline and punish: The birth of the prison.* New York: Pantheon.

Fox, J. R. (1964). Witchcraft and clanship in Cochiti therapy. In A. Kiev (Ed.), *Magic, faith, and healing* (pp. 174-202). New York: Free Press.

Fox, J. W. (1984). Sex, marital status, and age as social selection factors in recent psychiatric treatment. *Journal of Health and Social Behavior, 25,* 394-405.

Fox, R. W. (1978). *So far disordered in mind: Insanity in California 1870- 1930.* Berkeley: University of California Press.

Frank, J. (1930). *Law and the modern mind.* New York: Brentano's.

Frank, J. D. (1973). *Persuasion and healing* (2nd ed.). Baltimore: Johns Hopkins University Press

Frank, N. (1983). From criminal to civil penalties in the history of health and safety laws. *Social Problems, 30,* 531-544.

Friedman, L. (1985). *A history of American law* (2nd ed.). New York: Simon and Schuster.

Friedman, S. R., Des Jarlais, D. C., Sotheran, J. L., Garber, J., Cohen, H., & Smith., D. (1987). AIDS and self-organization among intravenous drug users. *International Journal of the Addictions, 22*, 201-220.

Friedman, S. R., de Jong, W. M., & Des Jarlais, D. C. (1988). Problems and dynamics of organizing intravenous drug users for AIDS prevention. *Health Education Research, 3*, 49-57.

Friedson, E. (1970). *Profession of medicine: A study of the sociology of applied knowledge.* New York: Harper & Row.

Friedson, E., & Rhea, B. (1972). Processes of control in a company of equals. In E. Freidson & J. Lorber (Eds.). *Medical men and their work* (pp. 185-199). Chicago: Aldine-Atherton.

Frolic, B. (1980). *Mao's people.* Cambridge: Harvard University Press.

Furer-Haimendorf, C. V. (1967). *Morals and merit: A study of values and social controls in South Asian societies.* Chicago: University of Chicago Press.

Galanter, M. (1974). Why the "haves" come out ahead: Speculations on the limits of legal change. *Law and Society Review, 9*, 95-160.

Galanter, M. (1983). Reading the landscape of disputes: What we know and don't know (and think we know) about our allegedly contentious and litigious society. *UCLA Law Review, 31*, 4-71.

Garnsey, P. (1968). Legal privilege in the Roman Empire. *Past and Present: A Journal of Historical Studies, 41*, 3-24.

Garrison, V. (1977). Doctor, espiritista, or psychiatrists? Health-seeking behavior in a Puerto Rican neighborhood of New York City. *Medical Anthropology, 1* (entire issue).

Geerken, M. R., & Gove, W. R. (1975). Deterrence: Some theoretical considerations. *Law and Society Review, 9*, 497-515.

Geertz, C. (1973). *The interpretation of cultures.* New York: Basic Books.

Gelles, R. J. (1972). *The violent home: A study of physical aggression between husbands and wives.* Beverly Hills: Sage.

Gerson, S., & Bassuk, E. (1980). Psychiatric emergencies: An overview. *American Journal of Psychiatry, 137*, 1-11.

Gibbs, J. (1975). *Crime, punishment, and deterrence.* New York: Elsevier.

Gibbs, J. (1981). *Norms, deviance, and social control.* New York: Elsevier.

Gilligan, C. (1982). *In a different voice: Psychological theory and women's development.* Cambridge: Harvard University Press.

Gillis, L. S., & Keet, M. (1965). Factors underlying the retention in the community of chronic unhospitalized schizophrenics. *British Journal of Psychiatry, 111*, 1057-1067.

Ginsberg, S., & Brown, G. W. (1982). No time for depression: A study of help seeking among mothers of preschool children. In D. Mechanic (Ed.), *Symptoms, illness behavior, and help seeking* (pp. 87-114). New York: Neale Watson.

Gluckman, M. (1963). Gossip and scandal. *Current Anthropology, 4*, 307-315.

Gluckman, M. (1967). *The judicial process among the Barotse of Northern Rhodesia.* Manchester: Manchester University Press.

Goffman, E. (1961). *Asylums: Essays on the social situation of mental patients and other inmates.* Garden City: Doubleday.

Goffman, E. (1971). The insanity of place. In *Relations in public* (pp. 335-390). New York: Harper & Row.

Goldberg, D., & Huxley, P. (1980). *Mental illness in the community: The pathway to psychiatric care.* London: Tavistock.

Goldhamer, H., & Marshall, A. W. (1953). *Psychosis and civilization: Two Studies in the frequency of mental disease.* New York: Free Press.

Goldschmidt, W. (1971). Independence as an element in pastoral social systems. *Anthropological Quarterly, 44*, 132-142.

Goode, W. J. (1971). Force and violence in the family. *Journal of Marriage and the Family, 33*, 624-636.

Gottfredson, M. R., & Hindelang, M. J. (1979). A study of the behavior of law. *American Sociological Review, 44*, 3-18.

Gove, W. R., Hughes, M., & Geerken, M. (1985). Are Uniform Crime Reports a valid indicator of the index crimes? An affirmative answer with minor qualifications. *Criminology, 23*, 451—501.

Grabowsky, P. N. (1984). The variability of punishment. In D. Black (Ed.), *Toward a general theory of social control: Volume 1—Fundamentals* (pp. 163-190). New York: Academic Press.

Graham, P., & Rutter, M. (1977). Adolescent disorders. In M. Rutter & L. Hersov (Eds.), *Child psychiatry*. Oxford: Blackwell Scientific.

Grasmick, H. G., Jacobs, D., & Mccollum, C. B. (1983). Social class and social control: An application of deterrence theory. *Social Forces, 62*, 659-374.

Green, T. A. (1972). Societal concepts of criminal liability for homicide in medieval England. *Speculum, 47*, 669-694.

Green, T. A. (1985). *Verdict according to conscience*. Chicago: University of Chicago Press.

Green, T. A. (1988). A retrospective. In J. S. Cockburn & T. A. Green (Eds.), *Twelve good men and true: The criminal trial jury in England, 1200-1800* (pp. 358-400). Princeton: Princeton University Press.

Greenberg, D. (1982). Crime, law enforcement, and social control in colonial America. *The American Journal of Legal History, 26*, 293-325.

Greenberg, D. F. (1985). Age, crime, and social explanation. *American Journal of Sociology, 91*, 1-21.

Greenberg, D. F. (1988). *The construction of homosexuality*. Chicago: University of Chicago Press.

Greenblat, C. (1983). A hit is a hit is a hit . . . or is it? Approval and tolerance of the use of physical force by spouses. In D. Finkelhor, R. J. Gelles, G. T. Hotaling, & M. A. Straus (Eds.) *The dark side of families: Current family violence research*. (pp. 235-260). Beverly Hills: Sage.

Greenhouse, C. J. (1982). Looking at culture, looking for rules. *Man, 17*, 58-73.

Greenhouse, C. J. (1986). *Praying for justice: Faith, order, and community in an American town*. Ithaca: Cornell University Press.

Greenley, J. R. (1972). The psychiatric patient's family and length of hospitalization. *Journal of Health and Social Behavior, 13*, 25-37.

Greenley, J. R., & Mechanic, D. (1978). Social selection in seeking help for psychological problems. *Journal of Health and Social Behavior, 17*, 249-262.

Griffiths, J. (1984). The division of labor in social control. In D. Black (Ed.), *Toward a general theory of social control, Volume l: Fundamentals*, (pp. 37-70). New York: Academic Press.

Griffiths, J. (1986). What do Dutch lawyers actually do in divorce cases? *Law and Society Review, 20*, 135-175.

Grob, G. (1973). *Mental institutions in America: Social policy to 1875*. New York: Free Press.

Grob, G. (1983). *Mental illness and American society: 1875-1940*. Princeton: Princeton University Press.

Gross, J. T. (1984). *Social control under totalitarianism*. In D. Black (Ed.), *Toward a general theory of social control: Volume 2—fundamentals* (pp.59-78). New York: Academic Press.

Guarnaccia, P., DeLaCancela, V., & Carrillo, E. (1989). The multiple meanings of "ataques de nervios" in the Latino community. *Medical Anthropology, 11*, 47-62.

Gulliver, P. H. (1963). *Social control in an African society: A study of the Arusha, agricultural Masai of Northern Tanganyika*. Boston: Boston University Press.

Gulliver, P. H. (1979). *Disputes and negotiations: A cross-cultural perspective.* New York: Academic Press.

Gurin, G., Veroff, J., & Field S. (1960). *Americans view their mental health.* New York: Basic Books.

Hagan, J. (1974). Extra-legal attributes and criminal sentencing: An assessment of a sociological viewpoint. *Law and Society Review, 8,* 357-384.

Hagan, J. (1982). The corporate advantage: A study of the involvement of corporate and individual victims in a criminal justice system. *Social Forces, 60,* 993-1022.

Hagan, J., Simpson, J. H., & Gillis, A. R. (1979). The sexual stratification of social control. *British Journal of Sociology, 30,* 25-38.

Hagan, J., Nagel, I. H., & Albonetti, C. (1980). Differential sentencing of white-collar offenders. *American Sociological Review, 45,* 802-820.

Hagan, J., Simpson, J., & Gillis, A. R. (1987). Class in the household: A power-control theory of gender and delinquency. *American Journal of Sociology, 92,* 788-816.

Haley, J. O. (1978). The myth of the reluctant litigant. *Journal of Japanese Studies, 4,* 359-390.

Haley, J. O. (1982). Sheathing the sword of justice in Japan: An essay on law without sanctions. *Journal of Japanese Studies, 8,* 265-281.

Hanawalt, B. A. (1979). *Crime and conflict in English communities 1300-1348.* Cambridge: Harvard University Press.

Harris, A. R. (1976). Race, commitment to deviance, and spoiled identity. *American Sociological Review, 41,* 432-442.

Hart, H. L. A. (1968). *Punishment and responsibility: Essays in the philosophy of law.* Oxford: Clarendon Press.

Hartman, M. S. (1977). *Victorian murderesses: A true history of thirteen respectable French and English women accused of unspeakable crimes.* New York: Schocken Books.

Harvey, Y. K. (1976). The Korean mudang as a household therapist. In W. Lebra (Ed.), *Culture-bound syndromes, ethnopsychiatry, and alternate therapies* (pp. 189-200). Honolulu: University Press of Hawaii.

Hasluck, M. (1954). *The unwritten law in Albania.* Cambridge: Cambridge University Press.

Hattie, J. A., Sharpley, C. F., & Rogers, H. J. (1984). Comparative effectiveness of professional and paraprofessional helpers. *Psychological Bulletin, 95,* 534-541.

Hay, D. (1975). Property, authority and the criminal law. In D. Hay, P. Linebaugh, J. G. Rule, E. P. Thompson, & C. Winslow (Eds.), *Albion's fatal tree: Crime and society in eighteenth-century England* (pp. 17-63). New York: Pantheon Books.

Hembroff, L.A. (1987). The seriousness of acts and social contexts: A test of Black's theory of the behavior of law. *American Journal of Sociology,* 93, 322-347.

Herrup, C. B. (1985). Law and morality in seventeenth-century England. *Past and Present, 106,* 102-123.

Hindelang, M. J., & Gottfredson, M. (1976). The victim's decision not to invoke the criminal justice process. In W. F. McDonald (Ed.), *Criminal justice and the victim* (pp. 57-78). Beverly Hills: Sage.

Hirschi, T. (1969). *Causes of delinquency.* Berkeley: University of California Press.

Hirschi, T., & Gottfredson, M. (1983). Age, crime, and social explanation. *American Journal of Sociology, 89,* 552-584.

Hirschman, A. O. (1970). *Exit, voice, and loyalty: Responses to decline in firms, organizations, and states.* Cambridge: Harvard University Press.

Hoebel, E. A. (1954). *The law of primitive man: A study in comparative legal dynamics.* Cambridge: Harvard University Press.

Hollander, P. (1982). Research on Marxist societies: The relationship between theory and practice. *Annual Review of Sociology, 8,* 319-351.

Hollinger, R. C., & Clark, J. P. (1982). Formal and informal social controls of employee deviance. *The Sociological Quarterly, 23,* 333-343.

Hollingshead, A. B. & Redlich, F. C. (1958). *Social class and mental illness.* New York: Wiley.

Holmes, O. W. (1881). *The common law.* Boston: Little, Brown, & Sons.

Holmes, O. W. (1897). The path of the law. *Harvard Law Review* 10: 457-478.

Homans, G. C. (1950). *The human group.* New York: Harcourt, Brace, & World.

Horowitz, R., & Schwartz, G. (1974). Honor, normative ambiguity, and gang violence. *American Sociological Review, 39,* 238-251.

Horwitz, A. V. (1977a). The pathways into psychiatric treatment: Some differences between men and women. *Journal of Health and Social Behavior, 56,* 86-106.

Horwitz, A. V. (1977b). Social networks and pathways into psychiatric treatment. *Social Forces, 56,* 86-106.

Horwitz, A. V. (1982). *The social control of mental illness.* New York: Academic Press.

Horwitz, A. V. (1982-1983). Resistance to innovation in the sociology of law: A reply to Greenberg. *Law and Society Review, 17,* 369-384.

Horwitz, A. V. (1984). The economy and social pathology. *Annual Review of Sociology, 10,* 95-119.

Horwitz, A. V. (1987). Help-seeking processes and mental health services. In D. Mechanic (Ed.), *Improving mental health services: What the social sciences can tell us* (pp. 33-45). San Francisco: Jossey-Bass.

Horwitz, A., & Wasserman, M. (1980). Formal rationality, substantive justice, and discrimination: A study of a juvenile court. *Law and Human Behavior, 4,* 103-115.

Hoskin, A. E. (1986). Preliminary accident report: 1985 work deaths decrease. *National Safety and Health News, 133,* 72-73.

Howell, P. P. (1954). *A manual of Nuer law: Being an account of customary law, its evolution and development in the courts established by the Sudan government.* London: Oxford University Press.

Hurst, W. J. (1945). The uses of law in four "colonial" states of the American union. *Wisconsin Law Review,* 577-597.

Hurst, J. W. (1980-1981). The functions of courts in the United States, 1950-1980. *Law and Society Review, 15,* 401-472.

Ingleby, D. (1983). Mental health and social order. In S. Cohen & A. Scull (Eds.), *Social control and the state* (pp. 141-188). New York: St. Martin's.

Jacoby, S. (1983). *Wild justice: The evolution of revenge.* New York: Harper & Row.

Janik, A., & Toulmin, S. (1973). *Wittgenstein's Vienna.* New York: Simon & Schuster.

Janowitz, M. (1975). Sociological theory and social control. *American Journal of Sociology, 81,* 82-108.

Jeffreys, M. D. W. (1952). Samsonic suicide or suicide of revenge among Africans. *African Studies, 11,* 118-122.

Jenkins, J. H., Karno, M., de la Selva, A., Santana, F., Telles, C., Lopez, S., & Mintz, J. (1986). Expressed emotion, maintenance pharmacotherapy, and schizophrenic relapse among Mexican-Americans. *Psychopharmacology Bulletin, 22,* 621-627.

Jensen, G. F. (1972). Delinquency and adolescent self-conceptions: A study of the personal relevance of infraction. *Social Problems, 20,* 84-103.

Jensen, G. F., & Erickson, M. (1978). The social meaning of sanctions. In M. Krohn & R. Akers (Eds.), *Crime, law, and sanctions: Theoretical perspectives.* Beverly Hills: Sage.

Jones, S. (1974). *Men of influence in Nuristan: A study of social control and dispute settlement in Waigal valley, Afghanistan.* New York: Seminar Press.

Kadushin, C. (1969). *Why people go to psychiatrists.* New York: Atherton.

Kagan, R. L. (1983). A golden age of litigation: Castile, 1500-1700. In J. Bossy (Ed.), *Disputes and settlements: Law and human relations in the West* (pp. 145-166). Cambridge: Cambridge University Press.

Kalmuss, D. S., & Straus, M. A. (1983). Feminist, political, and economic determinants of wife abuse services. In D. Finkelhor, R. J. Gelles, G. T. Hotaling, & M. A. Straus (Eds.), *The dark side of families: Current family violence research* (pp. 363-376). Beverly Hills: Sage.

Kalven, H., & Zeisel, H. (1966). *The American Jury*. Boston: Little, Brown.

Kaplan, B., & Johnson, D. (1964). The social meaning of Navaho psychopathology and psychotherapy. In A. Kiev (Ed.), *Magic, Faith, and Healing* (pp. 203-230). New York: Free Press.

Katz, J. (1988). *Seductions of crime: Moral and sensual attractions in doing evil*. New York: Basic Books.

Kawashima, T. (1963). Dispute resolution in contemporary Japan. In A. T. von Mehren (Ed.), *Law in Japan: The legal order in a changing society* (pp. 41-72). Cambridge: Harvard University Press.

Kessler, R. C., Brown, R. L., & Broman, C. L. (1981). Sex differences in psychiatric help seeking: Evidence from four large-scale surveys. *Journal of Health and Social Behavior, 22*, 49-64.

Kiev, A. (1964). The study of folk psychiatry. In A. Kiev (Ed.), *Magic, faith, and healing* (pp. 3-35). New York: Free Press.

Kiev, A. (1972). *Transcultural psychiatry*. New York: Free Press.

King, D. W., & McEvoy, K. A. (1976). *A national survey of the complaint handling procedures used by consumers*. Rockville: King Research.

Kleck, G. (1981). Racial discrimination in criminal sentencing: A critical evaluation of the evidence with additional evidence on the death penalty. *American Sociological Review, 46*, 783-805.

Klerman, G. (1988). The current age of youthful melancholia: Evidence for increase in depression among adolescents and young adults. *British Journal of Psychiatry, 152*, 4-14.

Kobler, A. L. (1975). Police homicide in a democracy. *Journal of Social Issues, 31*, 163-184.

Koch, K. F. (1974). *War and peace in Jalemo: The management of conflict in Highland New Guinea*. Cambridge: Harvard University Press.

Koch, K. F. (1984). Liability and social structure. In D. Black (Ed.), *Toward a general theory of social control, Volume 1: Fundamentals* (pp. 95-130). New York: Academic Press.

Koch, K. F., & Sodergren, J. A. (1976). Political and psychological correlates of conflict management: A cross-cultural study. *Law and Society Review, 10*, 443-466.

Kohn, M. L. (1959). Social class and parental values. *American Journal of Sociology, 64*, 337-351.

Kramer, M. (1983). The continuing challenge: The rising prevalence of mental disorders, associated chronic diseases and disabling conditions. *The American Journal of Social Psychiatry, 3*, 13-24.

Krohn, M. D., Curry, J. P., & Nelson-Kilger, S. (1983). Is chivalry dead? An analysis of changes in police dispositions of males and females. *Criminology, 21*, 417-438.

Kruttschnitt, C. (1981). Social status and sentences of female offenders. *Law and Society Review, 15*, 247-265.

Kruttschnitt, C. (1984). Sex and criminal court dispositions: The unresolved controversy. *Journal of Research in Crime and Delinquency, 21*, 213-232.

Kruttschnitt, C., & Green, D. E. (1984). The sex-sanctioning issue: Is it history? *American Sociological Review, 49*, 541-551.

Kruttschnitt, C., & McCarthy, D. (1985). Familial social control and pretrial sanctions: Does sex really matter? *The Journal of Criminal Law & Criminology, 76*, 151-175.

LaBarre, W. (1964). Confession as cathartic therapy in American Indian tribes. In A. Kiev (Ed.), *Magic, faith, and healing* (pp. 36-49). New York: Free Press.

Ladinsky, J., & Susmilch, C. (1982). *Community factors in the brokerage of consumer problems*. Paper presented for Conference in Honor of Morris Janowitz, Chicago.

LaFree, G. D. (1980). The effects of sexual stratification by race on official reactions to rape. *American Sociological Review, 45*, 842-854.

LaFree, G. (1981). Official reactions to social problems: Police decisions in sexual assault cases. *Social Problems, 28,* 582-594.
LaFree, G. D., Reskin, B. F., & Visher, C. A. (1985). Jurors' responses to victims' behavior and legal issues in sexual assault trials. *Social Problems, 32,* 389-407.
Lambek, M. (1980). Spirits and spouses: Possession as a system of communication among the Malagasy speakers of Mayotte. *American Ethnologist, 7,* 318-331.
Lambert, M. J. (1979). *The effects of psychotherapy, Volume 1.* Montreal: Eden Press.
Landman, J. T., & Dawes, R. M. (1982). Psychotherapy outcome: Smith and Glass' conclusions stand up under scrutiny. *American Psychologist, 37,* 504-516.
Lane, R. (1967). *Policing the city: Boston-1822-1885.* Cambridge: Harvard University Press.
Lane, R. (1980). Urban police and crime in nineteenth-century America. In N. Morris & M. Tonry (Eds.), *Crime and Justice: An Annual Review of Research, Volume 2* (pp. 1-43). Chicago: University of Chicago Press.
Langbein, J. H. (1983). Albion's fatal flaws. *Past and Present, 98,* 96-120.
Lasch, C. (1977). *Haven in a heartless world.* New York: Basic Books. Laslett, B. (1973). The family as a public and private institution: An historical perspective. *Journal of Marriage and the Family, 35,* 480-492.
Lauderdale, P. (1976). Deviance and moral boundaries. *American Sociological Review, 41,* 660-676.
Leaf, P. J., & Bruce, M. L. (1987). Gender differences in the use of mental-health-related services: A reexamination. *Journal of Health and Social Behavior, 28,* 171-183.
Leaf, P. J., Livingston, M. B., Tischler, G. L., Weissman, M. M., Holzer, C. E., & Myers, J. K. (1985). Contact with health professionals for the treatment of psychiatric and emotional problems. *Medical Care, 23,* 1322- 1337.
Lederman, E. (1985). Criminal law, perpetrator and corporation: Rethinking a complex triangle. *The Journal of Criminal Law and Criminology, 76,* 285-339.
Lefley, H. P. (1987). Culture and mental illness: The family role. In A. B. Hatfield & H. P. Lefley (Eds.), *Families of the mentally ill: Coping and adaptation* (pp.30-59). New York: Guilford Press.
Lefley, H.P. (1989). Family burden and family stigma in major mental illness. *American Psychologist,* 44, 556-560.
Leff, J., & Vaughn, C. (1985). *Expressed emotion in families: Its significance for mental illness.* New York: Guilford Press.
Leifer, R. (1969). *In the name of mental health: The social functions of psychiatry.* New York: Science House.
Lempert, R., & Sanders, J. (1986). *An invitation to law and social science.* New York: Longman.
Lenski, G. (1988). Rethinking macrosociological theory. *American Sociological Review, 53,* 163-171.
Lerman, P. (1982). *Deinstitutionalization and the welfare state.* New Brunswick, NJ: Rutgers University Press.
Lesse, S. (1968). Patients, therapists, and socioeconomics. In S. Lesse (Ed.), *An evaluation of the results of the psychotherapies,* (pp. 239-253). Springfield, IL: Charles C Thomas.
Lewis, I. M. (1959). Clanship and contract in northern Somililand. *Africa, 29,* 274-293.
Lewis, I. M. (1961). *A pastoral democracy: A study of pastoralism and politics among the Northern Somali of the Horn of Africa.* London: Oxford University Press.
Lewis, I. M. (1966). Spirit possession and deprivation cults. *Man, 1,* 307-329.
Lewis, I. M. (1976). *Social anthropology in perspective.* Middlesex: Penguin.
Levi, E. (1949). *An introduction to legal reasoning.* Chicago: University of Chicago Press.
Levi-Strauss, C. (1964). The effectiveness of symbols. In *Structural anthropology* (pp. 181-201). Garden City: Doubleday Anchor.
Lieberman, J. K. (1981). *The litigious society.* New York: Basic Books.

Liebman, R., & Polen, M. (1978). Perspectives on policing in nineteenth-century America. *Social Science History, 2*, 346-360.

Lilly, J. R., & Ball, R. A. (1982). A critical analysis of the changing concept of criminal responsibility. *Criminology, 20*, 169-184.

Lin, T., Tardiff, K., Donetz, G., & Goresky, W. (1978). Ethnicity and patterns of help seeking. *Culture, Medicine, and Psychiatry, 2*, 3-14.

Link, B., & Dohrenwend, B. P. (1980). Formulation of hypotheses about the ratio of untreated to treated cases in the true prevalence studies of functional psychiatric disorders in adults in the United States. In B. P. Dohrenwend, B. S. Dohrenwend, M. S. Gould, B. Link, R. Neugebauer, & R. Wunsch-Hitzig (Eds.), *Mental illness in the United States: Epidemiological estimates* (pp. 133-149). New York: Praeger.

Link, B., & Milcarek, B. (1980). Selection factors in the dispensation of therapy: The Matthew effect in the allocation of mental health resources. *Journal of Health and Social Behavior, 21*, 279-290.

Linsky, A. S. (1970). Who shall be excluded: The influence of personal attributes in community reaction to the mentally ill. *Social Psychiatry, 5*, 166-171.

Lipton, D., Martinson, R., & Wilks, J. (1975). *The effectiveness of correctional treatment: A survey of evaluation studies.* New York: Praeger.

Liska, A. E. (1987). A critical examination of macro perspectives on crime control. *Annual Review of Sociology, 13*, 67-192.

Liska, A. E. & Tausig, M. (1979). Theoretical interpretations of social class and racial differentials in legal decision-making for juveniles. *The Sociological Quarterly, 20*, 197-207.

Little, C. B., & Sheffield, C. P. (1983). Frontiers and criminal justice: English private prosecution societies and American vigilantism in the eighteenth and nineteenth centuries. *American Sociological Review, 48*, 796-808.

Lizotte, A. J. (1978). Extra-legal factors in Chicago's criminal courts: Testing the conflict model of criminal justice. *Social Problems, 25*, 564-580.

Lofland, J. (1969). *Deviance and identity.* Englewood Cliffs, NJ: Prentice-Hall.

Loizos, P. (1978). Violence and the family: Some Mediterranean examples. In J. P. Martin (Ed.), *Violence and the family* (pp. 345-352). New York: John Wiley.

Loring, M., & Powell, P. (1988). Gender, race, and DSM-III: A study of the objectivity of psychiatric behavior. *Journal of Health and Social Behavior, 29*, 1-22.

Lowenthal, M. F. (1964). *Lives in distress: The paths of the elderly to the psychiatric ward.* New York: Basic Books.

Lowie, R. H. (1927). *The origin of the state.* New York: Harcourt.

Lowy, M. J. (1978). A good name is worth more than money: Strategies of court use in Urban Ghana. In L. Nader & H. F. Todd (Eds.), *The disputing process: Law in ten societies* (pp. 181-208). New York: Columbia University Press.

Lunbeck, E. (1984). *Boston Psychopathic Hospital and other origins of American Social Psychiatry, 1900-1925.* Unpublished doctoral dissertation, Harvard University.

Luckenbill, D. F. (1977). Criminal homicide as a situated transaction. *Social Problems, 25*, 176-186.

Lundman, R. J., Sykes, R. E., & Clark, J. P. (1978). Police control of juveniles: A replication. *Journal of Research in Crime and Delinquency, 15*, 74-91.

Lundsgaarde, H. P. (1977). *Murder in space city: A cultural analysis of Houston homicide patterns.* New York: Oxford University Press.

Macaulay, S. (1963). Non-contractual relations in business: A preliminary study. *American Sociological Review, 28*, 55-67.

Macaulay, S. (1966). *Law and the balance of power: The automobile manufacturers and their dealers.* New York: Russell Sage Foundation.

Macaulay, S. (1979). Lawyers and consumer protection laws. *Law and Society Review, 14*, 115-171.

Macdonald, M. (1981). *Mystical bedlam: Madness, anxiety, and healing in seventeenth-century England.* Cambridge: Cambridge University Press.
Mahoney, A. R. (1974). The effect of labeling upon youths in the juvenile justice system: A review of the evidence. *Law and Society Review, 8,* 583-614.
Maine, H. S. (1861). *Ancient law: Its connection with the early history of society and its relation to modern ideas.* Boston: Beacon Press.
Manderscheid, R. W. & Barrett, S. A. (1987). *Mental health, United States, 1987.* Washington, DC: U.S. Government Printing Office.
Marmor, J. (1975). *Psychiatrists and their patients: A national study of private office practice.* Washington DC: American Psychiatric Association.
Marx, G. (1988). *Undercover: Police surveillance in America.* Berkeley: University of California Press.
Marx, K. (1890) *Capital: A critique of political economy.* New York: International Publishers.
May, M. (1978). Violence in the family: An historical perspective. In J. P. Martin (Ed.), *Violence and the family* (pp. 135-168). New York: John Wiley.
Maybury-Lewis, D. (1967). *Akwe-Shavante society.* New York: Oxford University Press.
Mayhew, L. (1968). *Law and equal opportunity: A study of the Massachusetts commission against discrimination.* Cambridge: Harvard University Press.
Mayhew, L., & Reiss, A. J. (1969). The social organization of legal contacts. *American Sociological Review, 34,* 309-318.
Maynard, D. W. (1982). Defendant attributes in plea bargaining: Notes on the modeling of sentencing decisions. *Social Problems, 29,* 347-360.
McCarthy, J. D. & Hoge, D. R. (1987). The social construction of school punishment: Racial disadvantage out of universalistic process. *Social Forces, 65,* 1101-1120.
McDowall, D., & Loftin, C. (1983). Collective security and the demand for legal handguns. *American Journal of Sociology, 88,* 1146-1161.
McEwen, C. A., & Maiman, R. J. (1984). Mediation in small claims court: Achieving compliance through consent. *Law and Society Review,* 18, 11-50.
McFarlane, W. F. (1983). *Family therapy in schizophrenia.* New York: Guilford.
McLeod, M. (1983). Victim noncooperation in domestic assault. *Criminology, 21,* 395-416.
Mechanic, D. (1989). *Mental health and social policy* (3rd ed.) Englewood Cliffs, NJ: Prentice-Hall.
Mechanic, D., & Hansell, S. (1987). Introspection and illness behavior. *Psychiatric Medicine, 5,* 5-14.
Mechanic, D., & Rochefort, D. (1990). Deinstitutionalization: An appraisal of reform. *Annual Review of Sociology, 16,* forthcoming.
Meier, R., & Johnson, W. (1977). Deterrence as social control: The legal and extralegal production of conformity. *American Sociological Review, 42,* 292-304.
Mendel, W., & Rapport, S. (1969). Determinants of the decision for psychiatric hospitalization. *Archives of General Psychiatry, 20,* 321-328.
Mennel, R. M. (1983). Attitudes and policies toward juvenile delinquency in the United States: A historiographical review. In N. Morris & M. Tonry (Eds.), *Crime and Justice: An Annual Review of Research, Volume 4* (pp. 191-224). Chicago: University of Chicago Press.
Merry, S. E. (1979). Going to court: Strategies of dispute management in an American urban neighborhood. *Law and Society Review, 13,* 891-925.
Merry, S. E. (1982). The social organization of mediation in nonindustrial societies: Implications for informal community justice in America. In R. L. Abel (Ed.), *The politics of informal justice, Volume 2: Comparative Studies* (pp. 17-46). New York: Academic Press.
Merry, S. E. (1984). Rethinking gossip and scandal. In D. Black (Ed.), *Toward a general theory of social control, Volume 1: Fundamentals* (pp. 271-302). New York: Academic Press.

Messing, S. D. (1959). Group therapy and social status in the Zar cult of Ethiopia. In M. Opler (Ed.), *Culture and mental health* (pp. 319-332). New York: Macmillan.

Middleton, J. (1965). *The Lugbara of Uganda*. New York: Holt, Rinehart & Winston.

Miller, R. E., & Sarat, A. (1980-1981). Grievances, claims, and disputes: Assessing the adversary culture. *Law and Society Review, 15*, 525-566.

Mintz, S., & Kellogg, S. (1988). *Domestic revolutions: A social history of American family life*. New York: Free Press.

Monkkonen, E. (1981). *Police in urban America: 1860-1920*. Cambridge: Cambridge University Press.

Mnookin, R. H., & Kornhauser, L. (1979). Bargaining in the shadow of the law: The case of divorce. *Yale Law Journal, 88*, 950-997.

Murashin, W. A. (1976). The social-control theory in American History: A critique. *Journal of Social History, 9*, 559—569.

Murphy, H. B. M., & Raman, A. C. (1971). The chronicity of schizophrenia in indigenous tropical peoples: Results of a 12-year follow-up on Mauritius. *British Journal of Psychiatry, 118*, 489-497.

Murphy, J. M. (1964). Psychotherapeutic aspects of shamanism on St. Lawrence Island, Alaska. In A. Kiev (Ed.), *Magic, faith, and healing* (pp. 53-83). New York: Free Press.

Myers, M. A. (1980). Predicting the behavior of law: A test of two models. *Law and Society Review, 14*, 835-857.

Myers, M. A. (1987). Economic inequality and discrimination in sentencing. *Social Forces, 65*, 746-766.

Myers, M. A., & Hagan, J. (1979). Private and public trouble: Prosecutors and the allocation of court resources. *Social Problems, 26*, 439-451.

Myers, M. A., & LaFree, G. D. (1981). The uniqueness of sexual assault: A comparison with other crimes. *Journal of Criminal Law and Criminology, 73*, 1282-1305.

Myers, M. A., & Talarico, S. M. (1986). The social contexts of racial discrimination in sentencing. *Social Problems, 33*, 236-251.

Nader, L. (1964). An analysis of Zapotec law cases. *Ethnology, 3*, 404-419.

Nader, L. (1965). Choices in legal procedure: Shia Moslem and Mexican Zapotec. *American Anthropologist, 67*, 394-399.

Nader, L. (1969). Styles of court procedure: To make the balance. In L. Nader (Ed.), *Law in culture and society* (pp. 69-91). Chicago: Aldine.

Nader, L. (1984). From disputing to complaining. In D. Black (Ed.), *Toward a general theory of social control, Volume l: Fundamentals* (pp. 71-94). New York: Academic Press.

Nader, L., & Metzger, D. (1963). Conflict resolution in two Mexican communities. *American Anthropologist, 65*, 584-592.

Nader, L., & Todd, H. F. (1978). Introduction. In L. Nader & H. F. Todd (Eds.), *The disputing process: Law in ten societies* (pp. 1-40). New York: Columbia University Press.

Nagel, I. H. & Hagan, J. (1983) Gender and crime: Offense patterns and criminal court sanctions. *Crime and Justice, 4*, 91-143.

Nagel, S., & Weitzman, L. (1971). Women as litigants. *Hastings Law Journal, 23*, 171-181.

Nelson, W. E. (1975). *Americanization of the common law: The impact of legal change on Massachusetts society, 1760-1830*. Cambridge: Harvard University Press.

Newman, K. S. (1983). *Law and economic organization: A comparative study of preindustrial societies*. Cambridge: Cambridge University Press.

Oberg, K. (1934). Crime and punishment in Tlingit society. *American Anthropologist, 36*, 145-156.

Obeysekere, G. (1970). The idiom of demonic possession: A case study. *Social Science and Medicine, 4*, 97-111.

Oppenlander, N. (1982). Coping or copping out: Police service delivery in domestic disputes. *Criminology, 20*, 449-465.

Otterbein, K. E., & Otterbein, C. S. (1965). An eye for an eye, a tooth for a tooth: A cross-cultural study of feuding. *American Anthropologist, 67,* 1470-1482.

Palmer, T. B. (1973). Matching worker and client in corrections. *Social Work, 18,* 95-103.

Parnell, P. (1978). Village or state? Communication legal systems in a Mexican judicial district. In L. Nader & H. F. Todd (Eds.), *The disputing process: Law in ten societies* (pp. 315-350). New York: Columbia University Press.

Parsons, T. (1937). *The structure of social action.* New York: McGraw-Hill.

Parsons, T. (1942). Propaganda and social control. *Psychiatry 25,* 551-572.

Parsons, T. (1951). *The social system.* New York: Free Press.

Parsons, T. (1966). *Societies: Evolutionary and comparative perspectives.* Englewood Cliffs, NJ: Prentice-Hall.

Paternoster, R. (1984). Prosecutorial discretion in requesting the death penalty: A case of victim-based racial discrimination. *Law and Society Review, 18,* 437-478.

Paternoster, R., & Iovanni, L. A. (1986). The deterrent effect of perceived severity: A re-examination. *Social Forces, 64,* 751-777.

Patterson, O. (1982). *Slavery and social death: a comparative study.* Cambridge: Harvard University Press.

Perry, M. E. (1980). *Crime and society in early modern Seville.* Hanover: University Press of New England.

Peters, E. L. (1967). Some structural aspects of the feud among the camel-herding Bedouin of Cyrenaica. *Africa, 37,* 261-282.

Petersilia, J. (1985). Racial disparities in the criminal justice system: A summary. *Crime and Delinquency, 31,* 15-34.

Peterson, R. D., & Hagan, J. (1984). Changing conceptions of race and sentencing outcomes. *American Sociological Review, 49,* 56-70.

Peyrot, M. (1982). Caseload management: Choosing suitable clients in a community health clinic agency. *Social Problems, 30,* 157-167.

Phillips, D. (1964). Rejection of the mentally ill: The influence of behavior and sex. *American Sociological Review, 29,* 679-687.

Phillips, D. (1977). *Crime and authority in Victorian England: The black country 1835-1860.* Totowa: Rowman & Littlefield.

Phillips, D. M., & DeFleur, L. B. (1982). Gender ascription and the stereotyping of deviants. *Criminology, 20,* 431-448.

Piliavin, I. M. & Briar, S. (1964). Police encounters with juveniles. *American Journal of Sociology, 70,* 206-214.

Pitts, J. R. (1961). Social control: The concept. In D. L. Sills (Ed.), *International Encyclopedia of the Social Sciences, 14,* 381-396. New York: Macmillan.

Platt, T. (1969). *The child savers: The invention of delinquency.* Chicago: University of Chicago Press.

Pleck, E. (1987). *Domestic tyranny: The making of American social policy against family violence from Colonial times to the present.* New York: Oxford University Press.

Polyani, K. (1957). *The great transformation: The political and economic origins of our time.* Boston: Beacon Press.

Popenoe, D. (1988). *Disturbing the nest: Family change and decline in modern societies.* New York: Aldine de Gruyter.

Posner, R. (1980). A theory of primitive society with special reference to law. *The Journal of Law and Economics, 23,* 1-53.

Pound, R. (1942). *Social control through law.* New Haven: Yale University Press.

Prince, R. (1964). Indigenous Yoruba psychiatry. In A. Kiev (Ed.), *Magic, faith, and healing* (pp. 84-120). New York: Free Press.

Quinney, R. (1974). Critique of legal order: Crime control in capitalist society. Boston: Little, Brown.

Radcliffe-Brown, A. R. (1922). *The Andaman Islanders.* New York: Free Press. 1964.

Radcliffe-Brown, A. R. (1933a). *Structure and function in primitive societies: Essays and addresses.* New York: Free Press.

Radcliffe-Brown, A. R. (1933b). Social sanctions, in *Encyclopedia of the Social Sciences, 13,* 531-534. New York: Macmillan.

Radelet, M. L. (1981). Racial characteristics and the imposition of the death penalty. *American Sociological Review, 46,* 918-927.

Radelet, M. L., & Pierce, G. L. (1985). Race and prosecutorial discretion in homicide cases. *Law and Society Review, 19,* 587-621.

Rafter, N. H. (1983). Chastising the unchaste: Social control functions of a women's reformatory, 1894-1931. In S. Cohen & A. Scull (Eds.), *Social control and the state* (pp. 288-311). New York: St. Martin's Press.

Rafter, N. H. (1984). *The punishment of women: State prisons and their inmates 1790-1935.* Boston: Northeastern University Press.

Redfield, R. (1967). Primitive law. In P. Bohannon (Ed.), *Law and warfare: Studies in the anthropology of conflict* (pp. 3-24). Garden City: The Natural History Press.

Reid, J. P. (1980). *Law for the elephant: Property and social behavior on the Overland Trail.* San Marino: The Huntingdon Library.

Reiman, J. H. (1979). *The rich get richer and the poor get prison: Ideology, class and criminal justice.* New York: John Wiley and Sons.

Reiss, A. J. (1971). *The police and the public.* New Haven: Yale University Press.

Reiss, A. J. (1984). Selecting strategies of social control over organizational life. In K. Hawkins & J. M. Thomas (Eds.), *Enforcing Regulation* (pp. 23-35). Boston: Kluwer-Nijhoff.

Reskin, B. F., & Visher, C. A. (1986). The impact of evidence and extralegal factors in jurors' decisions. *Law and Society Review, 20,* 423-438.

Reuter, P. (1984). Social control in illegal markets. In D. Black (Ed.), *Toward a general theory of social control, Volume 2: Selected problems* (pp. 29-58). New York: Academic Press.

Richards, P. (1979). Middle-class vandalism and age-status conflict. *Social Problems, 26,* 482-497.

Rieder, J. (1984). The social organization of vengeance. In D. Black (Ed.) *Toward a general theory of social control: Volume 1—Fundamentals* (pp. 131-162). New York: Academic Press.

Rieff, P. (1961). *Freud: The mind of a moralist.* Garden City: Doubleday Anchor.

Rieff, P. (1966). *The triumph of the therapeutic.* New York: Harper.

Roberts, S. (1979). *Order and dispute: An introduction to legal anthropology.* New York: St. Martins Press.

Robinson, C. D., & Scaglion, R. (1987). The origin and evolution of the police function in society: Notes towards a theory. *Law and Society Review, 21,* 109-153.

Rock, P. (1983). Law, order and power in late seventeenth and early eighteenth-century England. In S. Cohen & A. Scull (Eds.), *Social control and the state* (pp. 191-221). New York: St. Martin's.

Rogler, L. H., & Hollingshead, A. B. (1965). *Trapped: Families and schizophrenia.* New York: Wiley.

Rojek, D. G. (1979). Private justice systems and crime reporting. *Criminology, 17,* 100-111.

Rose, A., & Prell, A. (1955). Does the punishment fit the crime? A study in social valuation. *American Journal of Sociology, 61,* 247-259.

Rosen, G. (1968). *Madness in society.* New York: Harper.

Rosenberg, S., Prola, M., Meyer, E. J., Zuckerman, M., & Bellak, L. (1968). Factors related to improvement in brief psychotherapy. In S. Lesse (Ed.), *An evaluation of the results of the psychotherapies* (pp.82-100). Springfield, IL: Charles Thomas.

Rosenfield, S. (1983). Sex roles and societal reactions to mental illness. *Journal of Health and Social Behavior, 23,* 18-24.

Ross, E. A. (1901). *Social control.* New York: Macmillan.

Ross, M. H. (1985). Internal and external conflict and violence: Cross-cultural evidence and a new analysis. *Journal of Conflict Resolution, 29,* 547-579.

Ross, L. H. (1970). *Settled out of court: The social process of insurance claims adjustment.* Chicago: Aldine.

Ross, L. H. (1986). Social control through deterrence: Drinking and driving laws. *Annual Review of Sociology, 10,* 21-35.

Ross, L. H., & Foley, J. P. (1987). Judicial disobedience of the mandate to imprison drunk drivers. *Law and Society Review, 21,* 315-323.

Ross, L. H., & Littlefield, N. O. (1978). Complaint as a problem-solving mechanism. *Law and Society Review, 12,* 199-216.

Rossi, P, Waite, E., Bose, C. E., & Berk, R. E. (1974). The seriousness of crimes: Normative structure and individual differences. *American Sociological Review, 39,* 224-237.

Rothenberger, J. E. (1978). The social dynamics of dispute settlement in a Sunni Muslim village in Lebanon. In L. Nader & H. F. Todd (Eds.). *The disputing process: Law in ten societies* (pp. 152-180). New York: Columbia University Press.

Rothman, D. (1971). *The discovery of the asylum: Social order and disorder in the new republic.* Boston: Little, Brown.

Ruane, J. (1987). *The behavior of tolerance and social control: A test of social space versus social learning.* (Unpublished doctoral dissertation, Rutgers University.)

Ruffini, J. L. (1978). Disputing over livestock in Sardinia. In L. Nader & H. F. Todd (Eds.), *The disputing process: Law in ten societies* (pp. 209-247). New York: Columbia University Press.

Ruggiero, G. (1980). *Violence in Early Renaissance Venice.* New Brunswick, NJ: Rutgers University Press.

Rusche, G., & Kirchheimer, O. (1939). *Punishment and social structure.* New York: Russell and Russell.

Safilios-Rothschild, C. (1968). Deviance and mental illness in the Greek family. *Family Process, 7,* 100-117.

Safilios-Rothschild, C. (1969). "Honour" crimes in contemporary Greece. *British Journal of Sociology, 20,* 205-218.

Salas, L. (1979). *Social control and deviance in Cuba.* New York: Praeger.

Samara, J. (1974). *Law and order in historical perspective: The case of Elizabethan England.* New York: Academic Press.

Sampson, R. J. (1986). Crime in cities: The effects of formal and informal social control. In A. J. Reiss & M. Tonry (Eds.), *Communities and crime* (pp. 271-311). Chicago: University of Chicago Press.

Sarat, A. (1977). Studying American legal culture: An assessment of survey evidence. *Law and Society Review, 11,* 427-488.

Sarat, A., & Felstiner, W. L. F. (1986). Law and strategy in the divorce lawyer's office. *Law and Society Review, 20,* 93-134.

Sarri, R. C. (1983). Gender issues in juvenile justice. *Crime and delinquency, 29,* 381-397.

Sartorious, N., Jablensky, A., & Shapiro, R. (1978). Cross-cultural differences in the short-term prognosis of schizophrenic psychoses. *Schizophrenia Bulletin, 4,* 102-113.

Sartorius, N., Jablensky, A., Korten, A., Ernberg, G., Anker, M., Cooper, J. E., & Day R. (1986). Early manifestations and first-contact incidence of schizophrenia in different cultures. *Psychological Medicine, 16,* 909-928.

Scheper-Hughes, N. (1979). *Saints, scholars, and schizophrenics: Mental illness in rural Ireland.* Berkeley: University of California Press.

Schlossman, S. L. (1977). *Love and the American delinquent: The theory and practice of "progressive" juvenile justice 1825-1920.* Chicago: University of Chicago Press.

Schneider, D. M. (1957). Political organization, supernatural sanctions and the punishment for incest on Yap. *American Anthropologist, 59,* 791-800.

Schneider, J. (1971). Of vigilance and virgins: Honor, shame, and access to resources in Mediterranean society. *Ethnology, 10,* 1-24.

Schur, E. M. (1971). *Labeling deviant behavior.* New York: Harper & Row.

Schur, E. M. (1984). *Labeling women deviant: Gender, stigma, and social control.* New York: Random House.

Schutz, A. (1967). *Collected papers I: The problem of social reality* (M. Natanson, Ed.). The Hague: Martinus Nijhoff.

Schwartz, R. D. (1954). Social factors in the development of legal control: A case study of two Israeli settlements. *Yale Law Journal, 63,* 471-491.

Schwartz, R. D., & Miller, J. C. (1964). Legal evolution and societal complexity. *American Journal of Sociology, 70,* 159-169.

Shannon, L. W. (1982). *Assessing the relationship of adult criminal careers to juvenile careers: A summary.* Washington, DC: U.S. Office of Juvenile Justice and Delinquency Prevention.

Shapiro, S., Skinner, E. A., Kessler, L. G., Von Korff, M., German, P. S., Tischler, G. L., Leaf, P. J., Benham, L., Cottler, L., & Regier, D. A. (1984). Utilization of health and mental health services. *Archives of General Psychiatry, 41,* 971-978.

Sharpe, J. A. (1983). Such disagreement between neighbours: Litigation and human relations in early modern England. In J. Bossy (Ed.), *Disputes and settlements: Law and human relations in the West* (pp. 167-189). Cambridge: Cambridge University Press.

Shearing, C. D., & Stenning, P. C. (1983). Private security: Implications for social control. *Social Problems, 30,* 493-506.

Sherman, L. W., & Berk, R. A. (1984). Deterrent effects of arrest for domestic assault. *American Sociological Review, 49,* 261-271.

Sherman, L. W., & Cohn, E. G. (1989). The impact of research on legal policy: The Minneapolis domestic violence experiment. *Law & Society Review, 23,* 117-144.

Shilts, R. (1987). *And the band played on: Politics, people and the AIDS epidemic.* New York: St. Martin's Press.

Shinnar, R., & Shinnar, S. (1975). The effects of the criminal justice system on the control of crime: A quantitative approach. *Law and Society Review, 9,* 581-612.

Showalter, E. (1985). *The female malady: Women, madness, and English culture, 1830-1980.* New York: Pantheon Books.

Silberman, M. (1976). Toward a theory of criminal deterrence. *American Sociological Review, 41,* 442-461.

Silberman, M. (1985). *The civil justice process: A Detroit area study.* Orlando, FL: Academic Press.

Skogan, W. G. (1976). Citizen reporting of crime: Some national panel data. *Criminology, 13,* 535-549.

Skogan, W. G. (1986). Fear of crime and neighborhood change. In A. J. Reiss & M. Tonry (Eds.). *Communities and crime.* Chicago: University of Chicago Press.

Skolnick, J. K. (1965). The sociology of law in America: Overview and trends. *Law and society.* Published as a supplement to *Social Problems, 12,* 4-39.

Smith, D. A. (1984). The organizational context of legal control. *Criminology, 22,* 19-38.

Smith, D. A. (1987). Police response to interpersonal violence: Defining the parameters of legal control. *Social Forces, 65,* 767-782.

Smith, D. A., & Klein, J. R. (1984). Police control of interpersonal disputes. *Social Problems, 31,* 468-481.

Smith, D. A., & Uchida, C. D. (1988). The social organization of self-help. *American Sociological Review, 53,* 94-102.

Smith, D. A., & Visher, C. A. (1981). Street level justice: Situational determinants of police arrest decisions. *Social Problems, 29,* 167-177.

Smith, D. A., Visher, C. A., & Davidson, L. A. (1984). Equity and discretionary justice: The influence of race on police arrest decisions. *The Journal of Criminal Law and Criminology, 75,* 234-249.

Smith, M. L., Glass, G. V., & Miller, R. H. (1980). *The benefits of psychotherapy.* Baltimore: Johns Hopkins University Press.

Smith-Rosenberg, C. (1985). *Disorderly conduct: Visions of gender in Victorian America.* New York: Oxford University Press.

Sparks, R. F. (1980). A critique of Marxist criminology. In N. Morris & M. Tonry (Eds), *Crime and Justice: An Annual Review of Research, Volume* 2 (pp. 159-210). Chicago: University of Chicago Press.

Sparks, R. F., Genn, H. G., & Dodd, D. J. (1977). *Surveying victims.* New York: John Wiley.

Spence, J. T., & Helmreich, R. L. (1978). *Masculinity and femininity.* Austin: University of Texas Press.

Spierenburg, P. (1984). *The spectacle of suffering: Executions and the evolution of repression.* Cambridge: Cambridge University Press.

Spitzer, S. (1975). Punishment and social organization: A study of Durkheim's theory of penal evolution. *Law and Society Review, 9,* 613-635.

Spitzer, S., & Scull, A. T. (1977). Privatization and capitalist development: The case of the private police. *Social Problems, 25,* 18-29.

Spohn, C., Gruhl, J., & Welch. S. (1981-1982). The effect of race on sentencing: A re-examination of an unsettled question. *Law and Society Review, 16,* 71-88.

Srole, L., Langner, T. S., Michael, S. T., Opler, M. K., & Rennie, T. A. C. (1962). *Mental health in the metropolis: The midtown Manhattan study.* New York: McGraw-Hill.

Stables, W. G. (1984). Toward a structural perspective on gender bias in the juvenile court. *Sociological Perspectives, 27,* 349-367.

Stables, W. G. (1986). Restitution as a sanction in juvenile court. *Crime and Delinquency, 32,* 177-185.

Stables, W. G. (1987). Law and social control in juvenile justice dispositions. *Journal of Research in Crime and Delinquency, 24,* 7-23.

Stables, W. G., & Warren, C. A. B. (1988). Mental health and adolescent social control. In A. Scull & S. Spitzer (Eds.), *Research in law, deviance, and social control, Volume 9* (pp. 113-126). Greenwich: JAI Press.

Stall, R. D., Coates, T. J., & Hoff, C. (1988). Behavioral risk reduction for HIV infection among gay and bisexual men. *American Psychologist, 43,* 878-885.

Stanko, E. (1981-1982). The impact of victim assessment on prosecutor's screening decisions: The case of the New York County district attorney's office. *Law and Society Review, 16,* 225-238.

Steadman, H. J., & Cocozza, J. J. (1974). *Careers of the criminally insane.* Lexington: Heath.

Steffensmeier, D. (1980). Assessing the impact of the women's movement on sex-based differences in the handling of adult criminal defendants. *Crime and Delinquency, 26,* 344-357.

Steinberg, A. (1984). From private prosecution to plea bargaining: Criminal prosecution, the district attorney, and American legal history. *Crime and Delinquency, 30,* 568-592.

Stenross, B. (1984). Police response to residential burglaries: Dusting for prints as a negative rite. *Criminology, 22,* 389-402.

Stern, M. S. (1977). Social class and psychiatric treatment of adults in the mental health center. *Journal of Health and Social Behavior, 18,* 317-325.

Stinchcombe, A. L. (1963). Institutions of privacy in the determination of police administrative practice. *American Journal of Sociology, 69,* 150-160.

Stone, L. (1983). Interpersonal violence in English society 1300-1980. *Past and Present, 101,* 23-33.

Sudnow, D. (1965). Normal crimes: Sociological features of the penal code. *Social Problems, 12,* 255-270.

Sviridoff, M., & Thompson, J. W. (1983). Links between employment and crime: A qualitative study of Riker's Island releasees. *Crime and Delinquency, 29,* 195-212.

Swanson, G. (1971). An organizational analysis of collectivities. *American Sociological Review, 36,* 607-623.

Szasz, T. S. (1961). *The myth of mental illness.* New York: Harper.

Taube, C. A., & Barrett, S. A. (1985). *Mental health, United States, 1985.* Washington, DC: U.S. Government Printing Office.

Tentler, T. N. (1977). *Sin and confession on the eve of the Reformation.* Princeton: Princeton University Press.

Thomas, C. W., & Cage, R. J. (1977). The effect of social characteristics on juvenile court dispositions. *Sociological Quarterly, 18,* 237-252.

Thomas, W. I., & Znaniecki, F. (1918). *The Polish peasant in Europe and America* (V1). Chicago: University of Chicago Press.

Thompson, E. P. (1975). The crime of anonymity. In D. Hay, P. Linebaugh, J. G. Rule, E. P. Thompson, & C. Winslow (Eds.), *Albion's fatal tree* (pp. 255-344). New York: Pantheon.

Tischler, G. (1966). Decision-making process in the emergency room. *Archives of General Psychiatry, 14,* 69-78.

Tittle, C. R. (1980). *Sanctions and social deviance: The question of deterrence.* New York: Praeger.

Toby, J. (1981). Deterrence without punishment. *Criminology, 19,* 195-209.

Todd, H. F. (1978). Litigious marginals: Character and disputing in a Bavarian village. In L. Nader & H. F. Todd (Eds.), *The disputing process: Law in ten societies* (pp. 86-121). New York: Columbia University Press.

Tomes, N. (1978). A "torrent of abuse": Crimes of violence between working-class men and women in London, 1840-1875. *Journal of Social History, 12,* 328-345.

Tomes, N. (1984). *A generous confidence: Thomas Story Kirkbride and the art of asylum-keeping, 1840-1883.* Cambridge: Cambridge University Press.

Tonnies, F. (1887). *Community and society.* New York: Harper & Row.

Trice, H. M., & Roman, P. M. (1970). Delabeling, relabeling and Alcoholics Anonymous. *Social Problems, 17,* 538-546.

Trubek, D. M., Grossman, J. B., Felstiner, W. L. F., Kritzer, H. M., & Sarat, A. (1983). *Civil litigation research project: Final report.* Madison: University of Wisconsin Law School.

Trumbad, R. (1977). London's sodomites: Homosexual behavior and western culture in the 18th century. *Journal of Social History, 11,* 1-33.

Tseng, W. (1976). Folk psychotherapy in Taiwan. In W. Lebra (Ed.), *Culture-bound syndromes, ethnopsychiatry, and alternate therapies* (pp. 164-178). Honolulu: University Press of Hawaii.

Tudor, W., Tudor, J. F., & Gove, W. R. (1977). The effect of sex role differences on the social control of mental illness. *Journal of Health Behavior, 18,* 98-112.

Turkel, G. (1979). Testing Durkheim: Some theoretical considerations. *Law and Society Review, 13,* 721-739.

Unger, R. M. (1976). *Law in modern society.* New York: Free Press.

U.S. Bureau of the Census (1986a). Current population reports, Series P-20 No. 411, *Household and family characteristics: March 1985.* Washington, DC: U.S. Government Printing Office.

U.S. Bureau of the Census (1986b). Current population reports, Series P-20 No. 410, *Marital status and living arrangements: March 1985.* Washington, DC: U.S. Government Printing Office.

Vaughn, C. E., & Leff, J. P. (1976). The influence of family and social factors on the course of psychiatric illness: A comparison of schizophrenic and depressed neurotic patients. *British Journal of Psychiatry, 129,* 125-137.

Veroff, J., Kulka, R. A., & Douvan, E. (1981). *Mental health in America: Patterns of help seeking from 1957 to 1976.* New York: Basic Books.

Visher, C. A. (1983). Gender, police arrest decisions, and notions of chivalry. *Criminology, 21,* 5-28.
Wagatsuma, H., & Rosett, A. (1986). The implications of apology: Law and culture in Japan and the United States. *Law and Society Review, 20,* 461-498.
Waldorf, D. (1973). *Careers in dope.* Englewood Cliffs, NJ: Prentice-Hall.
Wallace, A. F. C. (1972). Mental illness, biology, and culture. In F. Hsu (Ed.), *Psychological anthropology* (pp. 363-402). Cambridge: Schenkman.
Wanner, C. (1974). The public ordering of private relations, Part 1: Initiating civil cases in urban trial courts. *Law and Society Review, 8,* 421-440.
Wanner, C. (1975). The public ordering of private relations, Part 2: Winning civil court cases. *Law and Society Review, 9,* 293-306.
Warner, W. L. (1958). *A black civilization: A social study of an Australian tribe.* New York: Harper and Brothers.
Warren, C. A. B. (1977). Involuntary commitment for mental disorder: The application of California's Lanterman-Petras-Short act. *Law and Society Review, 12,* 629-649.
Warren, C. A. B. (1981). New forms of social control: The myth of deinstitutionalization. *American Behavioral Scientist, 24,* 724-740.
Warren, C. A. B. (1982). *The court of last resort: Mental illness and the law. Chicago: University of Chicago Press.*
Warren, C. A. B., & Guttridge, P. (1984). Adolescent psychiatric hospitalization and social control. In L. Teppin (Ed.), *Mental health and criminal justice* (pp. 119-138). Beverly Hills: Sage Publications.
Waxler, N. E. (1974). Culture and mental illness: A social labeling perspective. *Journal of Nervous and Mental Disease, 159,* 379-395.
Weber, M. (1925). *Max Weber on law in economy and society* (M. Rheinstein ed.). Cambridge: Harvard University Press.
Weiner, C. Z. (1975) Sex roles and crime in late Elizabethan Hertfordshire. *Journal of Social History, 8,* 38-61.
Weissman, M., & Paykel, E. S. (1974). *The depressed woman: A study of social relationships.* Chicago: University of Chicago Press.
Werthman, C., & Piliavin, I. (1967). Gang members and the police. In D. J. Bordua (Ed.), *The police: Six sociological essays* (pp. 56-98). New York: John Wiley.
Westermeyer, J. J. (1973). Assassination and conflict resolution in Laos. *American Anthropologist, 75,* 123-131.
Wheeler, S., Weisburd, D., & Bode, N. (1982). Sentencing the white-collar offender: Rhetoric and reality. *American Sociological Review, 47,* 641-659.
Wilkins, L. (1964). *Social deviance.* London: Tavistock.
Williams, K. M. (1976). The effects of victim characteristics on judicial decision making. In W. F. McDonald (Ed.), *Criminal justice and the victim* (pp. 177-214). Beverly HIlls: Sage.
Williams, K. R., & Flewelling, R. (1988). The social production of criminal homicide: A comparative study of disaggregated rates in American cities. *American Sociological Review, 53,* 421-432.
Williams, K. R., & Hawkins, R. (1986). Perceptual research on general deterrence: A critical review. *Law and Society Review, 20,* 545-572.
Williams, L. S. (1984). The classic rape: When do victims report? *Social Problems, 31,* 459-467.
Wilson, W. J. (1987). *The truly disadvantaged: The inner city, the underclass, and public policy.* Chicago: University of Chicago Press.
Wimberly, H. (1973). Legal evolution: One further step. *American Journal of Sociology, 79,* 78-83.
Witty, C. J. (1980). *Mediation and society: Conflict management in Lebanon.* New York: Academic Press.

Wolfgang, M. (1958). *Patterns in criminal homicide.* New York: John Wiley.
Woodson, R. (1981). *A summons to life: Mediating structures and the prevention of youth crime.* Boston: Ballinger.
Worden, R. E., & Pollitz, A. A. (1984). Police arrests in domestic disturbances: A further look. *Law and Society Review, 18,* 105-119.
Wrightson, K. (1980). Two concepts of order: Justices, constables, and jurymen in seventeenth-century England. In J. Brewer & J. Styles (Eds.), *An ungovernable people: The English and their law in the seventeenth and eighteenth centuries* (pp. 21-46). New Brunswick, NJ: Rutgers University Press.
Young, M. W. (1971). *Fighting with food: Leadership, values and social control in a Massim society.* Cambridge: Cambridge University Press.
Yngvesson, B. (1976). Responses to grievance behavior: Extended cases in a fishing community. *American Ethnologist, 3,* 353-373.
Yngvesson, B. (1978). The Atlantic fishermen. In L. Nader & H. F. Todd (Eds.), *The disputing process: Law in ten societies* (pp. 59-85). New York: Columbia University Press.
Yngvesson, B., & Hennessey, P. (1975). Small claims, complex disputes: A review of the small claims literature. *Law and Society Review, 9,* 219-274.
Ziegenhagen, E. (1976). Toward a theory of victim-criminal justice system interactions. In W. F. McDonald (Ed.), *Criminal justice and the victim* (pp. 261-280). Beverly Hills: Sage.
Zimring, F., & Hawkins, G. (1973). *Deterrence: The legal threat in crime control.* Chicago: University of Chicago Press.
Zingraff, M., & Thompson, R. (1984). Differential sentencing of women and men in the U.S.A. *International Journal of the Sociology of Law, 12,* 401-413.

Index